The Political Agenda of Organizations

The Political Agenda of Organizations

Yitzhak Samuel

Transaction Publishers
New Brunswick (U.S.A.) and London (U.K.)

Copyright © 2005 by Transaction Publishers, New Brunswick, New Jersey.
www.transactionpub.com

This book is printed on acid-free paper that meets the American National Standard for Permanence of Paper for Printed Library Materials.

Library of Congress Catalog Number: 2004051783
ISBN: 0-7658-0260-0
Printed in the United States of America

M/L

Library of Congress Cataloging-in-Publication Data

Samuel, Yitzhak
    The political agenda of organizations / Yitzhak Samuel.
        p. cm.
    Includes bibliographical references and index.
    ISBN 0-7658-0260-0 (cloth : alk. paper)
        1. Organizational effectiveness—Political aspects.   2. Power (Social sciences) I. Title.

HD58.9.S26   2004
302.3'5—dc22   2004051783

To the memory of my parents

Contents

Acknowledgments   ix

Preface   xi

Introduction   xv

1.   The Essence of Power   1

2.   The Theoretical Basis   25

3.   The Political Layout   45

4.   The Political Agenda   65

5.   Perceived Politics   87

6.   Political Games   107

7.   Interpersonal Politics   127

8.   Intergroup Politics   147

9.   Interorganizational Politics   171

10. Managerial Politics   193

Conclusion   215

References   221

Index   229

Acknowledgments

It is my pleasure to express my gratitude to the people who encouraged and assisted me to turn the original Hebrew version of this book into an English one. First and foremost, I would like to thank Rebecca Toueg for her professional translation of the Hebrew into English, saving me a great deal of time and effort.

I am grateful to my colleagues at the University of Haifa: Rector Aaron Ben-Zeev; Dean for Research, Moshe Zeidner; Dean of the Faculty of Social Sciences, Arye Rattner; and Chair of the Department of Sociology and Anthropology, Gustavo Mesch for providing me with the necessary financial means to complete this project.

My research assistant Orit Shamir helped me greatly with her library search, checking of references, quotations, and similar tasks. The editor, Anne Schneider carefully polished the text, paid attention to every detail, and nicely arranged the layout of this volume. Paul Corrington prepared the index for this volume. My thanks are also due to Irving Louis Horowitz for his confidence in my work and for the prompt to publish it once the manuscript was completed.

Published book reviews of the Hebrew version, written by my colleagues Ephraim Yuchtman-Yaar, Boas Shamir, and Eran Vigoda contributed useful comments and suggestions, which I have taken into consideration in the present version of the book. Michael Harrison shared with me his publishing experience with American publishers. Warner Burke, Stewart Clegg, and Jim Taylor kindly agreed to review the English manuscript for potential publishers.

The University of Haifa Press and Zmora-Bitan publishers kindly allowed me to publish this volume abroad in English. Special thanks to Miriam Zeidan for her cooperation and assistance in this matter.

Last but not least, I am grateful to my family—Yael, Sigal, Amir, Gil, and Tal for their encouragement and support. My wife Yael closely followed my work, offered her advice and extended her assistance throughout this project, as she has done in all my academic endeavors.

Preface

The history of this book begins about thirty years ago. As a doctoral student at the University of Michigan, I wrote a seminar paper on organizational effectiveness from the point of view of power and exchange relations, and was awarded a prize for the paper and a contract for writing a book on the subject. For different reasons the writing of the book was delayed for a long time and it was never published. In the course of time, some of the ideas presented in that seminar paper were adopted by organization theory, and some of the terms which I employed at that time became current in research and industrial circles.

During the past decade, I returned to address the phenomenon of organizations from the perspective of power and politics. As a lecturer in the Department of Political Sciences and the Department of Sociology and Anthropology, as well as in the College for National Security of the University of Haifa, I taught several classes on this subject. I also gave lectures on the basics of organization politics to executives and managers in various organizations. In my teaching experience, quite often I encountered the same response from my students and trainees, which confirmed that the use of power and politics is deeply rooted in organizational life everywhere. In addition, I noticed that my audience felt uncomfortable discussing this political phenomenon openly and in public, for in their opinion, this subject seemed to cast a shadow over the image of their organization and indirectly on themselves.

Hence, I reached the conclusion that there is a need to address the issue of organization politics, to discuss its causes and to assess its effects. In the light of the knowledge and experience I had gained in organizational politics through my academic and practical work, I decided to put it in writing in a much more detailed and expanded manner than previously, in the form of a reference guide and textbook. This volume is different in content and format from the book that was not published earlier, but it is based on the same thoughts and theoretical ideas that had begun to form since then.

This volume examines all kinds of organizations from a political perspective, analyzing them in terms of social power and politics.[1] For the purpose of simplification, it employs the concept of political games to describe organizational politics in terms borrowed from the realm of sports, such as contesters, playgrounds, and encounters, as well as rules of the game, strategies and tactics, scores, victories and defeats that refer to various aspects of political games. The main purpose of such political games is the maximization of benefits for the participating players or for their dispatchers.

The book analyzes the concepts of social power and social influence from several viewpoints. It presents and compares several theories of power and politics as developed in the disciplines of sociology, psychology, and economics. It draws upon comcepts and ideas taken from Game theory, and also scrutinizes the political layout of organizations.

The main political issues that emerge in conjunction with the organizational agenda are examined in the book. One chapter deals with the notion of "subjective politics," as it is perceived and described by internal participants and external observers. The book outlines the variety of political games that are played in the realm of organizations, listing nine types of games and specifies the ways in which individual level politics, group level politics, and organizational level politics take place. Power based, self-serving relationships between managers and executives are discussed under the title of "Managerial Politics" in chapter 10.

It should be noted that this volume deals with organizational politics and not with national or international politics. Broadly speaking, organization politics is here perceived as a power-based web of relationships conducted for the purpose of maximizing benefits. This is known in professional terminology as *micropolitics*, which frequently occurs in business corporations, factories, communal and governmental offices, hospitals and clinics, schools and universities, military and police organizations, communication networks and newspaper offices, art and cultural institutions, professional unions, voluntary associations, and many other organizations.

Those who participate in micropolitics may be individuals, groups, departments and organizational units, entire organizations or multi-organizational networks. In contrast with the wider scene of politics designated as *macropolitics,* organizational politics does not deal with political parties and factions. It is not the type of politics conducted according to socio-political points of view as declared in political party platforms. Moreover, active participants of micropolitics are executives, supervisors, workers, investors, clients and the like, who are neither politicians nor those whose main occupation is politics. As will be discussed in more detail, political behavior is in essence an informal, non-sanctioned, some times illegitimate, organizational behavior, which does not correspond to the rules and procedures of organizations.

The Political Agenda of Organizations should serve a variety of readers. It is intended mainly for students in the social and behavioral sciences as well as for students of business and/or public administration. It may assist lecturers and teachers who give courses on organization theory and the basics of organizational behavior. Managers, commanders, supervisors and officers can consult this book for an informal analysis of organizational structures and processes, such as budgeting and decision processes, from a political viewpoint. It can also serve as a tool for practitioners engaged in the management and development of human resources. Organizational consultants are likely to find in this volume some clues and directions for diagnosing organizations; reporters dealing with public and business organizations can obtain a better understanding of the organizational reality on which they report; public representatives who run governmental and municipal agencies can find a systematic and comprehensive analysis of organization politics in the institutions that they have been elected to govern. And the volume may also serve educated readers, who have an interest in the ways that organizations are run and in their influence on the daily life of the organizational society in which we live.

I have made every effort to write this book in a friendly manner and to address a large variety of readers, including readers who are unfamiliar with organization theory and who do not deal professionally with organizational research. It also contains a large selection of references published on this subject, which were used as source material for writing the book. In order to illustrate professional terms and abstract arguments, examples of different events that occurred in various countries were quoted from the media.

I view the writing of this book as a kind of payment of a debt to myself, and a tribute to the memory of my mentor and colleague—the late sociologist Robert (Bill) Hodge, who encouraged me to write a book on this subject at that early stage of my career.

Note

1. The present English volume is a translated and revised version of the original Hebrew book, *The Political Game: Power and Influence in Organizations,* published in Israel by The University of Haifa Press & Zmora-Bitan, 2000.

Introduction

This introduction presents, in a condensed form, the conceptual and theoretical framework of organizational politics as it is discussed in the present volume. The emphasis in this brief chapter is on the introduction of a new theoretical approach to the study of organizations, which is intended to explain the pattern of political behavior of those participating in organizations and those who are in contact with them on the outside. The purpose of this theoretical framework is to provide a systematic analysis of the notion of *political game* in all its forms—a game that is conducted within organizations and among them.

Since the beginning of the twentieth century, the scientific effort to conceptualize the phenomenon of organizations has produced a series of paradigms, which have not yet been integrated into a general theory of organizations. Of the various perspectives on organizations, we shall focus briefly here on only two of them. The traditional view of organizations as rational systems[1] sees them as merely "social machines" —designed and operated like instruments for the attainment of predetermined goals.[2]

Ideally, organizational participants are the operators of those machines, requested to perform their jobs and tasks as they are prescribed by formal rules, procedures, job descriptions, and contracts. From this perspective, members' informal actions and interactions are perceived to be unauthorized activities that do not accord with the regime of the organization. This outlook tends to underplay the role of the "human factor" and its effect on the behavior of organizations in general and that of their participants in particular.

Like any scientific theory, the rational theory is based on certain basic premises. Its primary assumption argues that every organization has a defined ultimate goal or mission, which justifies its existence in human society. Its secondary assumption postulates that organizations are well-controlled apparatuses, striving to fulfill their function. Organizations, therefore, define objectives and tasks, set procedures, and direct themselves in such a way as to proceed in the right direction—the way that will lead them to their ultimate goals. From this perspective, it is of no importance who was the individual or group that set the organization's goal, when it was set, and how; what is important is that the goal is a constant factor by which its inputs are determined and its outputs are assessed.

According to this theoretical approach, organizations employ different means (such as job descriptions, contracts, rules, and procedures) to lessen uncertainty, to save resources, to set processes, to avoid arbitrariness and favoritism, to prevent friction and confrontations and to ensure the adoption of rational organizational decisions. In other words, to operate as effective and efficient machines targeted at a preset goal. Hence, the behavior of members in organizations is focused upon the good of the organization and is aimed at goal attainment.

Critique of the functionalist perspective in general and the rational theory in particular argues that it portrays a rather normative image of organizations that barely exist in real life. That is, it describes the best way to design and to manage organizations instead of explaining how they are actually built and operating. On the basis of this critique, a newer perspective in organization theory was advanced—known as the "critical perspective"—in which the "open system theory" was developed.[3] This theory assumes that organizations are systems similar to many other systems in nature. However, organizations are social systems—namely, systems that are created and operated by human beings. From the moment they are created, these systems do the best they can to ensure their continued existence despite the forces that cause them to erode and disintegrate. According to this perspective, the goal of organizational systems of all types is merely survival.

Open systems ensure their existence through frequent exchange relationships with the surrounding environment in which they operate. In these exchange relationships, open organizational systems nourish the environment and are nourished by it. For this purpose they produce a series of valuable products and services and export them to the environment. At the same time, organizations import from their external environment the essential resources that ensure their continued existence and proper functioning. Hence, this approach renounces the existence of a preset goal or ultimate mission, and negates the importance of organizational goals as an essential component for understanding the structure and operation of organizations. Since this perspective attributes a high degree of egoism, sentimentalism, and impulsiveness to participants of organizations, it distrusts the assertion that they behave rationally from the organization's point of view.

"The political theory," which evolved within the framework of this intellectual approach to the study of organizations, views organizations as arenas for political struggles. In every organizational arena, human beings work alone or as groups to gain the best benefit that can be extracted from the organization with which they are involved.[4] Thus, every stakeholder in this arena does have some objectives, ambitions, and goals of his own, which differ or even contradict those of other stakeholders in the organization. Therefore, in every organization there is an ongoing struggle over the organizational spoils between its competing stakeholders. Thus, "the political metaphor encourages us to see how *all* organizational activity is interest-based and to evaluate all aspects of organizational functioning with this in mind."[5] Organizational survival is a result of the common goal of all stakeholders to preserve the organization and to continue gaining benefits from it. Scott explains this common interest:

> One does not have to posit a survival need for the collectivity itself. It is sufficient to assume that some participants have a vested interest in the survival of the organization. Because it is a source of power, or resources, or prestige, or pleasure, they wish to see it preserved and include among their own goals that the organization itself be protected and, if possible, strengthened.[6]

The functional and the critical perspectives present two opposite views in respect to the way organizations should be perceived and studied. For the former perspective, organizational rationality serves as the key to an understanding of the structure and behavior of organizations; whereas for the latter perspective organizational politics is the main concept for understanding organizations and their dynamics. Both the rational theory and the political theory, like all the other theories that were developed in the area of organizations, are limited in their explanatory capacity and cannot fully cover the complexity of organizations. Therefore, a theoretical line of thought needs to be developed that combines the rational and the political aspects of the mutual relationships that exist in organizational life between individuals, groups, and organizations.

 The theoretical line of thought suggested hereby is an attempt to broaden the political theory and to add some new elements to it, derived in part from the rational theory. This proposal, which is described here for the first time, will be called at this stage *the theory of political shadows*. Drawing upon the open system theory, this theory defines organizations as human productive systems that produce certain products or render specific services for the surrounding environment. This definition does not presume nor does it rule out the existence of an ultimate organizational goal, a final aim, a mission or some loftier purpose as a built-in feature of every organization. Organizations differ from other social systems, such as families or communities, by being productive systems: that is, systems that continuously produce goods or render services. The ultimate purposes that seemingly dictate the production of certain products or services in all organizations, if any do actually exist, are not essential for the understanding of the ways in which organizations are structured and operated. This is because organizations change again and again in their lifetime, as they attempt to adapt themselves to the many conversions that occur in the environments within which they exist and function.

Like any other theory, the theory of political shadows rests on several assumptions regarding the character of organizational activity in general and its actors' behavior in particular.[7] The three basic assumptions of this theory can be noted as follows:

> *The organization-oriented assumption*: This assumption states that, irrespective of personal inclinations, all participants in a given organization work according to the rules and regulations of the organization; hence, they comply with most of the orders and

instructions of their supervisors and managers. Such functional behavior allows the organizations to accomplish their operational objectives, to advance their strategies, to produce goods and services, and to survive over time.

The self-oriented assumption: This assumption states that individuals join an organization and participate in its activities because it is their best alternative in terms of rewards and penalties. These individuals will continue to participate in that organization's activities as long as it is more profitable for them than participating in other organizations, or alternatively as self-employed actors.[8]

The benefit-oriented assumption: The third basic assumption states that actors in organizations use their power and influence over other actors in order to increase their own personal benefit above and beyond what is promised them in return for their activity, even if this political behavior is not regarded as appropriate in those organizations.

On the basis of these postulates, the main argument of the political shadows theory can be formulated as follows:

As a rule, for every organizational behavior there are two sides or faces: The official side which is manifested by compliance with the organizational rules and demands, and the unofficial side which is expressed by utilitarian behavior that exploits every chance to get the best for oneself. These two faces are linked together and complement each other. Thus, every official behavior,[9] namely, behavior performed for the purpose of serving the organization, necessarily consists of unofficial behavior as well. The latter behavior is intended to benefit the individual performer or the person who instructs him to behave in this manner.

Because the official side is usually overt and the political side is covert, this dual behavior may be compared to a figure in the light, accompanied by a vague and obscure shadow. Just like any shadow, so the political shadow changes in its intensity and shape. Sometimes it is long, and sometimes short. In certain conditions of illumination it is strong and visible to the eye, and in other conditions it is too weak and pale to be noticed. Sometimes it is cast behind the object and sometimes alongside it. It takes the same shape as the figure, but yet distorts it to a greater or lesser degree.

Like the behavior of shadows in physical reality, so the political shadows in organizational reality change according to the conditions surrounding them. Organizational conditions and factors that influence the intensity and shape of political shadows are discussed in several chapters of this book.

The political shadows theory takes into account the existence of a structured tension between two types of rational behavior in organizations, that is, organizational rationality and personal rationality. The first type is expressed in the decisions and conduct of active members of the organization to promote the goals of the organization as a whole and to be concerned for its interests, while the second type is expressed by the behavior of active members of the organization whose purpose is to promote their goals, and satisfy their needs for their own personal interests. In many organizational situations the two behaviors cannot coexist since they contradict each other. As a result, preference for one interest is liable to be at the expense of the other, thus creating a tension between the tendency toward conformism and the tendency toward opportunism in the behavior of members of an organization.

On the basis of these assumptions some general propositions may be posited now. The propositions may be later on examined empirically by a suitable research design. The following three hypotheses present typical examples of such theoretical propositions:

- *Mutuality hypothesis*: Given that a certain organizational activity is performed, there should be a positive relationship between the organization's benefit from this activity and the performer's benefit. That is, the more beneficial that activity is to the organization, the more beneficial it is expected to be for the performing actor as well.[10] An unsatisfactory ratio between organizational utility and personal utility may increase the tendency of organizational actors to close this gap in favor of their own by means of self-serving political activities.

- *Clarity hypothesis*: It is expected that in obscure conditions and in ill-defined situations in the organization, active members will adopt political behavior. Hence, situations of uncertainty, fuzziness, conflict and disagreement encourage the politicization of organizations, which is expressed in the propensity of organizational actors to exercise power, exert influence, and take political steps that will lead to clear decisions and to unequivocal definitions of responsibility and authority suitable to their priorities.

- *Stability hypothesis*: An increase in political behavior can be expected in organizations that encounter unstable conditions such as changes of status, decline, crisis or bankruptcy, that is, states in which the established system of rules in those organization are found to be in the process of disintegration. These are situations of transition in which the old order is no longer effective, and a new order has not been sufficiently established. These intermediate "liquidated" states encourage politicization, both because people do not know how they should behave and because people tend to take advantage of changing conditions for their own personal benefit before they miss the window of opportunity.[11]

It should be emphasized that from the present perspective, organizational politics is neither a marginal nor a negligible element of organizational reality—it is an inseparable part of it; hence, it deserves careful attention. By being interwoven within the organizational system and operating according to a certain code, it allows us to explain its place and role in this reality. The political shadows theory explains politics by using the concept of duality, which describes organizational behavior. This concept suggests that organizational behavior projects two conflicting propensities simultaneously: The first is the conformist propensity to obey the regulations of the organization, and the other is the opportunist propensity to exploit advantages for personal profit. This concept can be summarized in the following statement:

> *The Law of Political Calculation*: Whenever an organizational actor is authorized or obliged to choose between several alternative actions for serving the organization, that actor is most likely to choose the alternative that best serves the actor's self interests and own preferences. This "law" foresees that organizational actors—individuals, groups, and organizations—will accomplish their tasks, but in a manner that suits them in the best way. This kind of behavior thus may prove to be optimal for its performer but not necessarily best one for the organization.

This book focuses upon the political behavior of individuals, groups, and organizations that are geared for self-benefit by exercising power and exerting influence over others.[12]

The first chapter in this book discusses in detail the concepts of power and influence as well as the causes and results of these phenomena in organizational activity.

The theory of political shadows serves as an analytical framework for the study of organizations from a political viewpoint. Such an analysis shows that even unselfish behavior patterns that are in line with the organization's interests, contain hidden political self-serving agendas. Moreover, under certain conditions, organizational behavior, that is by no means political, is likely to be interpreted by other actors inside or outside the organization as genuine types of political behavior.

This mode of analysis may shed equal light on both sides of organizational behavior: namely, it's formal as well as its informal faces. The book focuses on the opportunistic aspect of organizations, specifically because this aspect gets less attention than the conformistic aspect in the study of organizations. In addition to the scientific contribution of this line of analysis, the discussion about the political aspect may also be useful for various practitioners such as executives, commanders, and consultants who want to better understand the internal dynamics of the specific organizations that they attempt to influence.

Notes

1.   Thompson, 1967.
2.   See, for example, Morgan, 1986; Scott, 1992; Daft, 2001; Hall, 1999.
3.   Katz & Kahn, 1978; Scott 1992; Clegg, Hardy, & Nord, 1996.
4.   Bacharach & Lawler, 1980; Pfeffer, 1981; Mintzberg, 1983; Morgan, 1986.
5.   Morgan, 1986: 195.
6.   Scott, 1992: 53.
7.   The term "actor" in sociology means the individual, the group, and the organization that is actively involved in a defined social system and conducts mutual interactions with actors who take part in the same system.

8. For a detailed discussion of this postulate see March & Simon, 1958.
9. The professional term "official behavior" means dictated behavior that is officially and requisitely demanded from the participants in the organization by order of the organizational authorities. "Un official behavior" means behavior that is the result of the personal initiative of a participant that does not tally with the organization's policy.
10. See, for example, Kipnis & Schmidt, 1988.
11. Mintzberg, 1985; Hardy, 1989.
12. The first chapter in this book discusses in detail the concepts of power and influence as well as the causes and results of these phenomena in organizational activity.

1

The Essence of Power

This book discusses organizational politics—namely, ways in which people work in different organizations and try to exercise influence upon organizational structures and processes as individuals or groups, in order to achieve specific results. In trying to understand how organizational politics works, it is necessary to study and to understand the phenomenon of power in social reality in general and in the organizational reality in particular.[1] Hence, this chapter deals with the notion of power.

Power is one of the foundations of social life among the human species, as it is for other living creatures of all kinds. In nature, power is embodied in the physical prowess of animals. In human society it assumes many forms. Power is the motivating force that causes diverse types of behavior among individuals, groups, organizations, governments, and nations.

Bertrand Russell, the well-known philosopher, wrote about sixty years ago: "I shall be concerned to prove that the fundamental concept in social science is Power, in the same sense that Energy is the fundamental concept in physics."[2] Since that time considerable intellectual effort has been expended on the part of social scientists in researching the roots of the power phenomenon in human society, and attempting to understand its dynamics and its implications for society and for social life.[3] In the study of organizations, social scholars have dealt with the concept of power from various theoretical viewpoints.[4]

The efforts to explain the phenomenon of power created many different definitions of the power concept. These definitions revealed the conceptual differences among the various social sciences—psychology, sociology, political science, and economics—with regard to the phenomenon of power. Presumably these differences are the result of philosophical interpretations given by various intellectuals and humanists. Nevertheless, in spite of the differences between the definitions, certain commonly accepted components might be found that can characterize the power phenomenon. Moreover, many studies conducted on this subject over recent decades, brought forward a significant number of findings that can delineate the character of the power phenomenon in human society. Agreement is gradually being formed among researchers with regard to the essential nature of power, its sources, expressions, and results.

Therefore, it is appropriate to introduce some of the definitions of the concept of power and to discuss the ideas that they express. This is because power is the key to understanding the phenomenon known as "politics" in social life in general and in organizational life in particular.

Before we commence with the discussion it should be clarified that politics, in its broadest sense, includes all the actions aimed at gaining power and the usage of this power to attain goals and promote interests. The concept of power in politics has somewhat the same meaning as the concept of money in economics. Just as money turns the wheels of economics, so power turns the wheels of politics.[5] Both power and money are valuable resources that are used as bargaining chips in conducting economic deals or political deals between *actors*.[6]

It is no wonder, then, that power and politics have been growing subjects of interest among students of organizations. In their preface to a recent volume of articles, Bacharach and Lawler refer to this trend:

> As organizational politics began to emerge as a specific field of organizational theory some 50 years ago, many empirical studies were published that voiced implicit, if not explicit, political themes. We can look back to such classic works as Selzinck's *TVA and the Grass Roots* (1949), Gouldner's *Patterns of Industrial Bureaucracy* (1954), Crozier's *The Bureaucratic Phenomenon* (1964), Tannenbaum's *Control in Organizations* (1968), Zald's *Organizational Change: The Political Economy of the* YMCA (1970), Allison's *The Essence of Decision* (1971) and even Max Weber's prototypical *Religion of China* (1951) and clearly recognize the examination of organizations from an interest group perspective.[7]

Concepts of Power

"Power is the probability that one actor within a social relationship will be in a position to carry out his wishes despite resistance, regardless of the basis on which this probability rests."[8] This old and famous definition, suggested by Max Weber, is still used today with regard to most of the explanations of the power phenomenon. According to this definition, power is essentially coercion.

This view distinguishes power relationships from other social relationships as being asymmetrical in nature; that is, it deals with a situation in which one actor is capable of fulfilling his or her will in spite of the opposition of others to that will. Such coercion is achieved by the use of negative sanctions; that is, prevention of rewards or application of penalties upon noncompliance:[9] "Power in the present sense means control over rewards and/or penalties that give one actor, A, the capacity to induce otherwise unwilling compliance by a second actor, B."[10]

As it could be expected, this perception of power in social life raised various kinds of critiques and hence different conceptions of power.[11] However, "This seemingly simple definition, which presents the negative rather than the positive aspects of power, has been challenged, amended, critiqued, extended, and rebuffed over the years but, nonetheless, remains the starting point for a remarkably diverse body of literature."[12]

Nonetheless, it is worth presenting here briefly some other views on the power phenomenon. For example, Harvey and Mills suggest expanding the definition of power so that it will include a larger scope of social relationships.

> The definition of power with which we operate here is clearly much broader than this and is motivated by a felt need to conceptualize the general force resting behind all attempts to affect outcomes in social relationships, whether these attempts take the form of outright coercion, influence, or the exercise of legitimate authority. [13]

According to this approach, power is defined on the basis of two main factors: The first is the ability to use negative sanctions (penalties), and the other is the legitimacy (justification) for using power. By means of these two factors, Harvey and Mills distinguish between four types of power.

a.   *Legal Authority*—Power that is based on a strong punishment capability and a high degree of legitimacy, that is to say, a willingness to comply because of a recognized, legally determined authority within a specific official framework.

b.   *Rational Authority*—Power that is based on a weak punishment capability and a high degree of legitimacy, which expresses recognition of the expertise, knowledge, and experience of the person in power.

c.   *Coercion*—Power that is based on a strong punishment capability for enforcing negative sanctions (penalties) and a low degree of legitimacy (repudiation).

d.   *Persuasion and Manipulation*—Power that is based on a weak punishment capability and a low degree of legitimacy that is attributed to power and its usage. [14]

In many cases, power is based on the principle of *deterrence*. The ability of one actor to threaten another with negative sanctions saves him from the need to use his power. The expected negative response is the deterrent factor because of which the demands of the person in power are obeyed. Another aspect of deterrence ability results from the recognition of the fact that one actor possesses power over others in a given system of relationships. This knowledge also decreases the use of negative sanctions since this is also a deterrent factor that prevents resistance against the person in power, especially when this power is legitimized. Whenever there is a conflict between opposing desires of actors in a social relationship, the ability of one actor to overcome the will of the other is a practical expression of power.

The needs, motives, or goals of an actor are generally expressed in certain types of behavior. Persons, groups, and organizations usually tend to fulfill their needs by purposive, goal-directed actions. In the same way, social actors avoid, as much as possible, any behavior that goes against their needs, or behavior that makes it difficult for them to achieve their goals. From this perspective, power reflects a causal factor in human relationships that results in a change of behavior. Therefore, as Dahl suggests, "A has power over B to the extent that he can get B to do something that B would not otherwise do."[15] This definition perceives power as one's control of another's behavior.

Factors that increase the chances that an actor could cause another actor to change his behavior can be "structural factors" such as the role those actors hold in the organization, their place in the hierarchy of authority, or their centrality in the communication network of the organization. As it will be discussed in the chapter on interpersonal politics, there are different levels of power among people who take part in organizational activity compared with others in the organization. These differences result from their degree of proximity to the decision makers of the organization (for example a secretary or an assistant). Similarly, those who are close to centers of power in the external environment, such as government institutions or newspaper networks are likely to have greater power than those who are in remote positions.

Alternatively, factors that determine the power of actors may be psychological factors, that is, factors that are linked to the motivations of actors such as their ambitious drives or their domineering attitude. Power-driven people tend to recruit all their resources to gain power that will enable them to obtain positions of command and control. Persons identified as "politicians" are those actors striving to reach positions of dominance and who make every effort to hold those positions as long as possible.

Talcott Parsons, who treated power as a system resource, addressed a social system perspective of power; like money in economics, power operates as a specific mechanism responsible for creating change in individual or collective actors, interacting within a wider social system. Power is thus a means of coercion as well as consensus for the attainment of collective goals.

> Power then is a generalized capacity to secure performance of binding obligations by units in a system of collective organization when the obligations are legitimized with reference to their bearing on collective goals and where in case of recalcitrance there is a presumption of enforcement by negative situational sanctions—whatever the actual agency of that enforcement.[16]

Michel Foucault contributes another conception of power in social life. From his point of view power should not be perceived as domination by one actor—individual, a group, a class or organization—over other actors. Power is never in any one's possession, since it is neither a commodity nor is it a certain kind of wealth. Instead, power is embedded in everyday details of normal life; it is mainly applied and enhanced by practices of surveillance—personal, technological, administrative, judicial, and so forth. Thus, power is accomplished by language, by cultural practices, by discourse, by moral, and by formal knowledge or expertise. By those means of control compliance becomes not only acceptable but to some extent even desirable.

> Power must be analyzed as something which circulates, or rather as something which only functions in the form of a chain. It is never localized here or there.... Power is employed and exercised through a net-like organization. And not only do individuals

circulate between its threads; they are always in the position of simultaneously undergoing and exercising this power. They are not only its inert or consenting target; they are always also the elements of its articulation. In other words, individuals are the vehicles of power, not its points of application.[17]

A different perspective, as presented by Hannah Arendt, sees the phenomenon of power as a communicative form of action. This conception makes a distinction between power, which rests on the common will of a group or population, and between force, which designates an individual property inherent in a person. Thus,

> Power corresponds to the human ability not just to act but to act in concert. Power is never the property of an individual; it belongs to a group and remains in existence only as long as the group keeps together. When we say of somebody that he is "in power" we actually refer to his being empowered by a certain number of people to act in their name.[18]

Following the communicative interpretation of power, Mats Alvesson maintains that "the power element in communication means a forming and fixing of ideas, the selves of the participants and the preconditions for social interaction."[19] In other words, power is regarded as a dimension of cultural organizing, which influences ideas in such a way that it reinforces asymmetric relations between actors.[20]

The psychological perspective states that a concept of power has to include the element of *intention* to change the minds and behavior of others. Hence, the exercise of power towards another refers to "the capacity to produce intended effects, regardless of the physical or psychological factors on which the capacity rests."[21] According to this approach, the person in power not only takes care to fulfill his intentions through influencing the behavior of others, but also deliberately prevents others from reaching their goals.[22] This perspective emphasizes the subjective aspect and this heightens the complexity of power in social relationships.

Power is far too complex a phenomenon to be explained only by objective terms of causality or by subjective terms of intentions. Power has also to be examined as the ability to bring about certain results via intentional influence over others within an interactive relationship between specific actors. That is, power is the ability to influence that is created in certain social conditions and personal circumstances that occur at the same time. People who attain power of one type or another in circumstances for which they are not responsible, such as a sudden gain in wealth, could translate their power into practical influence over others only if they have the will to influence, the motive to change, or the desire to control.

The common term that appears in many definitions of power is that of *ability*.[23] Ability refers to possible options and not necessarily to their actual implementation. Every actor who has certain capacities that enable him to enforce compliance over another actor enjoys a certain level of power over others. This ability has two aspects: (1) the objective aspect, that is, power which is measured by the quantity and quality of resources of a specific actor with which he or she can influence another actor; and (2) the subjective aspect, that is, the assessment made by one actor about the ability of another actor to enforce his will over him or her in spite of resistance.

The definition of power relationships between actors in terms of causality leads the discussion to the concept of *influence*. It is already forty years since the two psychologists John French and Bertram Raven defined the term 'social influence' as the result expressed by "change in the belief, attitude or behavior of a person—the target of influence, which results from the action, or presence, of another person or group of persons—the influencing agent. Social power is thus defined as the potential for such influence. [24]

There are scholars who interpret the term *influence* as a general expression for all the means aimed at creating a change in the behavior of people.[25] There are also those who distinguish between the term *influence* and the term *authority*, and others who differentiate between influence and *coercion*.[26] According to this distinction, influence can be achieved by various means of persuasion: explanation, propaganda, preaching, and manipulation.

Power is created and used in organizational reality in the interactive relationships between various actors: individuals, groups, and organizations. In most cases these relationships are neither one-time encounters nor are they random. Therefore, power relations between actors usually occur in repetitious patterns of social exchange that are intended to achieve specific goals by the purposive use of various resources. These relationships are designated here as *political games*, and those who are active participants in those games are referred to here as *players*.[27] These players are a part of a larger complex of interconnecting forces that form the "circles of power" in organizations.[28]

The success of the participants in these kinds of political games reflects their ability to bring about the results they desire; that is, to influence others into thinking and behaving in the way they want, especially in the process of decision making in the organization. Thus, the ability of an actor in any organization to influence an organizational decision in his favor despite opposition, expresses the power of that actor in the organization. As it will be seen in the following chapters, power plays a role in a large variety of relationships between individuals, groups, and organizations which are not necessarily connected to decision-making processes in organizations. This applies, for example, to power in a relationship between employees in an organization, or between two professional groups. In these cases, and in many other similar ones, the more powerful actor manages to force his will upon the weaker and to create a change of behavior in the latter.

The sample of definitions and interpretations briefly reviewed here indicates that the notions of power and influence are rather complex and subject to diverse interpretations. Additional treatments of power and influence illuminate these concepts from other viewpoints, raising questions and challenging various assumptions underlying them in which these social phenomena are conceptualized.[29]

The Bases of Power and Its Sources

In order that an actor may realize his ability to influence another, his power must rest upon a basis that is as solid as possible; that is, on an economic basis, a physical or military basis, a religious and ideological basis, and so on. This is an essential yet insufficient condition for the existence of power in a given relationship between two or more actors.

As it has been explained before, the effect of power depends on the ability of an actor to offer a reward of some kind in exchange for the compliance of another actor to his wishes, or by the ability of an actor to punish another in response to noncompliance. Therefore, the basis of any kind of power is contingent upon control over valuable resources that can benefit others, whether these resources are concrete (objects) or abstract (symbols). This control enables the empowered actor to adopt a political stance towards other people—namely, to employ inducements, to threaten penalties, to allow or deny access to resources, as well as to mislead those people.

Most students of power tend to classify the bases of power into different types in accordance with the classification introduced by French and Raven.[30] This classification distinguishes between five different bases upon which people build their power. Later on an additional basis was included.[31]

Coercion

This basis includes physical resources such as the physical power of a heavily built man, weapons and other combat means and control over armies and other armed forces. It enables the actor who holds this power to impose his will over another actor. The potential for destruction and killing of these resources and similar ones is used as a threat on the safety, and property, and even the life of others or of those dear to them. The term *force* describes this type of power in social relations. The beating of women and children, armed robberies, demand of protection money through threats on the safety and property of business people, cases of rape, and terrorist acts—all these are occurrences in which force is used to receive rewards, to protect interests or to maintain control over others through coercion.

The motive to comply when force is threatened or actually used is the fear of the negative outcome of noncompliance. Fear enables the person in power to impose his will upon others and force them to behave in the way he or she wants. This is exactly what a military occupation means. Certain criminal organizations, for example, are maintained by the collection of protection money through terrorizing businessmen and threatening to destroy their property.

Rewards

This power basis includes economic resources such as cash money, credit lines, securities, art treasures, and even assets such as buildings, equipment, and various installations. Such a basis allows the actor who owns the property to promise another actor some economic reward in exchange for compliance, or alternatively to delay the receipt of reward and even to withhold it from the other actor. The desire of people to receive financial rewards motivates them to perform illegitimate acts. Without these rewards it is doubtful if they would have performed such acts.[32]

Preferential treatment in return for bribes is one of the most widespread acts of corruption in government offices, municipalities, and other public institutes. False testimonies given in court, the leakage of classified information, slandering, spying and betrayal—all these are common examples of acts performed by people in exchange for rewards from the wealthy. Here the main motivation for compliance is the financial temptation. In the realm of organizations, too, one may find many examples of "gray" behavior on the borderline of the law. For instance, the appointment of a certain bank representative to a position on the board of directors of a business organization on the understanding that the bank will offer the organization a generous credit line or convenient payment conditions in exchange for the appointment.

Expertise

This basis includes information resources and experience in special fields—resources that are usually based on long-standing professional expertise. Such resources are usually in the possession of academic professionals: doctors, lawyers, architects, psychologists, accountants, engineers, and other professional experts. In the recent past it was the artisans who had a predominant knowledge of the various fields of craftsmanship, and in the more distant past, this was the basis on which sorcerers, witch doctors, soothsayers, fortunetellers, and those of suchlike professions depended.

The social recognition of the professional talents of these experts allowed them to acquire power over those who needed their special services, very often in times of distress. As specialists, they could order their clients to change their habits, to adopt modes of thought and patterns of behavior other than the ones they were accustomed to follow. Although in most cases the exercise of power was intended to benefit the clients such as curing diseases, their expertise was sometimes used also to gain personal benefits for themselves at the expense of the clients. Price extortion, sexual bribery, the illegal acquisition of information, the enjoyment of excessive privileges, and receiving personal service—all these are quite common phenomena of the wrongful exploitation of information resources in exchange for favors in defiance of professional ethics.

Information

This power basis presents one of the most important and valued resources of our times. Information is a commodity that is very much in demand nowadays. For many individuals as well as for most organizations, information is a critical resource for managing their affairs. At present, much more than in the past, every process of forecasting, planning, decision-making, and the like must rest on reliable information. An actor's access to required information gives him the opportunity to exercise power over other actors in need of it, with the intention of obtaining personal benefit. The more classified and rare the information is, the greater is the power of those who possess it. Therefore, it is no wonder that there are an increasing number of cases in which the 'information trade' motivates people to perform illegal and immoral acts, such as industrial espionage, in order to obtain information or to pass it on to others.

Sensitive information that affects privacy is usually found in the hands of doctors, lawyers, journalists, psychologists, and other such people. Professional ethics, and in certain cases even state laws, prohibits them from exposing this information. But classified personal information of this type is also found in our times in the possession of private investigators, of self-employed detectives, of usurers, of debt-collectors, and of the various kinds of intelligence services. For this reason, many people are subject to harassment, to intimidation, and even to blackmail by those who possess classified information about them, information that is sometimes acquired by questionable means. In such circumstances, those who possess the information are able to exercise their power over such people and to demand an exorbitant price, not necessarily in money, for their silence.

Authority

This power basis consists of the authorization granted to those holding positions of various kinds, especially in organizations, to exercise power over others. As opposed to other bases of power, this type of power is limited by definite constraints that restrict its quantitative and qualitative boundaries. In other words, authority is a power that may be used solely over specific actors, under precise conditions, in matters that are determined in advance, and with a limited use of rewards and penalties. Authority is attached to a specific office— it is not a personal trait or private possession of the person in office. Authority is a power that is granted legitimacy, which means it is given the prior consent of those subordinate to the person in authority to obey his/her instructions within a defined set of limitations, because that authority is an inseparable part of the office he or she holds.[33]

Since authority reflects not only ability but also legitimacy, it is often defined as legitimate power. In the organizational society of our time, authority is probably the most prevalent type of power.[34] The expression "exceeding authority" relates to situations where a supervisor in an organization commands his subordinates to perform an action or to refrain from performing it without having the authority to give such commands. In many instances the exceeding of authority is motivated by personal considerations and the desire to gain personal benefit. The so-called *sexual harassment* is a typical example of illegitimate demand made by a senior officer to a junior one for the purpose of gaining personal benefits that exceed the privileges of the senior officer's authority.

Charisma

This basis of power represents extraordinary personal qualities, real or imaginary that some people attribute to a particular person in a particular society and in a particular period. The belief in the existence of qualities such as heroism, wisdom, resourcefulness, and foresight causes people to sympathize with those individuals who are regarded as unique and to comply with their demands. Power of this kind is usually identified with *leadership*. With this type of power as well, people tend to acknowledge a leader's authority in advance, and obey his every demand, usually without question or doubt.

In contrast to authority based on an organizational position, in the case of *charisma* the legitimacy is given not to the position of the leader but to the leader himself because of the personal qualities ascribed to him. On the basis of this power, many leaders in the course of human history have been able to impel millions of people to behave in ways that deviate from universal norms and to carry out actions that would not have been done without the leader's influence, actions such as robbery and plunder, expulsion and exile, murder and torture, and even mass genocide.

In spite of the repeated use of this classification of power bases, there are other researchers who prefer to make another kind of distinction that differentiates between power bases and power sources.[35] However, it is doubtful if this additional distinction contributes to a better understanding of the concept of power. On the other hand, it is worth considering the following analysis that distinguishes between different sources of power in organizations—sources that originate from the characteristics of the organizations in which actors are to be found.[36]

Certainty

The ability of organizational actors (individuals, groups or organizational units) to reduce the level of uncertainty that the organization has to cope with is an important source of power. *Uncertainty* is an existential problem of organizations, which threatens their long-run survival. Hence, every solution that may help the organization to overcome uncertainty constitutes a source of power within it. The power of specialists, scientists, and similar experts, who closely interact with the organizational environment, lies in their capacity to decrease the amount of uncertainty that pervades in the organization.

Supply

The ability of an organizational actor to supply the organization with the essential resources for its operation enables him to gain power. Since organizations are open systems, they are dependent upon the external environment. They therefore need to import various resources that are used as input for the production processes of goods and services. The acquisition of resources, some of them critical for the maintenance of the organization, involves rivalry, power struggles, the search for supply sources, high costs, and other difficulties. That is why every actor who can provide the organization with a necessary resource acquires real power in that organization. Investors, suppliers, consultants, and purchasers gain power in the organization, proportionate to their access to such sources of supply.

Centrality

The location of actor's communication networks, or along the flow of organizational work, is an important source of power to the organization to which he or she belongs. An actor located in the center of organizational work flow or at the center of the organization's communication network is capable of influencing the activities of other actors due to their dependence on him for performing their jobs. This power, therefore, is not dependent on the authority of those actors, because its source is in their structural location. Secretaries, executive assistants, telephone operators, and military signalers represent some examples of employees who are located at various centers of communication networks in organizations. Similarly, supervisors of computerized consoles controlling flow of work and material through production lines are located in central junctions in the flow of work of the organization. Nevertheless, in spite of their centrality, none of them possesses official authority that allows them to use the information for decision-making purposes of their own. What they do have is informal power derived from their central locations in the organization structure.

Familiarity

Organizational actors who are capable of correctly depicting the social landscape, and who know the important people of the organization, are likely to use this familiarity as a valuable source of personal power. Such actors possess *social capital* derived from their interpersonal relationships with influential figures, and they are therefore able to foresee the behavior of those influential figures in critical situations (such as in strategic decision-making processes or in management of crisis situations). For example, specialists in labor relations know how to identify the key people standing behind labor strikes, and to reveal their motives, with whom they are collaborating, and how and what would be the next steps taken by the representatives of the employers and of the employees in such circumstances. Such skills of those specialists as well as of similar experts serve as a good source of power.

Reputation

Organizational actors, who once wielded power, enjoy their reputation as a source of power in the present. People tend to credit others with specific characteristics that they formerly possessed long after they have lost them. Such attribution creates an image that after a time is accepted as a social fact even if it is already irrelevant. This tendency also occurs in situations where the reputation is attributed to groups or organizations, and it serves as a continuous source of power for them. In many countries, union leaders can be identified as people of great power because of their past combativeness, even though they have long ceased to lead the public and have stopped fighting its battles.

Status

The official position of a person in the hierarchy of authority of an organization is a source of power. The higher one's position is in the organizational hierarchy the more power he has. Although people holding senior positions at the top of the organization enjoy high levels of managerial authority, the personal power attributed to them often exceeds their authority. Junior employees are inclined to believe that senior staff members are "strong people" with much influence, even outside the organization. The general tendency is to believe that those people who managed to attain high positions use their organizational status for augmenting their own personal power and this enables them to enforce their will far beyond what their position allows. Hence, people in high organizational positions enjoy a feeling of power derived from their official status and not particularly from the authority that comes with it. This attitude of lower participants in organizations is directed not only towards senior managers and commanders, but also towards their assistants and secretaries, and their professional staff.

Liability

The ability of an organizational actor to offer benefits to others serves as a source of power in organizations. People who see themselves as indebted to an actor who has benefited them, grant him power by their very readiness to fulfill his wishes and to obey his demands. An actor who had considerably benefited others in the organization in the past can count on the gratitude accumulated towards him as a source of power, even in the present. This is a type of power that is possessed by those actors who have an influence over the hiring of workers, the nomination of positions in the organization, promotion in status and wages, and the granting of various emoluments. The feeling of liability towards them is their source of power in organizations. In many countries, civil executives and military commanders, chairmen of boards of directors, government ministers, and members of parliament as well as leaders of political parties depend on this source of power whenever they need to put their power to the test.

These sources of power are not restricted to individuals only; they are used as structural sources of power for organizational units of all kinds. They account for the relative and time-altered power of marketing and sales units, of computer centers and data management units, of research and development units, and of public relations units in organizations. They also explain the power of organizational units such as logistics, transportation, acquisition or maintenance, which enjoy a significant power, even though they are not in the mainstream of the organization. This power is obtained by their control over essential services for the functioning of the organization. From this perspective, one may understand the continuing power of organizations that have lost nearly all their other assets, a power that is based on a reputation that had been built up over the years.

Expressions of Power and Its Symbols

Power is frequently expressed by actors' modes of behavior towards others. Such behavior patterns can be overt and explicit, or covert and implicit, but they all have a common goal, which is above all to convey to the intended audience a message of power. By this message, the person in power intends to influence others to comply with his demands. Since these expressions are an inseparable part of the essence of power, it is appropriate to present them here.

Threatening Actions

The exercise of power in the relationships between actors usually includes the use of different types of resources. With regard to the person in power, the use of any resource is an expense, because resources tend to lose their value after they have been used. Hence, actors in power are inclined to save their resources and obtain their objectives through other means. The most common and, in many cases, the most efficient and decisive way is to make a threat against another person.

The threat is intended to make a clear stipulation between the behavior of a person and the expected outcome that will follow. A threat offers a choice between obeying and disobeying a certain demand, in such a way as to make it clear that noncompliance can result in the receipt of a prescribed penalty. Through the threat of imposing penalties on criminals, the state or municipal authorities ensure the compliance of the population to its laws. Many organizations behave in the same manner, formulating internal rules and regulations that oblige all their members, and that are accompanied by negative sanctions applicable in cases of noncompliance.

The most common expression for this type of stipulation is the "fine option." An offender knows in advance that he will have to pay a fine of some kind if he does not obey a certain law, unless he denies the offense in court. Threats may consist of a warning that benefits will be delayed or denied as a result of noncompliance. From the perspective of an actor who expects a certain reward (such as payment), every delay in receiving it is regarded as an act of punishment towards him. For example, in one industrial firm, the employees had imposed illegal sanctions and prevented the supply of goods to customers. In response, the chief executive officer threatened to delay salary payments. To prevent this threat from being carried out, hundreds of workers gathered one day in the management offices and laid siege to the bureau of the chief executive officer for many hours, damaged office equipment, and harassed him ceaselessly until he yielded and recalled his intention to delay salary payments.

In relationships between actors, a threat is expressed in two ways: (1) *verbally*, and (2) *behaviorally*. These two expressions of threat are quite common, both in interpersonal relations and in interorganizational relations, including relations between countries and world powers. For example, parents and teachers tend to use verbal threats towards children, especially when they are at a young age, such as: "If you do not behave properly, you will be punished by…" Official verbal threats, usually formulated in writing, are the working tools for lawyers who often use them on behalf of their clients. Heads of state use public verbal threats towards rival states, towards terror organizations, and towards various kinds of criminal organizations. Threats of this type are usually expressed in the form of a warning, not necessarily in diplomatic language. Business corporations usually make threats in the form of a declaration of intent to move their enterprises to other countries that would be more convenient and profitable for them. In the era of globalization, these are real threats from the point of view of professional unions, of tax authorities, and of the regional councils where the factories are located.

> We have become increasingly aware of the fact that the effectiveness of an influence attempt, and the aftermath of influence, is a function not only of the basis of power but the mode, or manner, in which it is exercised. An influence attempt can be presented in loud, forceful, threatening, or sarcastic mode; or in a softer, friendlier, light-humored mode. The empirical evidence on the effects of mode is still quite limited, but there is good reason to expect that mode can be a very important component. Adolph Hitler was a master of presenting his coercive demands in a harsh, violent mode, adding emphasis to his threats. We have speculated that hard, sarcastic humor can sometimes increase the threatening quality in the use of coercion. It also appears at times that a clever influencing agent, who feels compelled to use coercion, will couple the coercive influence attempt with a light soft humor. This may avoid the negative and hostile aftereffects, and the undermining of referent and personal reward power, which may result from coercion. And there is, of course, evidence that effects of informational influence can sometimes be enhanced, sometimes reduced, if information is presented in a threatening or fear-invoking manner, as, for example, the use of a fear-appeal by a physician who attempts to convince a patient to stop smoking.[37]

Behavioral threats become explicit in certain actions that people with power apply in order to threaten others. Certain facial gestures, provocative poses, the display of fists, and the drawing of weapons, are only some of the varied actions that are easily recognized by human beings in most cultures as expressing a threat to act violently in case of noncompliance. In international relations, threats of this sort become explicit through the shifting of military forces, re-cruiting reserve soldiers, opening emergency depots, arming missiles, and con-ducting maneuvers near the borders that divide hostile countries. The United States, for instance, is accustomed to move its aircraft carriers, warships, and submarines in a demonstrative manner from their known and fixed locations at sea in order to threaten punitive action against "undisciplined" rulers like those of Libya, Iraq and Iran, North Korea, and other rulers in the wide world.

The practical test for any kind of threat is its level of deterrence. For the threat to really deter the person in question, the possessor of power must be prepared to carry out the threat as an act of punishment for noncompliance. In other words, the difference between a "true threat" and a "false threat" lies in the level of probability that the threat will be executed when required. During the first Gulf War, for example, the Israeli leaders threatened and warned pub-licly several times that if Iraq launched missiles against Israel, the IDF would respond with its full power and with a harsh counter-strike. The Iraqi ruler, Saddam Hussein, was not deterred by the Israeli threat and launched about forty missiles against Israel, which brought no military response in spite of the threats. From the Iraqi perspective, therefore, the Israeli threat was no more than a "false threat." As will be clarified later on, actors take into account the probability of the execution of the threats when deciding whether to comply or refuse to comply with the demands of rival actors.

Penalty Actions

The term *penalty* in the current context means any negative sanction that one actor applies to another in response to noncompliance. Negative sanctions include many different types of action that aim to harm resistant actors. Promi-nent among such negative sanctions are the following types of penalty:

Physical injury. These actions include intentional physical injuries such as beatings, different kinds of physical torture, imprisonment, starvation, and kill-ing inflicted on others. Beating as a punishment for noncompliance is still common in society today among large numbers of husbands towards their wives and fathers towards their children. Until a few years ago, teachers and educators in different cultures used to beat pupils who had committed an offense—with a ruler, a stick, or a whip—as a legitimate and educational act.

In various military organizations around the world it is common for military commanders to beat disobedient soldiers with a rifle butt as an act of punish-ment. Several years ago, there was a public uproar in the United States after a courthouse in Singapore sentenced an American student to be lashed for drugs found in his possession. In Asian and African countries it has been the practice for many years to truncate limbs and to physically mutilate law offenders. Even today there are several ethnic communities in which it is customary to execute moral offenders, especially "women who have desecrated their family honor." The execution of murderers and rapists is common today in several countries, including some states in America. It should also be noted that all governments around the world imprison criminals for lengthy periods. In the past, countries such as France, England, and Russia at one time banished criminals and political renegades to distant and desolate regions where living conditions were extremely difficult, such as Guinea, Australia, and Siberia.

In interorganizational and international relations there is a common tendency to hurt people physically as an act of punishment. Intelligence organizations tend to kidnap and secretly eliminate spies and traitors, assassinate rulers of other countries, and murder people they regard as instigators and rebels. The systematic elimination of those who plan terror attacks and carry them out is viewed by many people in the world as an act of punishment, not as a means to prevent terror attacks. The United States performed several penalty actions of destruction and killing against Libya, Iraq, Iran, Somalia, Sudan, and Afghanistan. These actions were mainly bomb attacks from the air and the sea and the launching of missiles at these countries. The United States' authorities had no compunction for capturing the former ruler of Panama, General Manuel Noriega, who had encouraged the smuggling of drugs, and did not hesitate to incarcerate him in an American prison for many years.

Economic injury. These actions generally take the form of monetary fines. Local and state authorities, civilian and military employers, academic institutions, leasing and renting companies, and moneylenders—all these and others usually impose fines as a penalty action for not respecting the law, for breaking a contract, or for disobeying the orders of superiors. The ability of an actor—individual or group—to impose a fine on another actor is an expression of power, which is proved when the fine is actually collected. Governments, municipalities, and local authorities that have failed to collect fines have lost power in the eyes of the public because they exposed their weakness and inability to enforce the laws and regulations in the area of their jurisdiction. This weakness is revealed once and again in various large cities all over the world, in which an enormous number of parking tickets are deliberately not paid by violators who take advantage of the difficulties of the law-enforcing authorities to collect the fines or to bring drivers to justice.

Another kind of economic injury that is inflicted in response to noncompliance takes the form of suspending the flow of funds or economic rewards. Shutting down credit lines, applying an economic blockade, closing off supply lines for goods, raising tariffs and limiting imports, the freezing of bank accounts and cancellation of financial contracts—all these represent some of the methods of this type of economic injury. The United States applies this kind of policy towards countries that they define as "rogue states" and terrorist organizations in order to "teach them a lesson." Among them are Cuba, the former Soviet Union, and the Republic of China at an earlier period, Libya, North Korea, Iran, Iraq, and others. All the Arab countries enforced an economic boycott against Israel for many years, and Egypt even blocked the passage of ships supplying goods to and from Israel through the Suez Canal. Israel conducted this kind of policy recently towards the Palestinian Authority in response to the rising terror attacks, acts of sabotage and shootings against Israeli citizens.

Business corporations apply explicit or implicit financial pressure on suppliers and contractors who do not live up to their expectations or upon those who give preference to their competitors. It is a known fact that wealthy parents sometimes deny their sons and their daughters financial means as well as legacies as punishment for behavior of which they do not approve. Associations and funds of all kinds also impose an economic ban on organizations that do not comply with their demands on issues such as environmental health, human rights and freedom, public health, and animal welfare. The difficulty inherent in the application of economic penalties of this type is in the need for it to be consistently upheld for a long period of time. Actors who apply economic penalties may soon discover that they have to change their policies as a result of internal or external pressure. Every enforced change of this kind damages the reputation of the powerful actors and decreases their actual power accordingly. The success of economic penalties depends, therefore, on the ability of the power holder (individual, group, organization or state) to maintain his or her policies of economic penalty for as long as necessary.

Bribery Actions

Many actors prefer the "carrot method" to the "stick method" when it comes to using their power to obtain compliance to their demands. Actions of this type are mainly expressed in two ways: *temptation*, and *compensation*. The carrot method is based on the offering of financial grants and other rewards which are of value and use to other actors who aspire to obtain them for themselves.

Temptation. One of the wittiest phrases on this subject is credited to the famous British dramatist, Oscar Wilde, who once said: "I can resist everything except temptation" (*Lady Windermere's Fan*, 1892). Most people obviously aspire to obtain more money and to increase the capital they possess. The financial motive impels people to commit actions that they would not have done if it were not for the financial profit promised to them in return for their behavior. Naturally, most people are willing to work for wages, salaries, or for other forms of remuneration. However, many people agree to engage in activities that are not respectable, such as the drug trade or prostitution, because they are tempted by a high financial reward. In extreme cases, the desire for profit leads to unusual acts such as surrender, treason, total commitment, self-abnegation, and abasement.

It is therefore no surprise that many actors take advantage of human greed to exercise their power over them and to obtain their desires in this way. One of the most widespread and efficient methods of this type is the promise of a monetary bribe in exchange for compliance with certain demands that are illegal or immoral. Many employees of public and private organizations become targets for this type of temptation: in exchange for a bribe offered to them, people are asked to supply classified information (spying) or to give preferential treatment in appointments to desirable positions or in tenders for the supply of goods and services (favoritism). In other instances, they are asked to denounce their colleagues at work (slander), to spread false information in the organization (deception), or to mislead their employers (fraud). Quite naturally, the chances of response to this kind of temptation increase with the amount of money offered as bait.

The promise of a monetary bribe is one of the most widely used instruments employed by espionage organizations, by organized crime, drug dealers, and even by police organizations throughout the world. Monetary bribes are an inseparable part of the business dealings of corporations that function in Third World states in Africa, Asia, and Latin America. In many cases bribes are promised to government ministers, to senior officers, to judges, and to public representatives. Even the economic powers tend to offer poorer states enormous sums in exchange for compliance with their demands. The administration of President George W. Bush, for example, promised the Turkish government billions of U.S. dollars as economic aid if it would allow American forces to attack Iraqi targets from Turkish soil.

The greed for profit is a human weakness that exposes people to temptation by those who are wealthy. Lust is another weakness. And an additional temptation in exchange for cooperation is a "sex bribe." This very efficient means is serviceable for various actors—individuals, groups, and organizations—including respectable state organizations (for example, foreign offices and embassies of different countries) to influence certain people to comply with illegitimate demands imposed on them. It has been found that very often women who work in organizations have promised sexual favors to their superiors in exchange for professional advancements in status or salary. Generally speaking, sexual services are part of the reservoir of resources available to actors in human society and are used to gain power and to assist political maneuvers inside and outside organizations. In this connection, it is worth mentioning the success of some Islamic religious leaders in tempting impoverished and hotheaded youngsters to serve as suicide bombers in exchange for the promise of eternal life with many beautiful women in Paradise after their death as martyred heroes (*shahid*).

Compensation. The method of compensation is based on the payment of revenue, the granting of monetary awards, or the giving of any other kind of recompense in exchange for obedient behavior. The very granting of an award expresses power. It demonstrates the real ability of a certain actor to generously repay anyone who cooperates with his wishes. The greater the value of the compensation, the greater is the corresponding attributed power of the actor who grants it. Compensation of this type is frequently given without any explicit promises in advance. Unlike the method of temptation, compensation is only given retroactively to the person who cooperates.

The granting of monetary awards as a sign of appreciation to members of an organization for their devotion, hard work, and excellence is widely practiced everywhere nowadays. Many such awards express, in effect, the ability and desire of the employers and wealthy owners to give appropriate public honor for compliance with their interests. This is therefore a clear message of economic power. Indeed, private organizations grant significantly large monetary benefits to some of their employees, mostly to managers, whereas public organizations limit themselves to symbolic sums of money.

The foreign aid that the United States grants annually to Israel, Egypt, and Jordan—aid that amounts to large sums of money, food surpluses, military equipment, research and development funds, and economic guarantees—is one example of the compensation method employed by an economic power to the benefit of poorer countries that cooperate with its international policy. The Japanese government does this by means of investments and loans, while Germany prefers to grant economic benefits through valuable gifts such as civilian and military vessels, medical and educational establishments, and industrial enterprises.

Governments generally grant compensation to residents who agree to live in remote areas that are politically sensitive or subject to attack such as border settlements, regions of sparse vegetation, districts with scanty population, and so on. Such compensation is expressed by exemption from taxes and municipal rates, by special grants, by exceptional investments in the development of infrastructure and the promise of jobs and housing. All these are given to those residents in exchange for their cooperation with government policy and their support for the interests of the state by residing in such places. The many benefits granted over many years to the settlers in Judea, Samaria, and the Gaza Strip is one example of the "carrot method" form of economic compensation. Other examples can be found, of course, in other countries.

Symbolic Expressions

Similar to symbolic expressions of social status, social power is also frequently expressed by demonstrative symbols. The symbols of power are an indispensable part of the political language through which *political discourse* takes place in various social frameworks, including different types of organizations.

Political language enables the assignment of appropriate meaning to political activities so as to become legitimate and thus acceptable to members of a given social system. Such justification allows the actors who possess power to enlist support for their decisions and actions and to buttress their power. Political language also helps to undermine the status of rival actors and to raise doubts as to their power. Words and phrases can be used as weapons in political struggles and as supplemental means to gain influence over the thoughts, emotions, and behavior of others.

Symbolic objects and behaviors also constitute part of the overall expressions of power and the political use made of them to achieve desirable goals. Due to their hierarchical and formal nature, most organizations make extensive use of power symbols for the purpose of creating a clearly established distinction among their participants.

> The provision of social actors with the symbols of power both ratifies their power position within the organization and provides them with power because of the symbols. In a situation in which social power may be difficult to assess, the provision of clear signals of power conveys to others the fact that social actors who possess these symbols have come to be valued and revered in the organization. This social definition of power becomes, through its physical manifestation in the form of symbols, a shared reality, which serves to convey power to those possessing the symbols.[38]

The use of title and rank, by a special term, method of address, salute, bow, nod of the head, and kiss of the hand, are some of the of verbal and bodily expressions of submission towards powerful people that are practiced in different cultures. Power holders take great care in demonstrating their power through both official and non-official symbols.

Throughout history, it was the practice for kings, rulers, military commanders, religious leaders, and other men of authority to decorate themselves with rank insignia, badges, special dress (such as uniforms, robes, crowns, helmets), with staffs and batons, jewelry (such as rings and bracelets), and with other trappings for the purpose of symbolizing their power to the ruled population. Ever since recorded time, those in power have resided in palaces, castles, and luxurious mansions, surrounded by walls and guards. The use of special vehicles (splendid carriages, official cars, private trains and airplanes) was also meant for the same purpose. The well-known excuse for using such symbols is the importance of the personal safety of these superior personages. In fact, all these practices represent some of the side benefits and the perks that these power holders enjoy.

In the different kinds of contemporary organizations, it is customary to symbolize the power of managers and executives by the size, location, and luxury of their offices, by their reserved parking lots, by private dining halls, and even by their exclusive restrooms. These symbolic expressions concretely emphasize the hierarchy of authority in the organization and the location of each actor in the rungs of power. This system of symbols is consistently applied in various subunits within the organization: divisions, departments, sections, and the like. The location of each of these units in the organizational compound, the size of the area assigned to each of them, the number of floors, and the luxury standard of the buildings and installations in which the workers are placed—all these symbolize their proportionate power in the organization. Even if this geographical layout cannot change at the same rate as the changes in the balance of power within the organization, it still constitutes part of the political discourse in organizations.[39]

Many countries demonstrate their power through military marches in which they display their sophisticated armaments, or by airplane fly-bys and naval vessels sailing by in procession. Another way for the symbolic demonstration of technological and economic power is participation in various international exhibitions where countries show off their best products. Even in world sport competitions, such as the Olympics Games or the World Cup, there are symbolic expressions of power—personal, educational, and cultural—in which many countries differentiate themselves from the others.

Business organizations, mainly the biggest and richest of them, occasionally hold extravagant displays of their products to a select invited audience, not necessarily from among its clients. Such displays are accompanied by lavish meals, cocktail parties, granting of gifts, arranging of organized tours, and so on. Beyond the business objectives of these events, there lies the hidden agenda of the organizations to demonstrate their economic strength and political power. Even the support for artistic and educational activities, the public funding of parks and outdoor statues, and other acts of charity, carry a symbolic meaning, which is to display for the public the power of the organization.

Some of the symbolic expressions of power are those of the social establishment, that is, symbols and ceremonies that are identified among the general public and accepted by most people as symbols of legitimate power. These consist, for example, of things such as pistols, truncheons, handcuffs hung on the belts of police officers. But there are also other symbols of power whose significance is not generally known to all, because they are incorporated within a certain subculture—for example, symbols of power that are common among criminal gangs, religious sects, or secret orders.

To sum up, in spite of the differences between the various symbols of power, all are intended to indicate to the other that the power holder is liable to use his power as needed in order to enforce his authority. Symbols of power serve, therefore, as deterrent mechanisms against rejection, opposition, rebellion, and complaint.[40]

Conclusion

The phenomenon of power holds a central position in social life everywhere. This form of energy takes many alternating forms in human society, and serves as a preventive force against numerous actions both at the level of individual and group behavior and at the level of all types of organizations. Therefore, actors of all kinds seek to amass power and tend to use it to acquire personal benefit, to derive something of value, and to gain control over others. It is no wonder, then, that power struggles are an important component in the system of relationships between social actors, both for individuals and for groups. The relations between parents and children, teachers and pupils, those in charge and those subordinate to them, all involve a continual challenge to acquire power and to employ it.

The study of power that has been conducted mainly in the twentieth century has produced many definitions and interpretations, none of which have been equally accepted among scholars. Nevertheless, there are some characteristics of the power phenomenon that allow for an understanding of its essential nature and its use in order to explain various social phenomena. These characteristics have been described and illustrated in this chapter.

Most of the definitions of the power concept see power first and foremost as ability, possibility or potential. Power is therefore the possibility afforded the actor to realize his wishes by means of others and to obtain the results he desires, even if the other shows resistance to it. According to this conception, power exists even when it is not actually exercised. This potential creates a causal connection between the behavior of social actors within given conditions.

Power is revealed in various forms in social life. One of the forms of power is physical coercion; another is authority acquired through its legitimacy; and a third form is deceit, obtained through misleading the other. Whatever the form, power acquires practical expression through the degree of influence it has on others, that is, in its very achievement of the goals for which it is exercised.

Power depends on a number of basic factors and is derived from several sources. The basic elements of power are the various resource reservoirs that actors control or have access to. These basic elements include physical resources, economic resources, and knowledge resources, resources of ideas, personal resources, and information resources. As we shall see in the following chapters, each type of resource enables its possessor to take the political steps aimed at influencing others to behave in the manner desired by the power holder in specific circumstances.

In various social frameworks, such as in different kinds of organizations, structural and existential problems are created that have no tested and prescribed solution. In such circumstances, those actors who are capable of supplying suitable solutions or assist in finding them will acquire power. This is the case also for actors who attain key positions in production processes, in the communications network, and in the role assignment system of the social frameworks within which they play an active part. These circumstances constitute sources of power from which the actors derive their ability to influence the decision-making processes and their results.

With the aim of successfully influencing their intended actors, the power holders perform various actions and activate a variety of means with the purpose of expressing the full weight of their power in an open and clear manner. These expressions of power include verbal and behavioral threats, penalty actions both physical and economic, temptations through the promise of benefits, and the granting of compensation and awards. Such expressions highlight the power of those in authority, helping them to enlist support for their position and activities, and make it easier for them to fight against those who oppose them inside or outside the organization.

In organizational reality, power serves as the main resource through which individuals, groups, and organizations can participate in power struggles of various kinds that are identified in this book as "political games." This indicates that power constitutes the main exchange means that social actors employ in organizational politics in order to derive the greatest possible value from their participation in the organization and from their investments in it. This value implies the obtaining of more rights, benefits, assurances, advantages, and pleasures than they are entitled to receive, if at all, by virtue of official regulations and contracts. Therefore, the political shadows that accompany most of the behavior of organizational actors are the key to understanding organizational dynamics and to interpreting the power struggles that are conducted among the various parties concerned within organizational reality.

Notes

1. The term "power" is not identical with the word "force," although many people err in using these words as though they were synonyms. The difference between these terms will be clarified and emphasized in various chapters of this book.
2. Russell, 1938: 18.
3. See, for example, Mills, 1956;
4. See, for example, Weber, 1947; Cyret & March, 1963; Thompson, 1967; and Pettigrew, 1973.
5. For a detailed comparison of the role of money in economics and that of power in politics, see Parsons, 1963.
6. The term "actor" is used in sociology to define individuals, human groups, organizations of all kinds and business corporations, states, and international institutions (such as the United Nations) which constitute clearly defined entities that conduct interactive relationships with other actors.
7. Bacharach & Lawler, 2000: ix.
8. Weber, 1947: 152.
9. Blau, 1964.
10. Samuel & Zelditch, 1989: 288
11. For a collection of articles presenting different interpretations of power, see Lukes, 1986.
12. Hardy & Clegg, 1996: 623.
13. Harvey & Mills, 1970: 202-203.
14. Harvey & Mills, 1970: 203.
15. Dahl, 1957: 201.
16. Parsons, 1963b.
17. Foucault, in Lukes, 1986: 234.
18. Arendt, 1970: 44.

19. Alvesson, 1996: 3.
20. On the communicative perspective of power, see also Habermas, 1984.
21. Wrong, 1996: 22.
22. Bates, 1970.
23. The ancient Latin root of the word "power" (in French pouvoir) is posse which means "to be able."
24. Raven, 1992: 218.
25. For example: Tedeschi & Bonoma, 1972; Wrong, 1996.
26. See, for example, Bacharach & Lawler, 1980.
27. Chapter 6 in this book is devoted entirely to the description and classification of political games in organizational life.
28. Clegg, 1989.
29. See, for example, Bachrach & Baratz, 1962, 1970; Goldman, 1972; Lukes, 1974; Clegg, 1979, 1989; Galbraith, 1983; Boulding, 1989; Reed, 1989; Nicolson, 1996; Gergen, 1999; Gabriel, Fineman & Sims, 2000; Weick, 2001.
30. French & Raven, 1960.
31. Raven, 1992.
32. It is unnecessary to note that many people choose to perform actions that are desirable and useful to society not only because of the benefits they derive from them, but also because of monetary inducements without which they would not be prepared to act. The entry of idlers into the work force, the rehabilitation of drug addicts, the reformation of criminals, and the agreement of rapists to undergo medical treatment are some of the examples of the influence of monetary rewards on the drastic changes in deviant behavior patterns.
33. Samuel, 1996: 107-132 (Hebrew).
34. It is worth noting here that among the researchers there are those that distinguish between the concept of power and the concept of authority, and between that and the concept of persuasion, since in their view these concepts represent three separate phenomena that are expressed in different ways in social life. See the discussion on these distinctions and the bibliographical references in Samuel & Zelditch, 1989.
35. See this kind of differentiation in Bacharach & Lawler, 1980.
36. Pfeffer, 1997: 145-146.
37. Sutton 1982, quoted in Raven, 1992: 223.
38. Pfeffer, 1981: 54.
39. Pfeffer, 1981.
40. Samuel & Zelditch, 1989.

2

The Theoretical Basis

In order to understand how power merges with politics and how politics is conducted in social life in general and in organizational life in particular, we should make use of some relevant theoretical tools. In light of the importance of the power phenomenon, and in consideration of the frequency and influence of politics in social life, social scientists have devoted a great deal of attention to such phenomena. As a result, during the past fifty or sixty years, a large number of books and scientific articles that deal with this subject have been published. In these studies various theoretical assumptions have been presented and discussed, some of which have been put to empirical test in scientific research. Many of the efforts that were devoted to the study of the causes and consequences of power were conducted in the form of laboratory experiments. Many were based on questionnaires and interviews, and a few were even tested through the computerized simulation of social processes.[1] In spite of these attempts, a tested and accepted general theory of power and politics has not yet been formulated.

At the present state of the art, there are several theoretical models, of which some have been more extensively tested than others, trying to explain the phenomenon of power and its political manifestations in social life. Most of these theories represent a variety of perspectives about the phenomena of power and politics. But despite the intellectual differences among scholars dealing with this subject, we now have several theoretical explanations, albeit partial ones, for the ways in which social actors amass power and use it for their political purposes. Moreover, these theoretical models allow us to predict, to some level of confidence, the chances of success of political measures that are applied in different situations. Therefore, we should first get to know the major theories of power and pay attention to their advantages and disadvantages. With the help of these theories we would better understand the political dynamics of organizations.

Before introducing some theories of power and politics, a distinction must be made between structural theories and behavioral theories. Structural theories suggest explanations of the ways in which certain social conditions enable some actors to generate power and enforce other actors to be dependent on other ones.

For example, power relations exist between military commanders and their subordinates regardless of the mode of behavior of the former toward the latter, and vice versa. On the other hand, behavioral theories assume that power relations are created as a result of behavioral patterns that people conduct towards others. An example for this kind of argument would be the power relations created between men or woman who behave in a violent and dominant manner towards their obedient spouses.

Dependence Theory

In essence, *dependence theory* suggests that power is a direct result of the mutual dependence among actors.[2] This theory rests on the following assumptions: (a) social actors (people, groups, organizations) develop mutual relationships with other actors for the purpose of gaining benefits (rewards, rights, advantages); (b) these relationships usually emerge within some established social framework (family, community, organization); and (c) the outcomes of these relationships are affected by the composition of the participating actors as well as by their behavioral patterns.

The main argument of this theory is that in a given social setting in which there are two or more actors, power relations are most likely to emerge among them. These power relations are mainly determined by the interdependence of these actors. That is, the more one actor (B) is dependent on another actor (A), the greater the relative power of A will be over B, and vice versa. In such a situation, the *power advantage* of every actor is proportional to the gap between the magnitudes of power possessed by all the participating actors.[3] Therefore, the utility that one actor expects to gain from his relationships with another actor is conditioned by his dependency on that actor and the relative power the other actor has over him.

Assuming that some actor wishes to attain a specific end result, the *dependence* of an actor upon another is the outcome of two factors. The first factor is *utility*, that is, the importance or necessity that the actor attributes to achieving this specific result, for instance, the obtaining of a resource such as money or information. The second factor is *exclusiveness*, that is, the extent that such an actor has to rely on one source of supply of the desirable resource. The greater the desire for or need of a certain actor to receive a specific benefit, the greater his dependence on the source which is capable of supplying him with the desired benefit. An example of such exclusiveness is the child whose livelihood is dependent solely on the single parent that provides for the family. However, the greater the number of sources from which an actor can obtain the benefit, the lesser will be his dependence on any one of them. This is the case, for example, of a client who is given many offers from suppliers for their goods. We see here that the dependence of one actor on another is determined by the influence of the two factors at one and the same time. Therefore, the power that an actor has over another is a direct result of the degree of utility attributed to the resource in his or her possession and also to the degree of exclusiveness that he or she possesses over that resource.

Power is expressed through demands made upon others to comply with the will of the power holder. That is, an actor who holds power instructs another actor to perform certain acts or to refrain from acting in a certain manner, against his or her will.

For example, during the course of the Gulf War that occurred in 1991, the former president of the United States, George Bush, demanded from the prime minister of Israel at that time to refrain from military response to the hail of ballistic missiles launched against the State of Israel by order of the Iraqi ruler, Saddam Hussein. And indeed, contrary to the views of several government ministers, army officers, and military experts, foremost among them being the then defense minister, Israel curbed itself and refrained from responding to the Iraqi aggression.

In practical terms, one's level of dependence on another is determined by the financial, physical, psychological, or social price that the former is required to pay to the latter in return for receipt of the desired reward. The higher the dependence, the more expensive is the price. For instance, the dependence of elected governors on their political partners is indicated by the sums of tax-payer money that they are forced to allocate to welfare purposes, contrary to their own preferences.

This is also the case with regard to punishment. Power relations and the dependence among actors determine the nature of the punishment for noncompliance or lack of cooperation, and this punishment might even be the delay or denial of rewards. The greater the power, the greater is the expected penalty. Therefore, the greater the dependence, the greater the expectation will be of compliance, even if the price is high. For example, in countries where a totalitarian regime is in power, the punishment for any deviation from the laws and regulations of the authorities is expected to be severe: imprisonment, persecution, exile or execution. Awareness of this fact causes citizens to behave with absolute obedience and to refrain from any public expression of political protest. The feelings of fear, alienation, and isolation are part of the socio-psychological price entailed by such compliance.

According to the *dependence theory*, the power-dependence relationships are essentially structural. These mutual relationships are embedded in social systems and constitute an inextricable part of them. The concepts of power and dependence in this context have two meanings: objective and subjective. In a given social system, the power or dependence of actors is derived from their roles (parent, manager, student, soldier), as well as their status in that social setting (seniority, primacy, position). However, the way in which those actors perceive and assess their interrelationships, determines their sense of power and dependence, and influences their patterns of behavior accordingly.

The use of power, therefore, is almost always based not just on the objective conditions of dependence but also on the judgments actors make about these conditions. The dimensions of dependence are the criteria by which actors synthesize and summarize the multitude of conditions underlying a power relationship.[4]

The participants in those social systems can affect the outcomes by their modes of behavior, and will tend to act in ways that will decrease their dependence on others.

The ways to change the level of dependence are: (a) finding alternative sources to obtain the sought for rewards, inside the system or outside it, under better conditions; (b) lessening the worth or importance of the desired reward in the eyes of the actor who wishes to obtain it; (c) compromise with a substitute instead of the sought for reward; (d) giving up both of the original reward and its substitute.

These decisions and actions represent only a few of the political measures that actors take to lessen their dependence and to increase their power over others. Dependence theory claims that the mutual relationship in which one actor has more power than the other is an asymmetrical relationship and therefore an unstable one. For that reason actors tend to alter in the direction towards greater symmetry. All the changes leading to lesser dependency represent possible ways to equalize the social system and to bring it into a state of stability.

Here is a concrete example of the dependence theory in organizational reality. The growing need of organizations for an ongoing flow of updated information, and their entry into the computer era, has given rise to organizational units dealing with data. The mounting dependency of managers, planners, scientists, accountants, and other professional workers on incoming data had raised the importance of these units in many organizations. By their control of the computer centers, the staff of these units had grown significantly, and they had begun to employ computer scientists, systems analysts, programmers, operators, and maintenance workers.

These units and their managers gradually began to acquire power in the organizations in which they worked. They took an active part in important organizational decisions such designing production processes, in formulating procedures, and in planning organizational structures. Moreover, they had determined for other functionaries within the organization what kind of information should be furnished to them. In knowledge-based organizations such as universities, research and development centers, and medical laboratories, such data-handling units actually controlled the flow of scientific information as well as the flow of administrative information. As a result of these developments, information workers obtained relatively higher salaries, and some extra fringe benefits. Furthermore, various organizations promoted the managers of such subunits to higher status jobs, as high as the level of vice presidents. It is no wonder then that their influence on important decisions increased considerably.

In recent years, following the accelerated development of computer technology, this situation has changed. Many organizations have bought and installed, in their various departments and units, small high-quality computers for local workstations. Today personal computers stand on every office desk. Scientific and professional information today is handled separately from the administrative information of the organization. Many computer centers have been taken apart, central computers have been eliminated, and most of their workers are scattered throughout the organization. Many organizations have transferred the management of their administrative data, such as salary calculations, to the hands of external sub-contractors. The number of laptop computers is swiftly increasing, and many workers use them at any place they need to be for their work. Worldwide-computerized communication networks supply to all who are interested enormous amounts of information in all fields in real time. In short, the handling of information has quickly entered the era of decentralization and globalization.

In these changing circumstances, the past dependence on central information units in organizations has decreased to a great extent. The multiplication of information sources has opened unprecedented supply possibilities. Working with computers and linking up with communication networks have become fairly simple, and therefore the dependence of users on the "computer experts" has diminished; by the same token, customers of information have become less dependent on exclusive specialists. In fact, the relative power of data management subunits is decreasing in organizations, exactly as expected by the *dependence theory*.

Exchange Theory

Exchange Theory in sociology views mutual relationships between human beings and groups as a process in which social transactions are being made and favors are transferred from one actor to another.[5] Unlike economic theories, social exchange theory argues that even expressions of love, esteem, respect, assistance, acceptance, and of support are valuable goods which people transfer from one to another in social life.

The sociologist, Peter Blau, explained, over forty years ago, how numerous kinds of acts taking place in everyday life display the real nature of social exchange.

> Neighbors exchange favors; children, toys; colleagues, assistance; acquaintances, courtesies; politicians, concessions; discussants, ideas; housewives, recipes.[6]

Since such transfers are simple rewards, they do not have fixed and uniform prices set in advance. Although every favor that is given by one actor to another obliges the receiver to reciprocate properly, in most cases there is no exact specification for the value of that payment. Economic theories tend to focus on specific transactions, considering them as deals made on one occasion, between buyers and sellers. Exchange theory, on the other hand, perceives social transactions as ongoing processes in which mutual relationships between actors are formed and behavioral patterns of the "give and take" kind emerge over time.

The primary assumption of exchange theory maintains that the needs of people exceed the resources at their disposal to satisfy them. *Needs* are the practical expression for goals, for aspirations, for desires, for preferences, and for similar wills. Therefore, the assumption is that people choose the partners with whom they form exchange arrangements for resources. In other words, exchange relationships are outcomes of desired rewards by their partners. The choice of partners for exchange purposes is based mostly on past experience or on the expected results of the exchange to occur in the future. Social actors tend to initiate exchange relationships without bargaining ahead about conditions, and generally without any prior agreement. Exchange relationships are also characteristic of groups and organizations interested in obtaining benefits and achieving desirable results that are not necessarily of economic value, such as prestige, political support, or favorable public opinion.

According to this theory one might expect that every actor would try to obtain the greatest possible value from his exchange relationships without having to pay an excessive price. The results of such exchange depend, on the one hand, upon the resources at the disposal of each actor, and upon the degree of urgent necessity of these results for both sides. That is to say, the participants in exchange relationships will continue to take part in them as long as they profit from them. The profit of the participants is the cumulative result of give-and-take over a period of time, and not of any single transaction per se. Therefore, even a decision to continue or to stop certain exchange relationship is based on a series of past transactions rather than on the appraisal of a single deal. In exchange relationships power differences between the participants are likely to develop. The power of each actor, according to this theory, is the direct result of the quantity and quality of physical, economic, social, political, and psychological resources at his disposal. Therefore, the richer the reservoir of resources, the greater is the power. And the greater the power of the actor, the better will be the results of the exchange relationship for him or for her. Research supports this assertion, and shows that power has a direct influence on the outcomes of the exchange.[7] This was, for example, the balance of the exchange relationship that prevailed in Europe for hundreds of years between owners of estates (feudal lords) and farmers (vassals) who were subordinate to them.

It is worth stressing that exchange relationships are not necessarily equal or balanced relationships. On the contrary, in most cases they are based on differences of power between the actors involved in them, such as parents and children, teachers and students, commanders and private soldiers, and even between couples. In cases like these, the more powerful actors are expected to obtain more and to give less, while the less powerful ones are expected to receive less and to give more. Power then determines the exchange ratio between the mutually transferred favors from side to side. The exchange ratio expresses what one side is required to give in a deal in lieu of what the other side will receive from it.[8]

So long as it concerns goods and services that can be measured in quantitative terms, the calculation of an exchange relationship is quite a simple matter. However, as we have already said, the participants in a social exchange relationship give and receive social and psychological benefits that cannot be quantified; neither are they measurable in monetary units. In such cases, the exchange relationship is a subjective matter that is determined by the feelings and the assessments of the participants.

In light of the importance of power in exchange relationships, it might be expected that every actor would take measures to improve his bargaining position. These measures would generally be political ones; that is, each participant will act to strengthen his position and establish his independence in the social system in which the exchange relationship is conducted, so that he can demand more and offer less in return. This improvement is possible if an actor is able to increase the quantity of resources in his or her possession, such as knowledge and skills, or to expand the reservoir of resources available to him or to her. In this way that actor will amplify his or her relative power in the social system in question. It is also not unusual for actors to take various cunning and deceptive measures. Such methods allow them to present an apparently strong bargaining position based on a power that does not actually exist.

People and organizations that possess great power, such as the rich and wealthy, tend to make use of it for their own benefit. However, the very use of power depletes it, for two main reasons: first, power consumes resources that deplete their quantity in the owner's possession. For instance, every military use of arms and ammunition to obtain a desired objective reduces the reserves of the organization using it. This applies also to the use of money, natural resources, advanced technology and secret information. Second, the repeated use of resources on which power relies creates an increasing dependency on the required exchange and on the actor that supplies it. This dependency changes the balance of power between the participants. Therefore, the more often power is used, the more balanced the exchange relationship will become in time. It is possible to predict then that unequal exchange relationships, in which one actor has a power advantage over another, are liable to change in the direction of a more balanced relationship. In other words, unequal exchange relationships are unstable and imply future change.[9]

The so-called labor relations in organizations serve as another example of the ways in which social exchange takes place. Employees and employers in most organizations are used to exchanging demands and counter-demands with regard to employment terms and conditions. This type of labor relations is meant to lead to an agreement on the results of this exchange—namely, to define the demands of the employer from the employees, and the benefits that will accrue to the employees in exchange for their contribution to the organization. For this purpose, representatives of both sides engage in a continuous process of discussion and bargaining between them. Some parts of this dialogue take place in the form of explicit and official negotiation, whereas other parts of it are merely transmissions of implicit messages through various channels and with the help of different intermediaries.

The issues under consideration naturally concern wages and salaries, fringe benefits, work hours, tasks and requirements, and so forth. Therefore, labor relations are based on a conflict of interests identified as *distributive conflict*. This is a conflict concerning the division of resources that are limited both in quantity and quality. The representatives of the employees and of the employers attempt to enlarge their share of the "organizational pie," leading to a political fight conducted in the form of repeated cycles of confrontation. Each actor who participates in this kind of a game tries to obtain the best result for himself at the expense of the other side. To weigh the balance in his favor, each actor amplifies his power against the other. For this purpose both employees and employers try to pull the support of their countrywide associations, governmental officials, parliamentary representatives, the media, and the public at large to their side. Participants in the game also try to improve their bargaining positions and to gain an advantage over the other side. The more power one side accumulates through a supporting coalition of forces, the greater are its chances of success, and the achievements will be better at the end of the confrontation.

Since the conditions are constantly changing, the employees will win in one confrontation and the employers will win in another. Therefore, according to this theory, achievements are assessed in terms of cumulative experience of these exchange relationships and not by the results of single events. In the ongoing process of these repeated encounters between the representatives of the sides, they create personal acquaintances, they develop interpersonal understandings, form unofficial accords, make tacit agreements; and they bind themselves to mutual commitments.

In this way social relationships are merged with professional relationships, and have an influence on the *political players* in these confrontations to reconsider, to compromise, to yield, and in many cases to refrain from applying their full power. This is the way that representatives of employees and employers maintain balanced and stable relationships, with the purpose of maintaining long-term exchange deals and of enjoying the continuing benefits that everyone derives from them. Therefore, only in rare cases does one side take the drastic stand of breaking off relations irreversibly.

Conflict Theory

According to this theory, mutual relations between actors are usually the result of interdependence. This dependence is expressed by the influence brought to bear on the aims of one actor through the behavior of another actor. Such actors are frequently faced with a lack of accordance between their own goals and those of their counterparts. This way there is a structural situation of *conflict of interest* in which the aim of one actor contradicts the aim of another actor. The degree of nonconformity between the goals determines the degree of opposition or conflict that prevails between the actors participating in a certain system of interrelations among two or more actors.[10]

This kind of opposition creates a competitive situation that might quickly develop into a conflict between the actors, since each assumes that fulfilling the goal of the other would necessarily lessen the chances for realizing his or her goal. This is a clear-cut situation, identified in mathematical game theory as a *zero-sum-game*, that is, a game in which the profit on one side is equal to the loss on the other side. Seen from this viewpoint, conflict is a situation that defines the preferences of the actors involved in it, irrespective of the actions they take. The degree of conflict affects the behavior of the actors in the given situation as well as its outcome.

Conflict Theory maintains that, in a state of conflict, the actors will try to exercise power against the other to enforce their will, to ensure the achievement of their goals, and to obtain the benefits they wish to get. Conflict situations are therefore fertile soil for the growth of power struggles, for the mutual exertion of force and for the application of various political measures.

> Interdependence of outcomes and at least partially opposed interests appear to be ubiquitous in social relationships; hence conflict (of greater or lesser degree) sets the problem for human interactions. The solutions for such social problems often require the use of various modes of communication. These modes include threats, promises, warnings and recommendations, all of which can be contingent or non-contingent, more or less explicit or tacit, and may refer to specific types and magnitudes of reinforcements, including sensory stimulation, rewards or costs, provision of gains or deprivation of expected gains, and social rewards or punishments.[11]

As the economist Kenneth Boulding[12] explains, activities of this kind entail a considerable price that each of the sides involved will have to pay. Therefore, it is hardly surprising that sometimes the cost incurred by the exercise of power and the taking of political measures is greater than the gains of the actors who used them. Nevertheless, rivals are often drawn into a prolonged and exhausting struggle in which each side tries to overcome the other by various applications of force. Such struggles intensify the conflict and drag the parties into a process of escalation in which every action by one side is faced with a more radical reaction by the other side. Many examples for this process can be seen in the struggles between gangs and criminal organizations, in labor disputes between employees and employers, in the clashes between citizens and the police during demonstrations, and in military provocations between hostile countries.

The alternative to the use of force in these conflict situations is a mutual agreement to compromise. But compromise is possible only if the actors on both sides of the barrier are prepared to redefine their goals and to give up some of their ambitions. Yet in many cases of conflict, the rivals express negative feelings and display inclinations such as hostility, hatred, resentment and revenge. In these conditions, the overpowering of the rival per se and his removal from the arena becomes an end in itself. As a result, the two sides find it difficult to make concessions and to agree to compromise. Every concession made by one side is seen as an indication of weakness by the other, and every proposal to compromise is interpreted as a means to utilize the weakness of a rival in order to gain an advantage over him or her.

This kind of confrontation frequently involves actors such as lawyers, consultants, tradesmen, and agents who are not party to the dispute but derive benefit from its existence. Therefore, it is quite natural that it would be in their interest to prolong the dispute and even to intensify it as much as possible. The Israeli-Palestinian dispute is a clear example of a longstanding and exhausting power conflict, accompanied by expressions of violence of various kinds, infused with negative feelings and a mutual lack of trust. Throughout its history, interested parties on the outside have gotten in the way of this dispute to gain political or economic advantages for themselves. Among those interested entities we can identify the Great Powers, The United Nations, the European Union countries, Arab and Muslim states, international oil companies, the arms industry, religious organizations and various kinds of terror organizations.

Conflict theory asserts that the intensity of conflict determines to a great extent both the frequency in the use of power and the manner of its use against the rival. Low intensity conflict is likely to arouse attempts of persuasion, especially through promises and benefits, so as to influence the other side to change its position. On the other hand, high intensity conflict is likely to arouse attempts to frighten the rival by the use of threats and punishments.

The use of power in itself does not necessarily settle the dispute as long as the actors involved do not change their aims and motives. An enforced solution, in which one side dictates the outcome to the other side, is a temporary and unstable solution of conflicts because the conflicting goals and opposing interests of the actors remain as they were. The way to settle the conflict to the satisfaction of all sides is the path of negotiations that will lead to mutual agreement on the basis of compromise between the rivals' ambitions.

According to Samuel Bacharach and Edward Lawler,[13] conflicts in organizations are an integral part of the ongoing negotiations among intra-organizational coalitions. Such negotiations reflect, in their view, both the mechanism for settling disputes as well as the process of identifying conflicts of interest. By so doing it is possible to outline the borders of agreement among the interest groups that take an active role in the political game in the organization. Open discussions and even secret ones among the stakeholders in an organization moderate the conflict, slow the pace of escalation and lessen the mutual use of coercive force. For this reason, negotiation allows rivals to redefine their goals, to navigate the conflict in the direction of compromise and reach an agreement among themselves. Negotiations in which the rivals focus on bargaining over the allocation of resources represent one kind of organization politics taking place in all types of organizations.

Utility Theory

One theoretical perspective perceives power relationships as merely a decision-making process; in this process, decision makers weigh their alternatives and choose the best ones for them under the given conditions. The *Utility Theory*, in its various formulations, represents this line of thought.[14] The theory is based on a number of fundamental assumptions, implying that the decision-making process is essentially a rational process—namely, a process that is calculated and balanced, taking into account the chances and the risks involved in every feasible choice. The utility theory assumes that every decision maker has a set of objectives that he or she wishes to realize or some outcomes that he or she seeks to obtain. Second, it assumes that every decision maker knows what the alternatives available for his choosing are. Third, the decision maker knows what the results of these alternatives are and what benefit can be expected from each of them. Fourth, for every possible outcome there is a known probability that it will actually occur, if the actor does decide to choose a certain alternative.

Under such conditions, the actor who decides will examine each of the alternatives in terms of the *utility* he will derive from it, that is, according to the degree of importance he ascribes to obtaining each of the possible results. On the basis of the assumption of *rational choice*, the theory claims that the decision maker will choose the alternative from which the *expected utility* is highest.[15] This expected utility is calculated from the sum of profits attached to each alternative against the sum of losses attached to it. In other words, the actor who is required to choose between alternative A and alternative B is expected to choose the better one of them. Such utility does not have a fixed value though, since it changes with time and circumstances. Each decision is weighed in light of the given conditions, in the time and place when it is taken.

The theory also posits that the expected change in value is subject to *the law of diminishing marginal utility*. This economic law maintains that the expected utility of every additional unit of profit gradually diminishes. For instance, the utility that a penniless individual can get from gaining certain amounts of money will gradually diminish the richer he or she becomes. Put differently, the relative importance of an additional standard sum of money for a certain actor is the direct result of the amount of money in his possession. This principle is valid even for non-material benefits, such as honor or esteem, although they are not counted in measurable units that are definable and accepted as in counting amounts of money.

Utility theory, as the previous theories, tries to explain the power relationships between actors and to predict their behavior. When actors compete with each other over the attainment of resources or on other acquirements, they behave in the same manner as decision makers. The main behavioral alternatives open to them are the exercise of power or, refraining from such exercise, compliance with the will of the other or, refusal to do so, reprisal or restraint. Each of these alternatives can be carried out in different ways that represent sub-alternatives of some course of action, such as the use of physical force, the imposition of a monetary fine or social ostracism. Each of these actors is hypothetically placed before a *decision tree* that contains various options, and he or she has to choose the best option.

For a given actor (A) to make the best decision, from the rational point of view, A must not only know his own decision tree but also the estimated decision tree of the rival (B) with whom A is competing. That is to say, A should know the power of B, what benefit A will receive if he or she obeys B, and what damage A will suffer for noncompliance. Actor A should also know in advance what the chances are that rival B will indeed exercise power against him/her. These data are essential for any actor engaged in power relations who wants to assess the expected utility of each alternative open to him or her.

According to this theory, it is possible to suggest a number of predictions. First, actors will exercise their power only when it is a better strategy than a self-restraining one; for example, when one of the actors is expected to overcome his rival by the use of force. Second, actors will obey the will of another only if the expected utility justifies the price of obedience; for example, when a soldier knows that the expected punishment for refusing to fulfill an order will be imprisonment in a military jail. Third, actors will choose restraint as long as the expected damage is less than the self-damage of reprisal; for example, a parent who restrains himself when faced with aggravation from a son or daughter, to prevent the futile worsening of hostility between them.

It is reasonable to hypothesize that the greater the quantity and quality of the benefits that an actor receives from another, the weaker will be the tendency of that actor to comply with demands from him or her accordingly; and the higher the price of exerting power, the lower will be the tendency of the power holder to use it against the other.

Probably the best example to illustrate the theory of utility is the one that repeatedly occurs in history: the confrontation between states or between their armies. In such confrontations, the leaders examine and weigh their range of options and those of their rivals. Each leader, of course, knows the facts about his military strength and his political and economic power. In order to acquire reliable and updated information about his rival and his intentions, each side employs espionage agents and secret service units. In light of their information, the leaders decide at each stage of the confrontation whether to exercise power against the rival or enemy, and if so—in what way. Those leaders have to decide whether to comply with the rival's demands and surrender to threats, whether to respond with an act of revenge, or whether it is better to restrain themselves temporarily until a better opportunity presents itself. At different points in time the leaders choose a line of action that promises the highest expected utility, based on the given facts, which change in the course of political or military confrontation.

The exercise of power in confrontations such as these ones does not necessarily involve armed clashes on the battlefield. Rival countries frequently employ economic sanctions such as boycotts, the freezing of bank accounts, suspension of debt repayments, or the imposition of high protective tariffs. Even in the military sphere, the exercise of power is often carried out without actual shooting. Instead, the power of a nation state is displayed by the deployment or reinforcement of armed forces at the borders, by a declaration of intent, by mobilizing reserves, by the use of psychological warfare and non-lethal weapons.

Even the surrender to the demands of a rival is presented in many cases as a well-thought-out free-will choice intended to avoid war. Similarly, countries sometimes prefer to restrain their armed forces in spite of attacks against them, since this strategy implies greater utility than that of military retaliation. In the realm of business, for instance, many commercial firms (e.g., fast food chains) occasionally refrain from acts of retaliation against violent demonstrators, to avoid greater damage to their reputation in the market. Similarly, authors and artists are usually reluctant to respond to critiques of their work, even when they are vicious ones.

Power struggles of this kind are highly frequent between business organizations competing over certain sections of the market. Business firms are likely to exercise their power against competitors by means of political maneuvers such as hostile takeovers, monopolization of supply sources and control of marketing channels. Those and similar measures, besides being motivated by economic considerations, are also derived from political motives, such as the amplification of the firm's power and influence. Thus, in trying to reduce situations of uncertainty, organizations attempt to take control over vital sections of their environment in order to manage them in accordance with their own preferences.[16]

State and public organizations tend to exert their power through legislation. In this way, by the protection of laws and regulations, they impose limitations and regulations of various kinds upon private organizations. One way or another, these examples are common occurrences in power relationships that can be presented as decision-making processes, in which the actors involved— individuals, groups, and organizations—choose the optimal line of action on the basis of changing conditions. In organizational reality, such courses of action are considered *political games* that are played within organizations and between them.

Expectation Theory

This theory, like the previous one, also views power relationships between actors as decision-making processes.[17] In the literature, this theory is identified as the *Subjective Expected Utility Theory*. According to this theory, decision making is a process directed by subjective expectations of the actors involved in that process. The expectation theory is thus based on two basic assumptions: (1) that any interrelationship between actors, each of the participants tries to obtain the greatest utility; and (2) that each of them estimates subjectively the value of the expected result and the chances that it will actually occur, if he chooses a certain course of action. These subjective estimations are derived from various information sources: first, from personal experience with those actors in similar circumstances in the past; second, from information about the results of similar occurrences that others have experienced; and third, from beliefs about the personality traits and cultural features of the actors involved. In this way, for each of the actors engaged in these relations, a series of expectations regarding the other participants is created.

When actors encounter a confrontation or competition among themselves, each of them subjectively evaluates the optional actions available to him or to her. That is, each side develops expectations about the utility he expects to gain, according to his estimate, from each alternative. Moreover, every actor assumes that the other one knows what he expects to receive from his rival in various situations. Each actor is also aware of the options that are open to the other side and the likelihood that the other will utilize every one of them. In this way a state of *shared awareness* does emerge between them, which can be simply described in the following manner: "I know what my situation is in this confrontation, and I also know that you know what my situation is, and you know that I know what your situation is." On the basis of this shared awareness mutual expectations develop in connection with the behavior of the other person: "I expect that you will behave in a certain manner, because you expect me to behave in a certain manner."

These expectations prevent, or at least lessen, the repeated need for the rivals in a given confrontation to present demands, to threaten penalties, to exercise power, to refuse to comply, to retaliate, and to bear the cost of an increasing escalation during the course of the confrontation. In the language of expectation theory, the actors behave according to the *law of expected reactions*. This law states that each actor reacts to what is expected of him, whether the other person expresses his expectations by explicit demands, or whether he refrains from doing so.[18]

A typical example of power relationships based on mutual expectations is the system of interrelations between superiors and their subordinates in most organizations. According to the expectation theory, employees of an organization, whatever their ranks or functions, know who their superiors are and what they expect them to do while at work. These expectations are formed in the course of time, in accordance with the personal experience of the subordinates during their work for their superiors, as well as on the basis of the information that they collect from their colleagues. The workers thus discover the priorities, the tendencies and the caprices of their superiors. They learn to assess the strength of the expected reactions of their superiors whenever their expectations are not realized: reprimands, castigations, disciplinary complaints, or the imposition of fines. They know how to calculate their chances of obtaining benefits, such as distinction awards, prizes or promotions in exchange for good performance. They also can subjectively estimate the positive and negative results they might expect from direct confrontation with their superiors, such as the esteem and support of their colleagues, suspension, dismissal or being fired from their jobs. Superiors also learn to recognize the behavioral patterns of those subordinate to them: to appraise their obedience and cooperation; to discover which one among them is liable to incite his colleagues to disobey orders, to present counter-demands and to set conditions for obedience; they can calculate what would be the result of confrontation between superiors and those subordinate to their command.

On the basis of these mutual estimations and expectations, interrelationships develop in a way that the power inherent in them is hidden, that is, interrelationships where the superiors do not exercise their power openly in daily life and the subordinates do not make complaints against their superiors. In most organizations, these power relationships are maintained simply because both sides appreciate the expected utility that they are likely to gain from this state of affairs. They presumably figure out the expected costs and benefits of these power relations, comparing them to other alternatives. Therefore, confrontations caused by refusal to obey orders are not common events in workplaces, and they are even less likely to occur in organizations such as in defense industries, the military or the police force.

The use of power is expected mainly in situations where managers or rank-and-file try to obtain favors exceeding the working conditions and benefits that accrue to them by their contracts of employment. In such deviating cases, illegitimate demands as well as compliance or noncompliance with such demands constitute part of the political game conducted in organizations, as it will be described at greater length in the next chapters.

Comparative View

The political phenomenon is conceived here as a system of social actors conducting prolonged interrelations among themselves on the basis of mutual power. These relationships are meant to ensure that the power holders receive a regular supply of various favors that they need to satisfy their desires. From this point of view, politics is based on the buildup of power and its application as a deliberate means to produce utility in social relationships. Power and politics go hand in hand, and therefore it is not surprising that many scholars treat them as two sides of the same coin.

The different theories presented in this chapter represent the attempts made in the social sciences to explain the phenomenon of social power and to predict its impact—namely, the ways in which power affects the behavior of individuals, groups, and complex social entities (e.g., business firms, education or health institutes). The systematic and comparative consideration of these theories leads to the conclusion that they all have a common denominator. This common denominator is the conception of power, in all its forms and expressions, as the outcome of interrelationships conducted between social actors in a given social setting, and a specific time frame. All theories assert that the notion of power refers to a relative and temporary advantage that one actor has over another actor with whom he or she interacts under certain conditions. In other words, this is a situation-dependent advantage that is maintained as long as the situation remains the same.

All the theories, therefore, try to identify the conditions in which power is created in social relationships and to locate the factors that motivate the power holders to exercise their power against other actors. The dissimilarity between the theoretical explanations that have been presented and discussed here lies in their answer to the question about what these conditions are. There are theories that point to the structural conditions of organizations, such as the layout of positions, as the causal factors accounting for differences in power. On the other hand, some theories explain variations in power as an outcome of behavior patterns, such as modes of bargaining in exchange relationships. And there are some theories that account for the dissimilarity in the magnitude of power by referring to the conduct of actors as a decision-making kind of behavior.

The various theoretical explanations for all kinds of power relationships among actors are based on a few common assumptions. First, power constitutes an advantage that allows its possessor to receive more benefits and to give less in relations with actors who have less power than he or she does. Second, actors in general tend to attempt to derive the greatest utility they can get from the power they hold. Third, actors employ courses of action intended to improve their situation, that is, to amplify their power and lessen their dependence vis-à-vis the actors with whom they interact.

These assumptions lead to the conclusion that power relationships between actors are essentially of a political character. These are interrelationships in which each participant attempts to gain profits at the expense of the other. Nevertheless, the theories of power presented here differ one from the other by the range of alternative courses of action that they can employ in their power struggles.

The "dependence theory" and the "utility theory," for example, give great weight to objective constraints and they thus leave relatively little space for such a choice. On the other hand, the "exchange theory" and the "expectation theory" emphasize the importance of subjective considerations; therefore, they allow the use of a true judgment and free choice among alternative courses of action.

Most theories of power agree with the assumption that in social relationships there is no absolute power and no absolute dependence. That is to say, even weak actors in a given situation have a certain amount of power in comparison to those stronger than them. Therefore, they all have the ability to maneuver in their relations with each other, and each side tries to draw the most utility he can from his power or his weakness.

Both the power holders and those dependent on them have ways and means that allow them to utilize the relative power they possess for making profit. It is plausible to suggest then that actors engaged in power relationships with their rivals will choose the courses of action that are most appropriate for them. The theories posit that actors in such competitive situations will tend to behave as rationally as possible and to take the best advantage in those situations. As we shall see later on, in power relationships between actors, it is possible to identify action patterns that are suitable to specific situations. Borrowing images from the realm of sport, we may describe these series of patterns as different types of political games.[19]

In spite of the various theoretical attempts, some of which have been presented and discussed in this chapter, the power phenomenon is still a complicated question and the subject of controversy in the social sciences. Therefore, no single theory gives a satisfactory answer to the open questions concerning the fundamental nature, the true sources, the real usage of power and its consequences in social life.[20] Nevertheless, as Garth Morgan, maintains:

> These problems aside, however, it is clear that our discussion of possible sources and uses of power provides us with an inventory of ideas through which we can begin to decode power plays and political dynamics in organizational contexts. Like our analysis of interests and our discussion of conflict, it provides us with a working tool through which we can analyze organizational politics and, if we so wish, orient our action in a politicized manner.[21]

Conclusion

This chapter dealt with several theories of power relationships among social actors—namely, among individuals, groups, and organizations. Each of the theories discussed was developed in the course of attempts to explain the behavior of actors participating in unbalanced interrelationships in which one actor has more power than another. These attempts have led to the formulation of a few socio-psychological theories, each one of which is based upon different assumptions.

The theory of dependence is focused on the structure of relationships between certain actors, from which it derives the level of interdependence among them and the amount of power that this dependence grants their counter-partners. This theory is essentially a structural one; hence, it gives less importance to the personal qualities of the actors and to their political talents. Accordingly, those actors can loosen their degree of dependence to a certain extent by changing the structural conditions so as to reduce the price they have to pay in exchange for the benefits they are interested in gaining.

The theory of exchange explains how people, who are motivated by their will to obtain desirable resources, are able to do so through give-and-take deals of "social goods," which are not measurable in economic terms. Since exchange relationships are based on the mutual transfer of resources, the power of each participant in an exchange relationship is determined by the quantity and quality of the resources in his or her possession. This power enables its holder to control the flow of benefits transferred to the other person in a given social setting, and to stipulate this transfer on the other's compliance to his or her demands. According to this theory, it is power that actually determines the terms of the social transactions and their outcomes.

The theory of conflict assumes that interrelationships in economics, society, and politics are accompanied by rivalry among the actors involved in them. This antagonism stems from the incongruence between the goals of the actors and from their opposing interests. As a result, the actors find themselves in a conflict situation in which each actor attempts to realize his or her goals and press forward self-interests in the face of the opposition of their rivals. According to the conflict theory, one of the two following processes is likely to emerge— either struggle or bargaining. The first process is characterized by the frequent use of power, and often by repressive force, in order to achieve the desired end result at the expense of the opponent. The use of such force intensifies the conflict to the point of violence in which each side radicalizes his or her reaction to the other. The greater the escalations, the lesser the opponents are ready to compromise and the lower the chances for an agreement between them. The second process is characterized by negotiation between the sides to the conflict. In the course of negotiations they are required to redefine their goals and to adjust their interests to the constraints of reality. In this process, the wider the agreement the greater will be the tendency of the participants to reach an agreed compromise. Both processes reflect the power play aspect and the bargaining aspect of the political game.

The theory of utility sees the various kinds of social behavior as decision-making processes of social actors, which allow them to choose the best course of action under given conditions. This theory attributes a certain level of rationality to individuals, groups, and organizations. This ability enables them to handle the information needed to make a rational choice among the alternatives. A rational choice is determined by the extent to which the decision maker selects the best alternative in terms of expected utility. According to this view, power struggles among actors are no more than a series of decisions intended to obtain maximal utility. The optional choices in such relationships are the exercise of power (in one way or another), the granting of rewards or their denial, promises or threats, compliance or resistance, reprisal or restrain.

Expectation theory is another example of the decision-making paradigm. Unlike the utility theory, this theory undervalues the rationality of social actors. Since these actors are not capable, or perhaps are not even willing to gather and process all the information needed to make the best decisions, they are satisfied with personal judgments and subjective estimations in the lack of factual data. These subjective estimates serve the decision makers as a basis for mutual expectations. Through overt and covert messages, each actor becomes familiar with the expectations that the other person anticipates from him. This shared awareness limits the frequency with which the actors make use of the power they hold against the others, and lessen the lack of cooperation between them. Thus, the power in social interrelationships that are not confrontational tends to go under the surface. In situations of confrontation, competition, and struggle, these expectations lose their validity. Therefore, in such situations, there is a rising tendency to unveil the actors' power and to exercise it against the others, so that forcefulness is amplified respectively.

In spite of the differences between these theories, they are based on some common assumptions. Among these assumptions one may include the following: Actors try to attain the highest utility from the interrelationships in which they take part; each actor tries to amass the greatest possible power to improve his bargaining stance; even a relatively weak actor has a certain degree of power that enables him to lower the price he has to pay to the person stronger than him; every actor tries to find ways that lessen dependence on another; and finally—actors tend to behave in a political manner, that is, to choose rational courses of action that take advantage of their power vis-à-vis their counter-partners under the given set of conditions.

Notes

1. Computerized simulation is today an accepted research method in science, and is used to examine various phenomena—physical, climatic, biological, and social—by means of a computerized imitation of real situations that cannot be viewed directly. This research method is based mainly on a mathematical formulation of estimated behavior models and their examination by computer in relation to changing data. See the example for computerized simulation of change processes in organizations in Samuel & Jacobsen, 1997.
2. Emerson, 1962, 1972; Cook & Emerson, 1978.
3. These claims are formulated in the following equations: $p(A) = d(B)$, $p(B) = d(A)$, and the power advantage between them is $p(A) - p(B)$, where p indicates power, d indicates dependency, and the letters A, B, indicate the identity of the two actors. See Emerson, 1962.
4. Bacharach & Lawler, 1980: 22.

5.   Blau, 1964; Homans, 1974.
6.   Blau, 1964: 88.
7.   Molm, 1990, 1997.
8.   Emerson, 1972; Boulding, 1989.
9.   Samuel & Zelditch, 1989.
10.   Axelrod, 1970; Tedeschi, Schlenker & Bonoma, 1973.
11.   Tedeschi, Schlenker & Bonoma, 1973: 52.
12.   Boulding, 1989.
13.   Bacharach & Lawler, 1980.
14.   Alker, 1973; Harsanyi, 1962; Thibaut & Kelly, 1961; March 1955.
15.   "Expected utility" is determined according to the multiplication of the value of the result (v) with the probability of its realizations (p). That is: $ex(u) = vp$.
16.   In chapter 9, which deals with interorganizational politics, there are detailed descriptions of the various uses by business organizations, especially large corporations, of the economic power in their possession in order to dominate their competitors and to dictate the conditions of the market.
17.   Tedeschi, Schlenker & Bonoma, 1973.
18.   Samuel & Zelditch, 1989.
19.   See the details and discussion in chapter 6 which deals in the different kinds of political games.
20.   Morgan, 1986.
21.   Morgan, 1986: 185.

3

The Political Layout

Organizations usually function in the form of socioeconomic entities that produce a wide variety of products and services to their human environment. They are constructed and operated according to a set of rules and official regulations, and are managed systematically by means of a series of formally defined and controlled functions. This is the rational perspective on organizations: they reflect the organizational regime according to which actions are performed and results are assessed. From this perspective, organizations are based on some kind of management system through which law and order are maintained.[1]

However, participants in a variety of organizations understand very quickly that their organization has another aspect—a political one—which is based on an explicit or implicit barter system that accompanies nearly every matter and issue in the organization. This aspect reflects the power struggle between the different stakeholders who strive to realize their objectives. The political aspect of organizations does not correspond to the organizational objectives and goals, and does not necessarily assist in achieving them. From this point of view, organizations can be regarded as political arenas where individuals and groups fight to advance their interests or the interests of those standing behind them, at the expense of the organization in general. Therefore, from the organization point of view, the political aspect represents the non-rational, non-sanctioned, and to a certain degree the more hidden side of the organization. In accordance with this approach, Tom Burns described this political aspect of organizations:

> Corporations are co-operative systems assembled out of usable attributes of people. They are also social systems within which people compete for advancement; in so doing they may make use of others. Behavior is identified as political when others are made use of as resources in competitive situations…. The hierarchic order of rank and power that prevails in them is at the same time a single control system and a career ladder…. Politics are the exploitation of resources, both physical and human, for the achievement of more control over others, and thus of safer, or more comfortable, or more satisfying terms of individual existence.[2]

The term *organizational politics* means any use of power to obtain a desired outcome, including the actual or promised application of rewards and penalties in certain relationships that coexist between different actors who are involved in organizational activity.[3] This usage of power for political purposes is a common feature of organizational reality. Individuals, various groups, and organizations apply power; and it primarily involves bartering in resources of different kinds, based on the relative power of the negotiating parties.

As explained in previous chapters, in most organizations, numerous actors participate in this kind of a *political game*. It is a game in which supervisors, subordinates, colleagues, representatives of other units and similar functionaries become involved. The actors participating in the game strive to gain the most and best rewards—concrete or symbolic—that are obtainable in the organization within which they are active. The game they play reflects the organizational politics with all its varied expressions. Therefore, as Garth Morgan says:

> In order to understand the day-to-day dynamics of organization, it is also necessary to explore the detailed processes through which people engage in politics. For this purpose, it is useful to return to Aristotle's idea that politics stems from a diversity of interests, and trace how this diversity gives rise to the "wheeling and dealing" negotiation, and other processes of coalition building and mutual influence that shape so much of organizational life.[4]

Before we focus on the political processes that occur in organizations, it is appropriate first to become familiar with the composition and structure of the *political layout* of the organization. Such layout contains all the participants of the organization, not only the various levels of managers. Moreover, the political layout of an organization involves representatives of labor unions, governmental agents, consumers associations, suppliers, and investors. Thus, the political layout connects the entire set of ongoing interrelations between an organization's members and its external environment. The political layout of an organization therefore consists of the web of relationships between the internal as well as external participants of the organization. In every organization, over a period of time, a network of interrelations is formed and stabilized among those who are engaged in its activities and those who drive its wheels. This organizational network contains a large number of loops and sub-connections that are bound together in a complex web of interpersonal relationships.

It is obvious that the political layout of an organization is not a random or temporary system of interpersonal relations. It emerges primarily on the basis of the formal organizational structure of that organization; that is to say, on the basis of the organizational division of labor, as well as on the basis of the hierarchy of authority. The structure of an organization creates the functional interdependence between participants that are acting in it in one way or another. This structure hands over different amounts of power to the various functionaries, and hence creates different patterns of interdependence between them.

In spite of the tight linkage between the organizational structure and the political layout, these two are not identical. The former is based on the underlying functional structure of the organization, whereas the relations formed between individuals and groups within the organization influence the latter. In other words, the structure enables organizational actors to occupy various bargaining positions in the political layout, while the latter determines their relative power vis-à-vis their counter partners. These two structures— the functional and the political—complement each other in the organizational reality. The British scholar, Andrew Pettigrew, describes this interdependence as follows:

> In the present study the organization is considered an open political system. The division of work in an organization creates sub-units. These sub-units develop interests based on specialized functions and responsibilities. Although such sub-units have specialized tasks, they may also be interdependent. This interdependence may be played out within a joint decision-making process. Within such decision-making processes, interest-based demands are made. Given heterogeneity in the demand-generating process and the absence of a clearly set system of priorities between those demands, conflict is likely to ensue. Sub-units with differential interests make claims on scarce organizational resources…. It is the involvement of sub-units in such demand-and-support-generating processes within the decision-making processes of the organization that constitutes the political dimension. Political behavior defined as behavior by individuals, or, in collective terms, by sub-unit, within the organization that makes a claim against resource-sharing system of the organization.[5]

Organizations are therefore constructed on arrangements and agreements between actors involved in them; agreements that are formed and changed as a result of constantly recurring negotiation processes. In other words, the political dynamics that occur in organizations determines their structure, forms their characteristics, and influences their ways of behavior. Bacharach and Lawler have described this very well, as follows:

> Organizations are neither the rational, harmonious entities celebrated in managerial theory, nor arenas of apocalyptic class conflict projected by Marxists. Rather, it may be argued, a more suitable notion lies somewhere in between those two—a concept of organizations as politically negotiated orders. Adopting this view, we can observe organizational actors in their daily transactions perpetually bargaining, repeatedly forming and reforming coalitions, and constantly availing themselves of influence tactics…. Survival in an organization is a political act. Corporations, universities, and voluntary associations are arenas for daily political action.[6]

The Political Arena

Sports contests are usually conducted in specially designed arenas, tailored to fit every kind of game or wrestling. Football fields, basketball courts, boxing and wrestling rings, racetracks, and swimming pools represent some outstanding examples of sport arenas. In politics as well there are specific types of "arenas" in which political struggles take place.

The perception of organizations as *political arenas* in which actors compete over valuable resources by means of political behavior presupposes that this kind of contest takes place within the limits of recognized "rules of the game." The organization, therefore, serves as a venue where various stakeholders reconcile their opposing interests by exploiting the organization resources for their own benefit—each one according to his or her relative power and bargaining skills. Every participant in the political game strives to overcome his competitors and to gain the largest slice possible of the "organization's pie." Mintzberg figuratively describes this struggle for benefits as follows: "The French have a graphic term for it—*un panier de crabes*. A bucket of crabs, each one clawing at the other to come out on top."[7]

Theoretically speaking, all of the organization's participants are stakeholders, who seek to gain the greatest possible utility from their engagement in it. Therefore, these actors enter the organizational arena to compete over the given reservoir of resources. In such a competition, the prize won is as large as the loss incurred by the other actors. We are dealing here with a kind of contest known in "game theory" as a zero-sum game, that is, a game where the total profit and the total loss cancel each other out so that the end-result is zero. The possibility of stakeholders gaining the desired winnings not at the expense of other competitors may be realized only in situations in which mutual cooperation increases the entire reservoir of resources, so that the share of each stakeholder becomes larger.

On the face of it, the increase of the reservoir of resources can prevent conflicts and confrontations, save the exercise of power and the application of force, increase the satisfaction of the organization members, and ensure peace and quiet. However, in reality, situations of peace and quiet are not common in organizational life. This reality is usually characterized by conflicts of interest, by a tendency to strive for the full realization of objectives and goals, by competition, by mutual distrust and greed for profit, by pursuit of prestige and the possession of authority. It is not surprising, therefore, that different participants in the organization, as well as the stakeholders outside it, tend to compete over the organization resources and over bargaining positions. This tendency propels the wheels of organizational politics, strengthens its influence upon the behavior of individuals and groups, cultivates conflicts, and encourages power struggles. For that reason, organizations actually serve as a sort of wrestling arena where frequent political games are held between various internal and external actors.

It should be noted here that a political arena is not a battlefield, and a political game is not a war. Usually the purpose of those involved in the political game is neither to destroy the competitors nor to put them out of action, as enemies at war try to do. The term *game* in contrast with the term *battle* is meant to express the essential difference between the actors taking part in it, at least as far as intra-organizational politics is concerned.[8]

Rivals in a political game are actually partners in the organizational activities, conducting continuous actions and interactions for the purpose of producing the goods and services of the organization. In general, stakeholders have different, and even conflicting, objectives and preferences. Therefore, they act in a competitive manner that motivates them to behave selfishly. Nonetheless, they all have one common interest—namely, the preservation of the organization and the maintenance of its orderly operation. In other words, they all want to ensure the organization's survival as a viable socioeconomic system.

This common interest comes from the utility that each stakeholder involved in its activity gets from the organization. According to game theory, participants prefer to remain in a given organization and to invest resources in its operations as long as the expected utility for them is greater than the expected utility that they could gain from other organizations. Therefore, the survival of the organization is a necessary, albeit not a sufficient, condition to obtain benefits from it. Actors who find that their losses in the political game are larger than their profits might cease their activities in the organization and withdraw from it as soon as possible. The motivations of outside actors, such as business competitors, might be destructive, and their activities have a certain similarity to military warfare. In this respect, both their motives and behavior differ from those of the organization members.

As in a sports arena, the political arena also has defined borderlines. Naturally, these borderlines run more or less parallel to the limits of the organization itself. However, the larger an organization is, and the more divergent and complex it becomes, the more blurred and penetrable its borderlines will be. Interorganizational mergers, multi-divisional giant firms, global business corporations as well as alliances of various kinds create a new organizational reality in which borderlines are rather vague. Therefore, the political arena of many organizations today cannot be clearly discerned, and it tends to be more of an abstract conception than a concrete construct. Nevertheless, most participants of an organization, each according to his or to her position, learn to identify the borderlines that enclose the organizational arena and to locate its recognized limits.

Political Goals

All the arenas in the world of sports contain sites that the actors strive to reach during the course of the game. These sites are, for instance, the hanging nets in basketball games. Reaching these sites is a necessary condition to score points, and a critical target for winning the game. In the political arena these sites are decision-making centers that are dispersed throughout the organization. Among them is the Board of Directors, the General Headquarters, the Cabinet, the Executive Council, the Central Bureau, the Plenum or the Senate. All these represent some of the major decision centers of organizations. Such centers of decision making constitute political goals, which actors are interested in controlling so as to sway those decisions in favor of their own interests. Once those goals are attained, stakeholders divide among them some part of the organization resources in the form of various benefits. Those individuals and groups see themselves as the *beneficiaries* of the organization, who deserve to get a recompense for their investment in it.

In these decision-making centers, negotiations are conducted and business deals are made in a give-and-take manner. The persons engaged in this activity— "the players" of the political game—are subject to the influence of the stakeholders standing behind them, which is to say, those actors who have no authority in the decision-making process but, nonetheless, attempt to persuade and/or manipulate decision makers such as executives, directors, and representatives.

The same pattern characterizes other kinds of decision-making centers such as planning committees, disciplinary committees, finance committees, nomination committees, and acquisition committees. These committees and similar ones are authorized to determine distribution of resources and rewards, the granting of rights and privileges, and the promotion or demotion of organizational participants. Such decisions directly affect the balance of power among stakeholders and thus arouse political acts of various kinds.

It should be noted here that all those who hold managerial positions constitute "decision centers" by virtue of their authority. Executives, directors, managers, commanders, and supervisors of all kinds are the ones who make decisions at all times on a variety of subjects in their scope of responsibility. This is the functional basis and organizational source of their relative power. From this platform they derive their ability to influence the behavior and to affect the fate of those who are subordinate to them as well as the organizational processes and outcomes under their control.

It is obvious that the larger the spoils at stake in every decision center, the greater its importance as a preferred site in the political arena. The political domain of an organization can be portrayed as a three-dimensional topographical space in which sites of various sizes are scattered around, some in the center and some on the margins. All of them are indicated by appropriate names and titles that refer to their importance and their power in the organization. These sites are, as we said earlier, the political targets that the various actors are trying to reach in different phases of the political game. The actors are therefore under frequent political pressure in which different kinds of power are exerted and a variety of political moves are made. A political game is conducted in each of these sites, where a struggle takes place over the distribution of the organizational resources.

Political Actors

Some of the people involved in organizational activity participate in the political game to promote themselves in the organization, to obtain benefits, and to achieve personal advancement. A typical example of personal activity of this sort is explicitly expressed by the attempts of individuals to be elected to various positions and committees in the organization, or to serve as its representative to other organizations, such as in professional associations and boards of directors. Other actors participate in the political game for the purpose of providing the groups to which they belong with the most and best achievements that can be obtained under given constraints. This political activity is rationalized as a public service on behalf of a specific social group, such as women or ethnic minorities, as well as for the realization of specific social goals, such as environmental protection. Obviously, organizational actors are less likely to admit that they are driven mainly by personal interests and for self-advancement.

In every organization one can identify some political actors acting as either overt or covert representatives of external stakeholders. Those actors have an interest in the decisions of the organization, and they therefore exert influence in decision-making processes in a direct or an indirect manner. Quite often their influence is enabled by the assistance of collaborators within the organization itself. One example for the involvement of outside influentials like these in the political game is the involvement of the State Treasury, Members of Parliament, and leaders of nationwide trade unions in decisions concerning salaries and fringe benefits of civil servants in various countries.

In the ongoing political game taking place in organizations there are usually two main types of participants: *In-house players* and *Outside players*. Henry Mintzberg calls these two types "the internal coalition" and "the external coalition," respectively.[9] One way or another, these two kinds of players of the political game in organizations should be scrutinized.

In-house Players

Among the in-house players in an organization are all those individuals employed by it, and identified by the organization as its "workers" or "members." In different organizations there are different kinds of workers: tenured workers, temporary workers, full-time workers and part-time workers, wage earners and salaried ones, and some times volunteers, too. Recently, there are increasing numbers of workers of a new kind—"external workers"—who are employed by the organization through outsourcing manpower agencies and by sub-contractors. This wide variety of workers makes it difficult for organizations to set clear boundaries between those who belong to the organization and those who are not part of it. Usually the people defined as the workers of the organization are considered as its members. These members form a substantial part of the in-house players participating in the political game at the political arena.

The overall body of employees of an organization typically consists of several kinds of vocational and professional groups. Each one of these occupational groups displays unique characteristics and interests. Thus, every group in the organization may be identified as an *interest group* that competes in the political arena of the organization with other interest groups.[10] In fact, in many organizations different occupational groups tend to get unionized in one form or another. Quite often such trade unions go one step further and form a coalition of several interest groups on a provisional basis. These and similar tactics of coalescence are applied for the purpose of using political means as part of their struggle for additional benefits and privileges.

The variety of occupations is too wide to be classified here. Nevertheless, it is worth noting that the classification of such groups is mainly based on their educational level and professional expertise. In this way groups such as doctors, teachers, engineers, technicians, and nurses are formed among employees. Another common distinction among employed groups is that between manual workers (blue-collar), office workers (white-collar), and technicians and foremen (gray-collar). In many organizations there are groups of employees that are classified according to their organizational status: supervisors, managers, officers, and the like. Employees associated with such groups constitute the middle management of the organization. Middle managers are essentially responsible for supervising the smooth workflow in different areas of the organization. Their interests differ from other employees, both their subordinates and their superiors in the chain of command.

In certain organizations even tenure and seniority are used as a criteria to distinguish between different groups of employees. It is no wonder that a variety of individuals and groups take an active part in the political game, aiming to maximize their utility above and beyond what they are officially entitled to get as part of their contract with the organization.

An additional sort of in-house political players is the group of executives who are situated in the organization apex, representing its elite. This relatively small but selective group includes the Chief Executive Officer, the Vice Presidents, the Divisions General Managers, and several senior staff members such as the Secretary, the Treasurer, the Legal Counselor, the Spokesman, etc. This group enjoys a great deal of authority, substantial power and influence, excessive privileges, high levels of prestige, and other unique advantages in the organization. Therefore, it is quite obvious that this particular group of actors serves as the main target of influence attempts for all the other groups involved in the political game. Yet, even this privileged group has its own agenda of personal, organizational, and occupational interests, which motivate its members as a group and as individuals to employ political means in the organization and outside it. Such outside politics is frequently used against members of the board, major shareholders, senior officials in the corridors of government and various social, political, and economic elites.

Another group of in-house players consists of the professional staff, distinguished as being the group of "specialists" of the organization. This group usually includes a variety of highly educated professionals whose main role in the organization is to advise managers and to assist them in making rational decisions on the basis of data, and on a systematic consideration of the pros and cons. Among this kind of specialists in most organizations nowadays one can find professionals such as economists and lawyers, statisticians, planners and design-ers, system analysts, market researchers and public opinion pollsters, organiza-tional consultants, quality assurance engineers, and so forth.

This group of professionals is usually in continuous conflict with the super-visors and managers who are in charge of producing the organization's goods and services. This conflict is identified in organization theory as the *line-staff conflict*. This conflict frequently leads to a power struggle around the issue of influence in the organization. The professional staff strives to widen its scope of influence, seeking to occupy positions of power in the major decision cen-ters of the organization. This interest, together with the benefits and privileges that come with such positions, motivates these professionals to participate in the political game as an interest group.[11]

Outside Players

Henry Mintzberg calls the entire group of outside stakeholders who partici-pate in the political game of the organization "the external coalition," to differ-entiate them from the in-house players that constitute "the internal coalition."[12] These outside players are divided into several groups, each of which act politi-cally to influence the division of organizational spoils in their favor. In other words, they attempt to influence the allocation of organizational resources in a way that benefits them or their collaborators in the organization.

The first and most important of these stakeholders is the group of the organi-zation owners and shareholders. The separation between ownership and man-agement that occurs in many organizations today legally places the owners outside the inner circle of the organization. Except for small family businesses or national organizations that are owned by the state, most of today's organiza-tions are owned by a varying number of shareholders who apportion among themselves different slices of the organization's property. The more sharehold-ers there are, the more dispersed is the ownership, and the control of the owners over the organization becomes more limited. Others frequently replace owners as a result of the buying and selling of the organization's shares on the stock exchange. These anonymous shareholders show little interest in the organization's goals, action plans, and its modes of operation. They are mainly interested in its business performance, because it affects the shares' market value, and the owners return on investment. On the other hand, financial corpo-rations, investment companies, banks, pension funds, trade unions, and similar organizations possess large packages of shares for long periods of time. By so doing, they have representation on the organization's Board of Directors on a regular basis, so as to make sure that they have ongoing control over the organization's major decisions.

A board of directors whose members participate in other organizations repre-sents the various owners of the organization. Although these directors are ap-pointed for the purpose of promoting the objectives of the organization, they take care of the particular interests of their patrons outside the organization. As members of the board of directors of the organization, they appoint the senior executives, and deal mainly with strategic issues, such as approval of heavy investments. They maintain a constant follow-up of the organization financial performance; they examine and authorize accounts balance sheets and profit and loss reports. This activity grants the members of the board a significant utility expressed in monetary bonuses, power and influence, business connections, and personal relations with people of affluence. The greatest advantage of this group comes from its being placed in a pivotal position between the organization and the surrounding environment, and from its role as a "shock absorber" in the clashes between the inside and the outside stakeholders participating in the political game.

Contractors, suppliers, and other external factors provide a variety of materials and services that surround most organizations, especially the larger ones. This circle of suppliers assists the organization and ensures that it is constantly provided with the major input it requires. Some of the suppliers are associated with the organization by long-term contracts (for example, suppliers of raw material), while others supply the organization with goods and services exclusively (for example, suppliers of energy and contractors for security and protection), and some others are even suppliers for whom the organization is the sole customer (such as food, cleaning and transport services). In recent years there is an increasing trend to transfer responsibility for the supply of services to outside contractors. This tendency widens the circle of external suppliers and varies the basket of services that organizations purchase from them on a regular basis: mail, printing and documentation, computerization, training and advanced studies, medical services, as well as construction and maintenance. These are merely a few examples of *outsourcing* in today's world of organizations.

It is easy to understand, therefore, the considerable interest these supplier groups have in the organization and its operations. Since their livelihood depends on the organization as a client, they have to compete to gain tenders and contracts, to meet the requirements of the organization, and to prove their ability to "deliver the goods" promised to the clients of the organization. These exigencies and other requirements turn the suppliers into primary stakeholders and impel them to enter into the organization's political game, to take measures such as lobbying, pressuring, tempting, and intimidating.

In contrast to the suppliers who are interested in the organization's inputs, its clients are interested in its outputs. The size of the clientele differs of course from one organization to another. Many organizations serve a very large, anonymous, and changing number of customers (like the retail chains of food, electrical products, household appliances, clothing, and footwear). On the other hand, many business organizations target their products to a small and selective set of customers (for example, elite fashion designers, companies for financial and legal counseling, clinics and defense industries). The smaller the clientele of an organization and the more continuous the exchange relations that these clients conduct with the organization, the greater is their interest in the organization, in its activities, and products. These stakeholders try to influence the policy of the organization that directly affects their interests, and even indirectly with regard to prices and payment conditions, quality of product, delivery times, and maintenance services. For this purpose they intervene in decision-making processes of the organization; they apply covert or overt pressures on its managers; they offer ameliorations and incentives in return for having their preferences met; and they cooperate with each other in order to promote their interests at the expense of the organization.

The armed forces, for example, are the primary customer of the defense industries in every country, and in certain periods and places they are the sole customer. For years the military used to prescribe detailed specifications for every weapon and every device it purchased from these industries. To ensure the complete and precise fulfillment of its demands, it placed its own representatives in these organizations. Their job was to monitor the organization activities and to intervene concurrently in the design process, in the manufacturing process, and in the testing of the equipment before it was used. Moreover, the economic power of such an exclusive customer enabled it to have significant impact on the ways in which the domestic defense industries were doing their job. This influence could be traced in the costs and prices of products, in timetables, in quality control, in technological investments, and in documentation. In some cases the sole customer had a say even in the placement of employees in key managerial and professional positions in various projects performed by the defense industries. This influence has been gradually decreased in various countries due to the process of globalization, which has enabled such industries to diversify their clientele by sales contracts with foreign military forces all over the world.

Another external entity that is recognized as an influential stakeholder in organizations is the government. In most states of our times the government has a special interest in organizations and corporations of various kinds. First of all, the government is interested in collecting taxes, duties, and promissory notes that the organization has to pay out. The government is also interested in overseeing the quality of the many different products to ensure public safety, health, and welfare. It also endeavors to prevent organizations from signing cooperation agreements that are intended to adversely exploit the client public (such as cartels); and it is interested in preventing damage to the environment (air, water, and ground pollution, and over-exploitation of natural resources) for the sake of excess profit. The government has to prevent violations of the law (for example, the distribution of illegal drugs), and to control the production and supply of some goods and services (such as the import of agricultural products, the licensing of alcoholic beverages and tobacco products, and the export of antiques and artifacts).

This responsibility of the government accounts for its intervention in the operations of many organizations and affects their course of action. Since government is a unique kind of outside political player, it has the power to use methods and techniques that are its sole prerogative to employ. Thus, governmental agencies do eavesdropping and wiretapping, confiscate documents, seizure property, close businesses and destroy illegal places, visit organizational premises by surprise, and impose indemnities. These are just a few of the methods and techniques at the disposal of the government in the political game. In other words, the government uses its monopoly over the means of coercion to influence in-house players in organizations to maintain the interests of society and to abide by the law.

In addition, we can easily identify other kinds of outside stakeholders having special interests in various industrial firms and business corporations; therefore, they are inclined to enter the political game for their own benefit. Among those outside players are, for example, Greenpeace, Amnesty International, the Feminist Movement, the Association of Russian Immigrants, the Rotary, and many others of this kind. By the same token, various political parties, trade unions, religious cults, and consumer associations are also likely to join the political game of any organization whenever it suits them, and to participate as outside players for their specific interests. All those interest groups frequently apply political methods and techniques used by pressure groups; and they prod their target organization to change its policies, to adjust its organizational structure according to their own preferences, and to adopt behavioral patterns that are consistent with their goals and convictions. Their political means include protests and demonstrations, recruiting of the media and public opinion in their favor, lobbying among parliamentary members and the affluent as well as recourse to violent means.

The circle of external political players participating in organizations is rounded off by the mass media of communication. Since the media are controlled by wealthy business financiers ("the barons of the media"), who have their economic and political interests, they are not free of selfish considerations. Therefore, in many organizations, even the media take part in the political game whenever such participation suits their interests or that of their owners. The many newspaper scandals that appear over and over again in all Western countries repeatedly point to this self-serving preference.

Newspapers, for example, have a significant business interest in advertisements for cigarettes and alcoholic drinks. They are also stakeholders in everything that is related to the paper industry, in printing press and color, in professional photography, and in various types of transportation. Another example is the owners of the electronic media. These undoubtedly have a stake in the cinema and music industries, and they work for their own interests by employing political measures in organizations related to these industries. All the forms of mass media—written and broadcast—show a special sensitivity to any legislation or legal rulings on issues such as personal privacy, citizen rights, protecting state secrets, freedom of speech, and political correctness. Since these issues are existential matters from the point of view of the press in a democratic society, the media employ many efficient measures aimed at affecting governmental agencies; they interfere in legislation processes and mobilize public opinion in their favor. Thus, the so-called "seventh power" does not hesitate to exercise its power against all those who oppose the way it operates, in order to ensure its interests wherever and whenever necessary.

This wide variety of stakeholders and political actors accounts for the difficulty that anyone is likely to encounter whenever he or she has to cope with the political game in an organization. Moreover, as in a theatrical group or a sports group, the players in the arena are constantly being replaced. There are those who step into the field or onto the stage, and some who step down in the course of time, according to their interests in the organization and their ability to compete with their rivals. The dynamic nature of the organization's political arena requires organizational actors to be flexible and adaptive players to survive this kind of contest. It means that they should enter and re-enter into relationships with changing partners; make agreements but not necessarily realize them; form and dissolve coalitions every so often; identify changing proponents and opponents; adopt different measures and maneuver in one way and then another from time to time.

The need to survive compels in-house players to have both political awareness and political insight—if they wish to ensure their future with the organization and derive the desired benefit from it. Outside players, too, need to have adequate political skills that will enable them to obtain the benefits they are interested in without having to join the organization as members and thus lose their political flexibility by being outsiders.

Rules of the Game

In contrast to the games of sport in which there are sets of obligatory rules for everyone, political games are based on "rules of the game" of a different kind. These rules are formulated and altered from time to time according to the events that occur during the course of the game and precedents that occurred in previous games. In the negotiations between actors, some agreements emerge with regard to acceptable and non-acceptable political acts; and these agreements determine the rules of the game until they are changed. This process resembles the games children play, in which the players create ad hoc rules and change them occasionally in response to the changing conditions of the game and the new preferences of its players.

Nonetheless, during the course of time, some principles of operation and certain normative rules of behavior have been set up in the political reality of organizations. Among these rules one should note the collective agreements between employers and workers that state in a detailed and mandatory way some of the principles of action such as the rules of behavior between employers and employees during a labor dispute. Another example is the agreed upon and obligatory rules concerning the dismissal of workers from their jobs, mainly in the public sector. In addition to the formal collective contracts, there are rules that each side tries to impose on the other in order to ensure fair competition. For example, there are employers who do not agree to negotiate with their employees as long as the latter are on strike. In many work organizations it has been agreed upon and accepted by all that no violent means should be employed (such as sabotage of property, physical injury to people, or verbal violence). This rule applies not only in labor relations between employers and employees, but also in quarrels among peers and work groups, and even between rivals who represent opposing interests.[13] The fear of the outcome of violence felt by many people encourages agreement on interaction and negotiation procedures; and it also leads people to define legitimate forms of communication that stand in contrast to behavior that is regarded as illegitimate. In light of such anxieties one can understand the public shock and profound agitation caused to the American people by the assassination of President John F. Kennedy.

Nevertheless, the history of industrial relations in various countries is filled with many violent events. Acts of violence in work organizations have taken the form of siege against chief executive officers, sabotage of property in corporate headquarters, destruction of raw materials and finished products, locking of factory gates, and violent fights with police officers. On the other hand, managements do not sit idly by during labor conflicts, and they also initiate acts of violence. One of the unprecedented cases of management violence occurred in Israel in a defense industry, where the general manager brought in special dogs to expel employees who had garrisoned themselves in the factory courtyard.

It should be stressed here that labor relations reflect only one kind of political struggle in organizations. The political game is diverse and it is conducted on several planes at the same time. As we shall show later on, different organizational problems such as privatization in the public sector or the transfer of factories to foreign countries in the private sector are controversial problems; hence, they become issues over which different stakeholders struggle, using political means to bring about their preferred outcome. Every attempt to gain an advantage over others by means of a unilateral change in the agreed rules of the game reflects a political move by the stakeholder that is geared to tilt the situation in his favor.

In view of the ongoing political struggles that take place in organizations, there is an obvious need to impose principles of operation and to establish behavior patterns that will ensure that the rules of the game agreed upon by all are preserved. Among the behavioral rules that have been institutionalized within work organizations over time, we can mention principles such as trust, secrecy, decency, and reciprocity.

The participants in the political game expect specific behavior from their competitors and rivals. Hence, they show resentment to behavioral patterns that are not in accord with the agreed upon conventions. For instance, disclosure of secrets, slandering colleagues, and desertion to the rival side betrays a breach of the rules of the political game and causes harsh reactions.

A famous example of a reaction to a breach of this kind can be seen in the hostile attitude of the public towards Jonathan Pollard who conveyed classified material to a foreign country while he was working as a civil servant. The severe punishment he was given for this act, and the strong objection of the authorities to set him free after so many years of imprisonment, demonstrate the deep resentment towards his act of betrayal.

In the internal culture of many organizations, there are some "red lines,' which participants are forbidden to cross under any condition. Regardless of the organizational actors' goals and motives, certain behaviors are ruled out, even if the rules were not written down in the legal form of official regulations. Military, security and police organizations invest a great many resources and make serious efforts to instill among their people the proper norms of behavior; and at the same time they insist on imposing deterrent punishments on those who intentionally or even unintentionally violate these norms. In such organizations, loyalty is a supreme value, and there is no justification to betray it. Hence, these organizations prevent their members from organizing themselves into groups that aim to promote their own interests, such as professional unions or workers' committees. Any grouping together of a few soldiers making certain collective demands (rights, benefit, or exemption) is regarded as an attempt at mutiny, and causes a harsh reaction by the military authorities.

In our times, many business organizations, especially advanced hi-tech firms, place the highest emphasis on secrecy. Everyone who is involved in the activities of such organizations learns very quickly the set of regulations and the norms regarding secrecy and the formal and informal mechanisms for enforcing them. Individuals and groups know that revealing professional secrets is regarded as an illegitimate act that is not included among the political means they are permitted to take in order to gain advantages by playing political games. The obligation of secrecy is required from employees, suppliers, contractors, advisers, and in some cases, even clients. In spite of this, the leakage of information is unavoidable even in organizations of this kind. The high turnover of hi-tech employees, which is typical of these organizations, causes a continuous "brain drain"—namely, the transfer of professional knowledge from one employer to another, despite all the safeguards.

Another principle that is common among organizations and is expressed in organizational politics is the norm of reciprocity. The tendency of political actors to form coalitions, make agreements, and set up various modes of cooperation is based, in effect, on the principle of reciprocity. These arrangements, even if they are temporary ones, are intended to benefit the participants and to increase their bargaining ability when confronting their rivals in the political arena. Therefore, an actor who joins such a partnership expects his associates to treat him as an equal partner with equal rights, that is, to share with him the information about options and risks, to include him in the planned political moves, to involve him in the decision-making process, and above all—to grant him his/her share of the profits gained by this cooperative effort. Such rules of the game have become normative both in intra-organizational as well as in interorganizational politics nowadays.

In our times, more and more business organizations belong to multi-organizational networks, most of which are spread over a number of countries all over the world. Among these organizational networks there is interorganizational cooperation of various kinds. The principle of reciprocity is intended, therefore, to ensure a fair division of inputs and outputs between the organizational actors. Its role is to prevent or at least reduce the opportunistic tendency of individuals and organizations to take an advantage in their favor, at the expense of the other partners. It is doubtful if the coalition phenomenon, which is so common in the political game, would be possible if it were not for the preservation of reciprocity. Most probably, without mutual expectations of this kind, political actors—individuals, groups, and organizations—would be reluctant to cooperate with others. The rules of the political game that allow actors to work together for certain political ends serve as the normative basis for alliances between rivals and competitors in the organizational reality, however temporary and variable they may be. In this matter as well, violation of the reciprocity principle by one of the participants is regarded as an intolerable offense and causes negative reactions and punitive measures by the other participants.

The principle of fairness is also commonly accepted in organizational politics. According to this principle, members of the organization are required not to evade responsibility and to contribute their share to the general activities of the organization. As part of the collective effort, opportunities are often created that can be abused by members of the organization to win a "free ride" or to "hitchhike," as the popular expression goes, at the expense of others. In other words, this norm deters the participants of the organization to opt for opportunistic behavior despite the tempting circumstances to do so. From an economic viewpoint, personal interests encourage opportunism. Therefore, human beings are likely to behave selfishly whenever they can do so because they are primarily motivated by personal needs, desires, and goals.[14]

However, as the sociologist Amitai Etzioni asserts, many social-psychological laboratory experiments show that human beings do not take a free ride at the expense of others.[15] The feeling that such exploitation is not right and unfair motivates many people to contribute their share in the collective effort and to behave with utmost decency towards their associates. But it would be naïve to think that everyone behaves decently, especially when it concerns competitors and rivals. People and organizations do tend to exploit their associates to obtain greater benefits at their expense. Many actors adopt methods intended to take "short cuts" and to "cut corners" in order to attain their objectives. There are those who employ a variety of fraudulent and deceptive techniques towards their associates, allies, and the authorities. Such "hitchhikers" do not merely avoid paying the fare, but they even try to steal the car. Evading income tax, cheating the customs authority, the smuggling out of capital and of classified information, deceiving partners by forging accounts, and spying on the plans of allies, are some of the examples of a lack of decency in organizational life.

Yet such offenses are not usually tolerated, and the mechanisms of social control apply various kinds of punishment against the offenders that prevent them from participating in the political game. People who have the label of mistrust attached to them find it hard to enlist allies, to engage cooperative agreements, and to form political coalitions. Suspicion towards them increases and respect towards them diminishes accordingly. For example, the chairman of the Palestinian Authority had been caught time and again in acts of deception, double talk, false declarations, and broken promises up to a point that he is no longer trusted by major leaders of the world. In the same way, organizations and businesses that are found to be untrustworthy are forced to pay the price of their improprieties in the image they present among the wider public in general and among their clients in particular. The public image of the giant software company Microsoft, for example, was severely damaged by the accusations of impropriety that were leveled against it by the American Department of Justice and in view of the serious conclusions of the judge who presided over the case at that time.[16]

Individuals, groups, organizations, and corporations mostly behave according to abiding rules and the social norms. Thus, the behavior of people in an organization is basically conformist behavior that fits in with the set of social values and behavioral procedures. In spite of the particular interests of the participants and despite their selfish tendencies to satisfy their desires and to care for themselves, the normative order restrains their behavioral patterns and channels them into legitimate courses of action. Therefore, the political arena is not an open field, accessible to everyone, where each actor can do whatever he wants without consideration for other actors or for the effects of his activities upon them. As in a sports field, the game in the political field is also played with a set of agreed upon and obligatory rules. As Jeffrey Pfeffer notes:

> The conclusion from this brief review of relevant empirical evidence seems inescapable: social and individual values matter in understanding behavior and are often more powerful predictors than simple conceptions of self-interest. In determining the normative order, both prevalence and the actions of legitimate authorities, such as governments, are important. Consequently, understanding the emergence of norms and moral conceptions in organizations, and examining their effects on behavior, are important research tasks.[17]

Conclusion

Organizations formalize their exchange relationships within and between themselves by means of agreements and contracts. However, official agreements of this type are not a sufficient guarantee for the full recompense that the different actors involved in this exchange relationship are interested in receiving all the time. Because organizations are subject to the influence of small and large changes that frequently occur within them, their actors shift their preferences accordingly. Therefore, most participants are likely to take steps that assist them in the accumulation of power and enable them to use it in pursuing their objectives. This struggle for power and its usage is the very essence of organizational politics. These measures give the organization the character of a political arena that is used as a sort of playground in which organizational actors play political games of various kinds. These games are essentially competition over the rights to valuable and useful benefits above those granted to them by contracts and agreements.

Outside actors, who are not members of the organization but have an interest in it, occasionally join in these political games. Among these external actors are individuals, groups, and organizations that try to influence from the outside the course of action taken by the organization and to channel it in the direction that maximizes their profits or minimizes damage. The external players collaborate with some of the internal ones in forming political coalitions to deal with various issues. This kind of cooperation, sometimes conducted beneath the surface, complicates the political game and intensifies the conflict between the rival parties. Hence, the distribution of the spoils among different beneficiaries becomes much more difficult. The frequent lack of resources vis-à-vis the increasing number of beneficiaries competing over them sharpens the political struggle into a zero-sum game. This is a game in which the profit of one side is as great as the loss on the other side, unless there is the possibility of increasing the reservoir of resources in the organization.

It is not surprising, therefore, that different actors try to ensure the results they fight for in the game by using coercive means; for instance, the imposition of preconditions, the application of physical force, and expression of threats against their rivals. Alternatively, players take misleading steps and deceptive measures; they disclose secrets, reveal classified information, and breach trust. These and similar actions represent a contravention of the rules in the political game, an infringement of the regulations, a violation of agreements, and a betrayal of principles and values. They are therefore considered as illegitimate actions that undermine the rules of the political game, damage its role as a mechanism for the allocation of benefits, and endanger its continuity.

Such courses of action might very well encounter verbal or behavioral resistance, counter-acts of reprisal, and the use punitive measures against the offenders. In this way, the rules of the political game are determined normatively, and the borderlines of what is permitted and prohibited in organizational politics are set down. Like any other normative system, this system is subject to changes and its duration depends on the efficiency of the social control.

The participants of the political game in the organizational arena have no choice but to accept, sooner or later, the mandatory rules and to act accordingly. Even when the struggle involves clashes and disputes over rare resources that each participant strives to obtain, and even when the conflict is over essential positions of power, organizational politics is kept under some control. Without rules there is no game, and there are no extra benefits. By restraining themselves to some degree or other, organizational actors take an active part in the formation and reformation of the rules of the game over time.

Nevertheless, it should be realized that organizational politics is neither an exchange of gestures nor is it an innocent children's game. The political game is a tough fight, aggressively and cunningly played by opposing rivals with essential interests over very high stakes.

Notes

1. Morgan, 1986.
2. Burns, 1961:257-281.
3. The term "politics" in connection with party or government represents only one aspect of the political phenomenon in its wider and more comprehensive sense. In order to distinguish between national politics and the politics that is conducted with organizations or between them, certain scholars are accustomed to call organizational politics "micro-politics," which means politics on a minor scale. See Pfeffer, 1978.
4. Morgan, 1986: 148.
5. Pettigrew, 1973: 17.
6. Bacharach & Lawler, 1980: 1.
7. Mintzberg, 1983: 421.
8. In the political struggles conducted between competing organizations, especially in the business sector, one may identify certain characteristics that are similar to wars between enemies. Even in such competitions there is generally no intention to destroy the rival physically as on a military battlefield. See chapter 9, which deals with interorganizational politics.
9. Mintzberg, 1983.
10. Chapter 8 deals in detail with inter-group politics that are conducted in organizations.
11. Samuel, 1996.
12. Mintzberg, 1983.
13. It is worth noting the differences that exist between various countries both in the field of legislation and in the enforcement of state laws regarding the use of violence towards others in different social frameworks.
14. See, for example, Williamson, 1975, 1981.
15. Etzioni, 1988
16. See chapter 9 for a more detailed discussion on Microsoft.
17. Pfeffer, 1997: 77.

4

The Political Agenda

Determinants of Organizational Politics

Organizations function on the basis of rules and procedures that regulate in a clear and mandatory fashion the behavior of participants. These rules determine the mutual relationships between members and their associates, suppliers, and clients both inside and outside the organization. The greater part of such regulated behavior is generally conducted routinely. However, once new conditions creating conflict and encouraging competition among the different stakeholders disrupt the current state of affairs, then the emergence of organizational politics is likely to take place. Such organizational changes give impetus to power struggles and political games.

In our times, numerous and rapid changes characterize the processes of production in most industries. These processes constitute the *technical core* of every organization, without which it cannot exist. The production process of any goods or services is composed of a well-defined series of stages that are carried out in a specific order and is linked to other processes taking place in the organization, such as procurement or maintenance. Throughout these processes, the organization utilizes some kinds of production technologies, and it uses a certain mixture of resources.

Thus, the "production technology" is a complex whole of means, methods, tools, and procedures through which the activity of transforming inputs into outputs is carried out; that is, the conversion of resources into products. These conversion activities are defined in most organizations by means of formal and mandatory procedures in the form of operational instructions or production techniques. The production workers of the organization are required to strictly adhere to these procedures, in many cases without authority to use personal discretion. The higher the level of technology, the more highly programmed and rather rigid become the processes of production. Hence, any deviation from the procedures may halt the entire workflow.

Since the processes of production are generally determined by production engineers, suppliers of machinery, and experts in the quality of the product, such prescribed operational instructions are usually set down on the basis of engineering considerations, technical constraints, and economic calculations. These organizational activities, despite their central importance to the organization, are presumably included in the framework of technical activities of the organization that are not meant to be a matter for the political game.

This relative immunity from political involvement by the stakeholders protects the technical core as long as it proceeds by prescribed methods, tools, and procedures. The political game in this connection is played whenever a real change is foreseen in production processes. Organizational change in such processes is usually implemented by the installation of new technologies (such as computerization or automation); and it is expressed by newly established working procedures and the revised definition of roles and authority. The implication of such changes is alteration in the status and employment of the so-called *direct employees* belonging to the technical core of the organization.[1] This kind of change presents a threat to such workers—to their expertise, their achievements, and their status in the organization—and therefore it rouses them to political action intended to protect them from damage, ensure their rights, and compensate them for every change they have to make as a result of the new working conditions.[2]

The harsh competitive conditions that many business organizations have to face compel them to make constant technological changes. It is no wonder that many disputes between employees and employers have occurred in recent years as a result of technological changes in production processes, both in manufacturing plants and in service organizations. Just recently, workers everywhere showed stubborn resistance to the induction of advanced technologies such as automated machinery, computerized workstations, assembly line robots, and closed circuit television.

As employees feel threatened by the application of technological changes, so do investors feel threatened by the additional costs that might cause a loss in their profits; and managers become fearful of a decrease in the production of the organization and of poor business dealings during the running-in period of technological change. Suppliers and contractors are deterred by the need to adapt to specifications they are not familiar with, and clients ask themselves how much the products will cost them as a result of these changes in production processes. The skepticism and the suspicions are strong motivations for taking steps to prevent the change or to minimize its estimated damage.

Stakeholders, therefore, employ preventive measures intended to assist them to cope adequately with the results of the change and to insure themselves again the dangers and damages that might hurt their interests. These steps are essentially political since they usually involve negotiations leading to agreements between those affected by the change, and they entail the exercise of power and the use of manipulations in order to secure their interests. The political game in this context is mainly bargaining—explicit or implicit, overt or covert—over the range and quality of the compensation due to each stakeholder as a result of the implementation of the organizational change. In this way the subject of change is placed on the agenda of the organization.

Since all organizational changes entail various risks, many see them as a threat that might be harmful to them, and therefore they arouse opposition. *Resistance to change* is one of the most common social phenomena that accompany every social change. In light of the many and frequent changes that occur in most organizations today, it is not surprising that many of them have pockets of resistance. Those resistors encourage a show of opposition and mutiny through political organizational activities. Their aim is preventing the implementation of the organizational change, or at least minimizing what they consider to be its negative implications.

Such expressions of opposition include protest activities, sanctions, total or partial strikes, disruption of the processes, and reduction of output. The resistance to change brings rivals together, at least temporarily, and encourages the creation of coalitions between home players and external players against the initiators of change and their supporters. All these are intentional exercises of power at the disposal of various actors that are meant to ensure results to suit their personal interests or those of certain stakeholders whom they represent in the organization. These manifestations of resistance to change are expressed in a variety of ideological, intellectual, and legal explanations; in fact, they are intended to mask the selfish motives and the utilitarian considerations of the opposers.

Organizational change can therefore provide fertile ground for the emergence of organizational politics since change means, first and foremost, a state of *uncertainty*, that is, a lack of knowledge about the results and their implications. Generally speaking, people are afraid of uncertain situations because most of them find it difficult to cope properly with the unknown. The amassing of power and its political exercise for obtaining advantages and assurances are to be seen as attempts by organizational actors to avoid situations of uncertainty or at least to cope with them.

Uncertainty is not only the problem of individuals who belong to an organization that is undergoing a process of change. Uncertainty is a major existential problem of every organization as a whole, at any time and in any place. The changes and innovations that occur in the environment of most organizations today challenge them with a wide range of unforeseen problems that the organizations have to resolve for the purpose of survival. In light of such unknown factors, anyone who can lessen the degree of uncertainty in an organization will have relatively greater power and his political bargaining abilities will be superior to those of his competitors and rivals.[3]

The control over resources that are vital to the organization and its members creates a dependency on these actors and allows them to influence organizational decisions in the direction they prefer. Situations of change and instability pave the way for organizational participants to identify new opportunities and attempt to "reshuffle the cards" for the purpose of gaining greater benefits. Presumably, the various stakeholders will not miss such opportunities, and will do all that they can to win the political game that is being conducted against the background of organizational change.

Another factor that encourages organizational politics is the factor of *ambiguity*. Ambiguity is typical to various organizational situations in which rules and procedures are poorly specified and unclear, and job definitions are rather vague. In general, organizations are founded on a systematic division of labor.[4] Areas of specialization, authority, and responsibility are generally determined by the formal definition of roles, by personal and group agreements, by business contracts, and by official regulations and procedures. However, organizations differ from each other in the quantity and quality of such formalization. New and small organizations, for example, are usually less formalized than old and large ones.

In every organization there are, of course, areas of activities that are arranged in a more precise manner than others, such as those areas that concern security or privacy. Nevertheless, in most organizations one can find ambiguous areas in which expected behaviors or interpersonal relationships are not well defined. This kind of *organizational ambiguity* is characteristic of changing conditions as well as situations in which there is no clear division of labor among those in charge. Similarly, there are situations in which authority and responsibility of organizational subunits overlap one another in ways that create a great deal of organizational ambiguity. Last but not least, ambiguity prevails whenever the organization's authorities define certain requirements that actually contradict or do not accord with other demands.

Ambiguous situations prod the "activists" to establish precedence in various areas of operation that accords with their preferences; in other words, whoever acts in the area of ambiguity tries to impose his own interpretation and to establish the definition of the situation to his liking. A prolonged *role conflict* is thus created which serves as an excuse for the political activity of the actors involved in it.[5] This is a conflict in which the relative power of the actors and their bargaining positions are subject to constant ups and downs resulting from various internal and external constraints. Nevertheless, the definition of the situation also changes in accordance with the passage of time.

Organizations cannot function for long only on the basis of coercion. Regardless of their rigid regime, and in spite of the supervision and control they impose, organizations need a certain amount of general consensus as to their particular quality and function among those that belong to them. The lack of social agreement on such essential matters for an organization is a hotbed for the development of political struggle among actors in the organization and outside it. Disagreements spur the organizational actors to take measures and perform actions to persuade the rest of the participants in the organization to agree with their views and to accept the solutions that they suggest to settle disputes.

Most likely, the differences in opinion on essential matters are expressions of value judgment for opposing interests. Individuals and groups tend to camouflage their basic interests in a series of ideological, religious, moral or intellectual "masks." At the same time, it is often impossible to rely only on persuasion, or it does not succeed as hoped, and the need arises to implement various political means such as bribery, inducements, threats, deception, and awe intimidation on the dissidents. The justification for such tactics is publicly explained by the need to preserve the integrity of the organization, its proper functioning, its success and its future progress. From the point of view of certain stakeholders, in these cases just as in other organizational cases, the end justifies the means. In this way, a political game develops within the organization during which each player tries to win the greatest advantage over his rivals.

Gerald Salancik and Jeffrey Pfeffer[6] claimed that organizational politics is the unavoidable result of a dearth of resources. When vital resources are found in abundance in an organization, there is no problem of allocating them to the various beneficiaries, and therefore there is also no need for a struggle over the way they are divided. In such cases, the stakeholders are not required to apply force to overcome their competitors in the struggle over the division of the spoils. However, most of the organizational resources that are important for stakeholders are by their very nature rare resources. They therefore serve as a target to be reached and a subject for continuous competition among stakeholders.

The lack of resources intensifies organizational politics and it supplies the political game with motives such as greed for profit, desire for domination and authority, and aspirations for esteem and honor. The competition over resources tends to develop into confrontation between competitors that often escalates towards violent power struggles. Disputes between employers and employees, contentions between political parties, wars between criminal organizations, and competition between espionage organizations represent some examples of power struggles over scarce resources. The political struggle over resources is a struggle over the allocation of limited resources to the different organizational units to carry out their activities. The actors participating in this competition, or at least some of them, represent the needs of these organizational units, the target public they serve, and the objectives that they try to achieve within the organization. Each organizational unit strives to increase the slice assigned to it from the *organizational pie*, obviously at the expense of the competing units, and not necessarily by violent means. The competition between various units in organizations is often conducted through political measures of other kinds, such as the manipulation of information or warnings about states of emergency, and false alarms about expected crises.

Focal Points of the Political Struggle

The political actors in an organization and outside it, however energetic and determined they may be, cannot conduct an endless struggle on every matter and issue. As in the world of sports, in the organizational arena as well, there is a tendency to mobilize resources and to focus efforts for exerting influence on specific locations in the arena and on events that might lead to political victory. In the arena of organizational politics, these selected locations are the decision-making centers, like the Board of Directors. The most important decision-making centers are those in which critical issues are resolved for the entire organization.[7]

The decision-making centers in organizations are numerous and varied because they are scattered in different parts of the organization. In most public and private organizations, the top management of the organization constitutes the most important decision center. Participants of this *strategic apex* are usually the Chief Executive Officer, the Vice Presidents, the senior staff professionals such as the Legal Adviser and the Chief Engineer. This small group of decision makers determines the organizational strategy, outlines the organization's policy and sets up business goals. The top management is also in charge of raising capital, heavy investments, and the signing of business contracts with major suppliers and clients. It is also responsible for on-going internal control of the main subsidiary units. Thus, the top management makes binding decisions for the entire organization. It is not surprising, then, that such executives are subject to frequent pressures by stakeholders interested in diverting decisions in the directions they desire.

In business firms, the top management is supervised by the Board of Directors, representing the stockholders, the general public, and other interest groups.[8] The Board of Directors examines the management decisions, reviews the financial results of the enterprise, decides on the allocation of dividends, appoints and dismisses the Chief Executive Officer, and approves appointments of the senior staff. According to the law, members of the Board must act solely for the benefit of the firm, that is, for success and advancement of the business company they were entrusted to guard. The authority of the Board of Directors provides its members with a significant amount of power, turning this small group into a very important decision-making center in any organization— whether private or public. But the Board consists of different stakeholders having different interests; hence it is a locus of built-in competition among its members over the organizational spoils. Thus, the decisions of the Board of Directors are usually influenced to a considerable degree, and sometimes even to a conclusive degree, by the interests of their clients and the desired results of the issues being discussed.[9]

One of the important decision-making centers of nonprofit organizations, which constitutes an object of influence for most internal and external stakeholders of every organization, is the house of representatives of various kinds such as the parliament, the senate, the municipal council, the board of trustees, and the like. Within those assemblies a large and widely varied number of members gather to hold intensive and practical discussions concerning the subjects on the agenda; and therefore plenum meetings are frequently characterized by declarative speeches meant for the voting public or for the sake of being registered in the protocols of the meetings and in statements intended for the media.[10]

It is not surprising that these houses of representatives serve as arenas for the obvious wheeling and dealing of actors participating in the political game. It is quite common that more than a few decisions in the plenum reflect the relative political strengths among the stakeholders represented in it; such decisions are influenced by the lobbying of external stakeholders, who have no representation in the composition of the house members, like associations for environmental protection or trade unions.

Additional focal points of decision making that are active at lower organizational levels often include coordination and liaison teams between divisions in business corporations, between governmental agencies, and between staff and line authorities within the organization. Since these delegates represent various organizational units, they tend to sway the decisions in favor of their own organizational units, and quite often at the expense of the other participating organizations. Furthermore, these decisions makers are also exposed to the influence of various external stakeholders not participating in such centers; those interest groups often take political measures to divert the outcomes in the direction desirable for their interests.

Finally, it is also worth including in the political layout those decision centers that are active in many different organizations in the form of committees; among them one may consider planning committees, budget committees, recruitment and appointment committees, license committees, appeals committees, and steering committees as arenas of political struggle. A large number of such committees have direct control over critical resources, such as budget allocations, which many people and organizations are interested in obtaining. Other committees, such as disciplinary committees, deal with and decide on issues that concern possible penalties; others deal with decisions that have significant commercial implications such as the granting of licenses. Needless to say, members of these committees are subjected to pressure by various stakeholders, whose tactics include lobbying, enticements, and threats—in the form of overt and covert attempts.

Political Issues

To begin with, it is worth noting that the political agendas of many business firms as well as public agencies are considerably influenced by outside social groups as well as by nongovernmental organizations. This influence is due to considerable political efforts of such stakeholders to raise issues that will be in line with their particular ideologies and preferences. This kind of political intervention is meant to ensure that most organizations will be constantly involved in certain socioeconomic problems beyond the internal issues with which they are concerned. Issues such as social justice, rights and freedoms, quality of the environment, moral standards, equality before the law, and similar issues, according to the outlook of social activists, should constitute the daily concerns of organizations, especially those in the public sector.

One of the well-known examples of such political efforts is the pressure of feminist organizations to place the issue of sexism on the agenda of public organizations as a permanent issue that cannot be ignored in today's organizational reality. According to this view, organizations are essentially genderized entities in which those who are in control intentionally neutralize any problem connected with the gender factor; and hence they systematically overlook the issue of inequality among the sexes in the organizational world. The reason for this discrimination lies in the fact that the leaders of organizations as well as the middle managers are mostly males.

> The early radical critique of sexism denounced bureaucracy and hierarchy as male-created and male-dominated structures of control that oppress women. The easiest answer to the "why so little debate" question is that the link between masculinity and organizational power was so obvious that no debate was needed. However, experiences in the feminist movement suggest that the questions are not exhausted by recognizing male power.[11]

In present times, the well-developed and deeply rooted feminist awareness does not allow for the disregard of the sexist problem in organizational discourse. Both researchers and activists in the organizational field have adopted the view that organizations are sexist social entities in which, and through which, the advantages and disadvantages of men and women in society are realized. In organizations, the differences between the sexes acquire both concrete and symbolic expressions. Those differences may be seen in the income levels of men and women, promotion opportunities, working conditions, modes of thinking, language and behavior, in power relationships and in the domination of men over women. The masculine character of organizations also dictates the character of the professions and the social interrelations between the sexes.

According to this interpretation, the problem of sexism must be an inseparable part of the political agenda of organizations per se. It commands an important place in the discourse that is conducted at all organizational levels and sectors. Even if the executives of certain organizations do not want to deal with this issue, they should be forced to consider it seriously. It is no wonder, then, that in every case associated with sexual harassment or assault, with seeming discrimination against a woman at her workplace, or an insulting expression towards women, public debate is once again aroused. This debate takes place in the media, in houses of representatives, in courts and in various political parties; and they encourage taking legal steps to protect the female population in general, and working women in particular.

Another example of the repeated attempts to determine the political agenda of organizations may be seen in the activities of trade unions in various countries. They raise over and over certain issues for the agenda such as minimum wage for unskilled workers, the employment of illegal immigrants, and the protection of workers' rights in processes of privatization of state-owned enterprises. Union leaders strive to place these and similar issues on the national level agenda in such a way that every work organization, whether public or private, will be forced to give them serious consideration in spite of internal objections to such issues.

Nongovernmental organizations (NGOs) around the world repeatedly attempt to include in the political agenda of business firms the issue of environmental quality. On this subject as well, there is a growing tendency to make demands on many and various kinds of organizations to consider the question of environmental quality in their main decision-making processes, and to give it suitable response through practical measures and to be accountable for the results. Beyond these issues, every organization has several "issues of significance," as Stuart Clegg calls them, which encourage political struggle.[12]

It is for the sake of such issues that stakeholders are willing to enter the arena of organizational politics, to exercise the power at their disposal against their opponents, and to apply political tactics in order to steer the decision makers towards supporting the resolutions they desire; in other words, to participate in the political game in the organization. All this is because these issues reflect the opposing interests of the different stakeholders who are involved in the organization. Such issues encourage the politicization of decision-making processes in organizations. In fact, they create conflicts of a political nature among actors—both internal and external—who represent opposing interests.[13]

Whenever this type of significant problem is placed on the organizational agenda, stakeholders tend to focus on their political activities before the decisions that are imminent are actually made. These actors assume that it would be more effective to influence decisions before they are ratified than to appeal their validity or to annul them after they have been accepted through legitimate processes by the relevant authorities. Thus, organizational politics is to a great extent a web of actions and interactions by people and groups who have no authority in the matter to influence decision makers. Nevertheless, in the organizational reality there are plenty of examples of political struggles intended to reverse undesirable decisions after they have been legally approved. Political measures in situations of this kind include protests (such as propaganda, rallies, and demonstrations), sanctions (such as refusal to sign documents, refusal to obey instructions), lobbying (signing petitions, enlisting the support of politicians and public figures), and legal activities (such as appeals to the Supreme Court). There are even cases where actors who were appealing decisions demanded the dismissal of the decision makers. Such activities are concrete evidence that the political game is fundamentally a power game in which forceful measures and the ways in which they are applied have a decisive influence on the outcome.

However, important issues that have been decided upon are difficult to annul and even hard to change. This difficulty arises because persons of authority are reluctant to admit their mistakes publicly and to repent their decisions, which were supposedly taken on the basis of facts and after lengthy consideration. Decisions have a dynamics of their own that make them, after a while, accepted social facts that cannot be questioned. Many actors in organizations adapt themselves sooner or later to the behavior demanded by certain decisions, and this creates a real difficulty for doubting or questioning its validity. Moreover, every strategic decision made by the higher echelon of the organization becomes the basis for a long series of operative and tactical decisions at the lower ranks, thus creating a state of mutual interdependence among them.

In light of the difficulties involved in annulling or even changing decisions, actors often choose to employ a political measure aimed at a 'show of muscle' against the *dominant coalition*—a symbolic measure that serves as a kind of warning. That is to say, "even if the battle has been decided against us, the war is not over yet." For a message to be persuasive, to express strength and not weakness, such measures tend to be forceful in nature; that is, they include the use of physical force, public disturbances, initiated brawls, vocal agitations, or the destruction of property owned by the organization.

We should now consider issues of significance that cause political struggles within organizations:[14] (a) organizational goals; (b) budgets and appropriations; (c) senior appointments; (d) organizational structures. These issues are constantly being placed on the organizational agenda, according to the periodicity practiced by the organization, such as an annual work plan or the length of term in office of senior officials. Each decision on one of these issues embodies a very complex organizational task, which requires handling of information, assessment of alternatives, setting up an appropriate time-table, and proper management of the decision-making procedure itself.

In many cases, these processes involve the preparation of position papers by various experts and consultation with internal and external constituents. In theory, these decision processes are based on pertinent considerations, on factual grounds, on professional thinking, and on a comprehensive view for the general good of the organization. In fact, these processes are generally tinged with personal and group interests, value preferences, prejudices, and with the commitments of the decision makers to the interests of various stakeholders.

Goals and Objectives

In addition to the list of *official goals* that many organizations declare publicly—goals that have a marginal degree of practical influence on organizational functioning—organizations are also required, from time to time, to define their *operational goals*, that is, goals that are intended to determine the direction and formulation of their activities.[15] These goals consist of a series of practical objectives that are viable and measurable, for instance, work plans for various lengths of time, financial or operational outcomes that have to be obtained, organizational changes that must be completed, interorganizational connections that need to be established, and similar decisions of strategic significance.

Henry Mintzberg classifies these organizational goals into four main types: (1) ideological goals that are derived from a certain aggregate of beliefs, commonly shared by the members of the organization—namely, goals that define the mission of the organization in the eyes of its participants; (2) official goals that reflect the wishes and preferences of whomever controls the organization by virtue of his or her authority. The head of an organization defines such goals for the organization that are binding on all its participants; (3) commonly shared personal goals, that is, goals that resemble each other, which the members of the organization strive to realize through organizational activity.

It is for those purposes that the organization was established by the founders in the first place, and it is for their sake that they actively participate in it; (4) systemic goals that stakeholders strive to realize due to the benefits they derive from the very existence of the organization and its activities. These goals focus primarily on the survival of the organization, on the improvement of its internal efficiency, and on its independence and growth.[16] According to this view, every organization has a certain aggregate of goals that can be seen as the goals of the organization, since they are the goals that most members of the organization commonly share.

> This is not to say that the organization's influencers do not have goals of their own, which they seek to impose on the organization at the expense of those pursued more consistently. One clearly does not preclude the other. Indeed, the two sets of goals—shared and non-shared, organizational and personal—coexist in all imaginable organizations.[17]

The practical importance of the goals and objectives of organizational activities lies first and foremost in the fact that it is these that in effect determine the agenda of the organization. Thus, the organizational goals and objectives express the priorities according to which the organization plans and carries out its activities; they influence the allocation of resources at its disposal to the various units and activities, and they determine the fate of projects and programs. Consequently, the goals affect the preferential order of the various recipients to receive benefits. In view of these implications, it is easy to understand the efforts invested by stakeholders in the organization to influence decisions concerning its goals and objectives. Therefore, operational goals represent an organizational issue of great importance, of the highest value, that anyone able to do so would try to divert in the direction he prefers.

The process of choosing the goals of the organization and its implementation objectives is basically a political one. This is a process in which there is real interest not only by the in-house players but also by the outside players. The supporters and opposers of a certain organization see the decisions regarding the goals and objectives as a touchstone for the essential orientation of that organization. Investors tend to see the immediate goals and objectives as components of a business plan that must be tested for its chances of success. From the point of view of the clients, the question of goals and objectives implies the contents of the organization's "basket of products." The value of these products is tested by their quantity, quality, availability, service, reliability, and price. Competing organizations show an interest in the operational goals and implementation objectives to which the organization is directed, since these goals have implications for their own objectives and implementations.

Given the sensitivities and implications of these issues, it is no wonder that stakeholders acting outside the organization also apply political measures to affect its decision-making processes. A typical form of political action for situations of this kind is the formation of a coalition with some in-house players whose interests fall in line with those of the outside ones. This kind of alliance is liable to arouse other stakeholders, such as managers and professionals, to form a counter-coalition. As a result, a power struggle against the internal "collaborators" is likely to take place and even to develop into a violent one. Therefore, these external actors often maintain secret contacts with internal ones, generally by means of go-betweens who hide the real participants in the coalition.

The struggle conducted in the Israeli defense industry is an outstanding example of a political struggle over the definition of goals and objectives that had been continuing since the mid-1980s up to a short time ago. The various agencies of this state-owned industry were established in the past with the aim of developing and supplying the best armament for the Israeli Defense Forces. These mostly high technology enterprises were meant to serve in the defense of Israel. As a result of the geo-political changes that have occurred over the last two decades of the twentieth century, the defense industry went into a deep recession and was forced to layoff thousands of workers, to minimize its development activities, to close production lines, and to forgo its regular clients. These difficulties and losses forced the top management of those enterprises to redefine their goals and objectives, so as to adapt to the new environmental conditions.

According to the new government policy, all the defense industries are expected to export modernized armament to foreign countries. They should also offer the international market their know-how and innovative technology, and form business partnerships with similar industries in the United States and Europe for business purposes. These changes in goals and objectives inflamed the employees of the defense industry, especially the scientists and engineers, who refused to have their workplaces turned into arms factories for the highest bidder, and to be treated as technological "mercenaries." Therefore, they conducted a grim and stubborn political struggle against the Government of Israel, the Treasury, and the Ministry of Defense. In the course of this long tug of war, they joined forces with politicians from various parties, with the press, with public figures, and with retired senior officers who endorsed the employees' cause, each for his own good reasons.

However, behind the ideological struggle over the goals and objectives, there was also the desire of those civil servants to preserve the rights and privileges they had been enjoying in the past under the new conditions of privatization and globalization. The political strategy employed by them was a "delay strategy," that is, a process of negotiations with the management and with the government intended to postpone as much as possible the implementation of the organizational changes that were detrimental to their interests. This power struggle lasted approximately ten years, during which time repeated labor strikes, blocking of main roads and airfields, walkouts, retention of products as well as other coercive measures were employed.

Budgeting and Financing

The organizational budget is the lifeblood of all subsidiary units at all levels and in all sectors. There is no need to explain the importance of the budget to anyone who is responsible for implementing organizational programs. At the same time, the political nature of the budgetary process should be made clear and this applies not only to the governmental budget, but to the budgets of all other kinds of organizations no less. The budget is the practical expression of the organization plans and of its order of priorities. The budget also indicates the economic strength of an organization and its capacity to finance various sorts of activities. In addition, the budget enables the organization beneficiaries (e.g., executives, employees, stockholders, and suppliers) to get an idea of the amount of money available for them. It is not surprising, therefore, that every stakeholder in the organization casts sidelong glances at the budget with the clear intent of influencing its size and the way in which it is distributed.

Every financial budget includes two main parts: sources and usages. Financial sources are those incoming funds that the organization raises, including the income from sales of goods and services, from the sale or lease of property, from contributions and loans, from capital profits on investment, etc. The political aspect of this part of the budget is implied by the power it grants to the actors responsible for obtaining income from the various sources. Jeffrey Pfeffer and his associates found in the studies they conducted that academic departments that successfully managed to gain large research grants from external funds were the departments with much greater power in universities as compared with other departments.[18]

Similarly, marketing and sales units in business organizations acquire greater organizational power in comparison to other units, and the same applies to units handling data systems.[19] Individual actors, who also succeed in raising funds for the benefit of the organization, advance themselves to positions of influence within it. Outside Stakeholders such as investors, donators, bankers, governmental officials in charge of appropriations, and fund-raisers become as powerful as the amounts of money they can channel into the organization. This power is transformed into influence over decision makers whenever the latter deal with *issues of significance*, that is, issues that are of great importance to those external actors or stakeholders who appointed them to their positions. It seems that the popular proverb: "He who pays the piper calls the tune" rightly expresses the essence of organizational politics, first and foremost on the subject of budgetary allocation.

The second and main part of every budget is the financial usages, that is, the allocation of funds to the subunits of the organization and to various organizational projects. Every budget includes at least two types of fund allocation: (1) the operational budget, namely, allocation to fund current needs, and (2) the development budget, namely, allocation to fund investments. The operational budget determines the range of activities that the organization carries out in the spheres of production, services, maintenance, marketing, and the like. This budget is earmarked to finance the manpower dealing with these activities, the payments to sub-contractors and suppliers, the acquisition of equipment and expendable materials, transfers to various creditors, and so forth. The development budget includes allocations of funds for the development of infrastructure. This part of the budget is devoted to finance plans such as construction, procurement of heavy equipment and new technology, installing new lines of production, opening new branches and extensions, funding of research, financing of mergers, acquisitions, and takeovers of other business firms.

On the face of it, these fund allocations are merely accounting activities that are meant to ensure financial coverage for plans, projects, and activities of the organization according to the goals and objectives that were set down. However, it soon becomes evident that the process of allocation is not just a matter of technical accountancy.

Therefore, budgeting is essentially a political cycle of complex negotiations that have to be accomplished at the same time with several parties, year after year. In the course of this allocation process, the power of the senior staff members such as economists and accountants, who are in charge of the organizational funds, is revealed to its fullest extent. On the basis of their estimations and by means of complicated calculations, they manage to deduct from the budgets of certain units and add to the budgets of others, to spread out payments over long-term periods, to hasten or delay the pace of advancement for projects, to put an end to various programs, and to increase or decrease the acquisition and construction budgets.

Under these conditions of the political game, it is understood that players will take advantage of their political skills to divert budget allocations in their favor. As said before, this game is mainly played by negotiation, in the style of "give-and-take." Generally speaking, every actor demands a greater slice of the budget than the people in the budget division are willing to allocate him or her.

In return for the increase in their budget, managers promise to streamline their units, to increase production, to improve performance, to enlist support or to preserve peaceful labor relations with their employees. The bargaining focuses on the way that the given budgetary pie is divided among the different beneficiaries, a division in which every slice of the budget that one beneficiary gains is at the expense of the slices received by the other beneficiaries. Thus, budgeting represents a clear case of *zero-sum game* in organizations—a game that by its very nature calls for political behavior on the part of all parties involved.

Senior Appointments

Every organization is managed by a limited number of senior officials who possess wide authority. These executives usually include the president or chairman, the Board of Directors, the Chief Executive Officer, Vice Presidents, senior staff specialists (e.g., the Legal Advisor), and the general managers of major divisions. This selective group controls the activities of the organization and its resources, and it constitutes the *strategic apex* of the organization by virtue of its authority to make major binding decisions. As can be expected, those in senior positions belong to a group that enjoys special rights and privileges above and beyond those of all other members of the organization, in return for bearing the main burden of responsibility.

It is easy to understand why there are many who desire such positions in both public and private organizations. Stakeholders are aware of the advantages that these senior positions can offer them by way of advancement of their interests and an increase in the utility they can gain from the organization. They are therefore interested in manning as many senior positions with people who are close to them in outlook and who share their ambitions. From the moment they are appointed to their positions, these loyal servers grant the stakeholders who sponsored their appointment with a considerable influence over decisions that are taken on important issues. In some way or another, they serve in practice if not in theory, as unofficial delegates of the stakeholders in the main focal points of decision in the organization.

Yet, there are many executives who are considered to be professionals appointed to these key positions on the basis of proven skills and experience. But even such professionals cannot ignore the interests of whomever acted in order to ensure their appointments. Those senior officials know that their positions are not guaranteed and that they must satisfy their sponsors, or at least take into consideration the goals and preferences of the stakeholders who support them behind the scene.

Since the demand for these positions is greater than those available, those who see themselves as qualified candidates tend to compete for obtaining them. Unlike the political campaigns of candidates who want to be elected by the voting public, competitions in organizations are conducted in a low key and even concealed manner. The political game in this context is mainly based on

lobbying and persuasion. For these purposes a variety of methods are conducted, such as personal meetings, telephone conversations, business lunches,
and social encounters between candidates and those having the authority to
appoint them to the desired office. These competitors are frequently assisted by
the services of go-betweens and influential persons. This kind of lobbying
activity is meant to obtain a majority of supporters in the decision-making
body in favor of their candidacy to the vacant positions.

Since these are political measures, the support gained by their means is not
given freely. The candidates are well aware of the price they will have to pay to
the stakeholders who supported their appointment to the desired position. The
more the fate of a candidate is dependent on the support of a certain decision
maker, the greater will be his or her commitment to that decision maker. In short,
the greater the dependency of the one, the greater is the power of the other.
Experience teaches that stakeholders do not forgo the remuneration they are
owed, and they will present the senior official with the "bill" (not necessarily a
monetary one), requesting payment of the debt whenever it suits them. This
aspect of political reality is well captured by the proverbial saying that "in
politics there is no such thing as a free lunch."

This practice of appointing "our people" to key offices appears most often
whenever there is a change in the government in various countries or in the
administration in the United States. Then thousands of new senior officials
replace those that were serving in upper positions, in governmental agencies,
in state-owned enterprises, in public institutions, in embassies and consulates
abroad, and in many other organizations supported by the state. Every new
minister or secretary (just as every new mayor or head of a regional authority)
takes care to fill the top positions with those loyal to him/her, in a variety of
organizations that are subject to his or her authority. New Chief Executive
Officers of business corporations also tend to gradually fill key positions with
new loyal individuals that he or she can count on personally. These recruits are
popularly termed "paratroopers," and are generally found to have background
and life experiences similar to those of the executives who recruited them to
senior offices. Such similarity of background is likely to be found either in their
education and professional training, race and ethnicity, religion, military service, work experience, or in their political party affiliation.

The appointment of people to key positions in organizations is a shrewd and
profitable political act, since it serves as a powerful lever to influence major
decisions of the organization. Therefore, whatever the degree of compatibility
between the personal talents and professional skills of the senior officials in
organizations, many of them have obtained their positions as a result of political maneuvers, during the course of which the stakeholders conducted negotiations over the gains and losses that they expected from these appointments.

In this kind of political game, the actors employ measures such as lobbying,
agreements on the definition of their jobs and their authorities, negotiations

regarding the benefits accruing to them, secret understandings on the manning of other senior positions, and similar deals. Naturally, in such appointment processes there is no lack of mutual threats and the use of various kinds of forceful means.

In nonprofit organizations such as political parties, social movements, trade unions, scientific associations, societies, universities, and various funds, the main position holders are chosen by secret ballot of all members, or by their representatives, for a fixed term. In such organizations the appointment process in entirely political: the different stakeholders join together in coalitions that are intended to lead to the election of their preferred candidate; at the same time these coalitions negotiate with rivals to agree on a candidate that may be widely acceptable. The candidates themselves conduct overt or covert propaganda among the electoral body, promising benefits to all those who choose them; they also intimidate opponents by sending explicit or implicit threats, mostly through their close associates, regarding the price that they would have to pay one day for not supporting their candidacy. Thus, processes through which individuals are appointment to high rank positions become catalysts of organizational politics.

Organizational Structures

The main advantage that organizations have as compared with every other social entity lies in their ability to produce goods and services with great efficiency, and to carry out complicated tasks of far higher quantity and quality than those done by individuals. This advantage is due first and foremost to the division of labor in organizations. The division of labor, or *functional differentiation*, enables many employees having a variety of skills to carry out a large number of tasks and assignments at one and the same time. Coordination and supervision serve as the main mechanisms of integration that unite the differentiated activities of an organization into one whole.[20]

The systems of differentiation on one hand and the system of supervision on the other combine together in different ways to form various organizational structures. Thus, every organization will have, at any one time, a certain organizational structure within and through which all the organizational activities are carried out.

> Social structures in general and organizational structures in particular do not differ from physical structures. They all use frameworks for human activities and they are patterned according to the molds that suit the needs of the people working within them. Organizational structures reflect the way in which organizational activities are divided into functions, sub-units at different levels, and spheres of authority and responsibility. These structures officially constrain and determine the traffic signals for personnel and materials in the organization and the mutual relationships among them. As in physical and biological structures, organizational structures are also meant to regulate organizational activity, set out its limitations, lay down its path of progression, and supervise it.[21]

Organizational structure meets the functional needs of each organization, and it creates the necessary fit between the organization and the environment in which it exists and acts.

According to the contingency theory, organizations have to design their structure to suit their specific needs and their own character. At the same time they must adapt themselves to conditions of the environment in which they act so as to survive over time. Therefore, the structure of an organization ought to fit its functional, operational, economic, and environmental features. However, the structure of an organization inevitably entails certain implications affecting the status, power, prestige, and income of the organizational members. These employees will do all they can to improve their organizational status, so as to increase the basket of benefits they are due to receive from the organization. For this reason they try to rise up the organizational ladder and to seize senior positions—whether administrative or professional. A large number of workers also take overt political measures to improve their organizational status. These measures are based on the exercise of personal power against their superiors and colleagues in the organization to obtain more rights and gain exceptional benefits.

Political activities in this specific context are focused to a great degree upon the recurring attempts of units heads in the organization to broaden the organizational territory that they oversee; to raise the importance of their units, as well as to consolidate activities and areas of responsibility under the organizational roof that they control; to mobilize resources for their units, and to enhance their authority and organizational autonomy.

The political game is characterized by demands for alterations in the organizational structure; it consists of attempts to turn any precedent into an established structure; it intends to create new opportunities for promotion by adding managerial ranks, by demands for the expansion of units' sizes and their number of available jobs. These attempts and others like them are often accompanied by various forceful measures, including threats and sanctions. Managers do not hesitate to get into tough bargaining for every change, even a marginal and symbolic one that might increase the utility they derive from being the heads of organizational units.

Organizational structures are thus seen as significant issues for the sake of which it is worth exerting influence on decision processes and diverting their outcomes into desirable directions. Therefore, a proposed structural change lays the groundwork for a political game, in which relevant actors confront one another for the purpose of tailoring the new structure to suit their interests. Every player in this game strives to enlist supporters for his position in this debate, to create temporary coalitions with rivals aiming to bring about the decisions he desires. For this purpose, participants in the game mobilize resources at their disposal to prevent the implementation of structural changes that are undesirable for them, and to have recourse to methods that will affect processes of change. In this political struggle even outside stakeholders of an organization, such as investors or clients, get involved to avoid changes in organizational structure that could be harmful to their interests.

The political influence of stakeholders on organizational structures accounts for the endurance of organizational units and staff positions that may be no longer necessary for the organization. Similarly, many organizations conserve the forms of outmoded organizational structures only because they are unable to bring about organizational change under internal political conditions. Both of these are the result of recurrent political games in every organization. In general, public sector organizations, which are financed by taxpayers, are more susceptible to political maneuvers than business organizations that are maintained by their profits.

Governmental agencies and departments all over the world are frequently established and later on maintained due to political considerations alone. Regardless of the alleged necessity of such organizational units, they are truly intended to provide key politicians with ministerial positions, with budgets, and with jobs tailored for their protégés. Even business organizations are not free of the political influences of stakeholders over their organizational structures. Since these organizations are not in the focus of the public eye, the politics conducted within them remains inside their four walls. This organizational politics is publicly revealed in the following circumstances: when a business firm of high prestige encounters serious economic difficulties; when senior executives are removed from their positions; in the wake of official announcements of expected strategic moves such as a merger or takeover; the issuance of shares on the stock exchange or the creation of strategic partnership.

Such events and similar ones raise real interest among investors, clients, suppliers, authorities, and other groups of stakeholders in the organization, and prompt them to take action of a political nature to protect their interests. So, for example, trade unions exert various political influences on the management of the organization to prevent a mass dismissal of employees; government agencies take measures to prevent the creation of business cartels; suppliers act to ensure that the organization honors its commitments to them; and clients join forces to ensure their interests. In this way, temporary coalitions are formed and a network of cooperative actions is set up between stakeholders within the organization and outside it.

Recently, many and frequent organizational changes have been conducted by the inspiration of some business school academics. Organizational consultants have spread what seemed to be innovative ideas to improve the organizational structure and its function. Some examples of such organizational changes and transformations are known as *organizational downsizing*, *organizational delayering*, and *re-engineering*. These and other examples of fashionable changes have become widespread in organizational reality since the turn of the twentieth century. Organizational consultants tend to find allies for them in order to carry out such changes in various organizations. These supporters, internal and external ones, are generally stakeholders who see organizational change as an opportunity to increase the benefits that they gain from the organization, as well as a means for the enhancement of their power in the organization. For this purpose they exert political pressure on decision makers to decide positively on organizational change and to be prepared to implement the change as early as possible. In this way the ideas of academic scholars are translated into political measures through the initiative of practical people.

Conclusion

In all organizations, decisions are made daily on a variety of matters. These decisions drive the *organizational machine* and impel it to function both effectively and efficiently. An organizational decision-making process is guided to a large degree by pertinent considerations: business, operational, economic, and technological. At the same time, these decisions are influenced by political considerations regarding their direct and indirect implications for the various beneficiaries of the organization, and the benefits they get. These political effects are not "random noises" interfering with rational processes; they are the direct outcomes of intentional efforts that stakeholders invest to divert the decisions in the direction they wish. Therefore, politics plays an integral part in decision-making processes in organizations.

There are four main factors that arouse and encourage the activation of organizational politics: uncertainty, ambiguity, dispute, and lack of resources. Each of these factors creates a situation that threatens the quantity and quality of benefits enjoyed by the organizational actors and, therefore, it compels the stakeholders to take measures to guard their rights and to prevent their competitors from taking advantage of the situation in order to increase their share of the organizational spoils.

The situations that intensify organizational politics are those in which there exists a relative lack of clarity and stability, that is, situations in which there is no normative guidance about required behavior and proper interpersonal relations between participants. Hence, they become fertile soil for a variety of political games with which the stakeholders of the organization get involved. Organizational changes of various kinds represent typical examples of situations in which politics flourish.

In light of the numerous matters that decision makers have to consider and settle, it is clear that only some parts of them serve as objectives for organizational politics. These are the specific matters in which any change or innovation is expected to cut the organizational pie in different ways for different participants than what it used to be. By the nature of things, these matters are considered *significant issues*, that is, issues that every stakeholder inside or outside the organization sees fit to intervene in and influence binding decisions. Some of them are even considered as *critical issues* on which the very fate of the organization is liable to be dependent.

Among the variety of such issues, there are four significant ones that represent the main political agenda of organizations. These issues are organizational goals and objectives, budgeting and allocation of organizational resources, appointments of personnel to senior positions in the organization, and design and change in organizational structure. Each such issue leads to a series of interconnected decisions that are taken at different levels and in different parts of the organization.

Every strategic decision taken by the top management necessitates a series of operative and tactical decisions to be taken by middle and lower level managers accordingly. The latter are necessary for practical implementation of the strategy. Therefore, the political activity is spread throughout the ranks of authority in the organization. At each organizational level there are actors who show personal or group interest in the decisions regarding such issues, and so they take an active part in the political game that is conducted throughout the organization.

The political aspect of these major issues is displayed in a variety of pressures, inducements, persuasion, threats, maneuvers, and other expressions of power used by the different actors aimed at influencing decision makers to cast their votes in the desired direction. In cases where final decisions have already been made, there is a tendency among some of the actors to "put off the evil hour" by shows of force and political measures designed to prevent the implementation of those decisions. Some of these measures are carried out secretly behind the scenes, and some are performed publicly in ways that cannot be or are not worth being hidden.

Organizations conduct administrative activities together with political activities and both constitute the two sides of the same organizational coin. Therefore, just as administrative activity is continuous and dispersed throughout the organization, so is political activity that accompanies it at all times and places like the shadow of an object. The interdependence between formal and informal conduct in organizations turns administrative agenda into political agenda. This is the very essence of the *theory of political shadows* for the description and analysis of organizational reality.[22]

Notes

1.   The term direct employee is used to define those workers in an organization who are personally involved in the production of the organization's products and its services intended for the clients. This sector of employees includes, for example, the production workers in factories, chefs in hotels, teachers in schools, and doctors in hospitals. On the other hand, the term indirect employee refers to the participants in an organization who assist the direct employees to carry out their work properly. This sector of employees includes, for example, managers, inspectors, clerks, storekeepers, guards and maintenance personnel.

2. March & Simon, 1958; Patti, 1974; Pichault, 1995.
3. Hickson et al., 1971; Hambrick, 1981.
4. Pfeffer, 1981.
5. Kahn et al, 1964.
6. Salancik & Pfeffer, 1974.
7. Pettigrew, 1973.
8. In state and public organizations, for example in state companies, there exist frame-works parallel to management councils which are called by various names such as "advisory council."
9. A detailed discussion of this subject is presented in chapter 10 which deals with management politics.
10. The practical work of the various houses of representatives is mostly carried out in select committees in charge of specific matters such as the financial committee, although even thee committees are also composed according to a "political code-key"—overt or covert.
11. Acker, 1990: 141.
12. Clegg, 1979: 147.
13. Morgan, 1986.
14. Samuel, 1996.
15. Perrow, 1961.
16. Mintzberg, 1983: 246-247.
17. Mintzberg, 1983: 248.
18. Salancik & Pfeffer, 1974; Pfeffer & Moore, 1980.
19. Sagie, 1990 (Hebrew).
20. Samuel, 1996 (Hebrew).
21. Ibid.
22. See the details in the introduction to this book.

5

Perceived Politics

Attitudes towards Organizational Politics

The concept of *organizational politics* was analyzed in the previous chapters from an objective viewpoint, that is, as a phenomenon that may be revealed to an observer who is neither a member nor a stakeholder of the organizations under consideration. This is the way in which a social researcher, for example, "measures" politics and assesses its strength, its prevalence, and its observable expressions in organizations. This perspective is typical for a school of thought that prefers to deal with the phenomenon of politics in the realm of organizations in terms of actions and interactions, rather than in terms of perceptions and interpretations of others' intentions and behaviors.

> Bacharach and Lawler (1996) recently defined organizational politics in terms of "the efforts of social actors (individual to corporate) to strengthen or defend their power positions and to exercise influence over goals, policies, rules, everyday routines, and events that are internal or external to organizations." Central to any conception of effective political behavior is the notion of adaptive or efficacious strategic choice (e.g., the use of social influence behaviors that promote individuals' goal attainment). This conceptualization of organizational actors as strategic decision makers who achieve their goals by successfully manipulating others has occupied a prominent place in organizational theory from it inception. (e.g., Bacharach & Lawler, 1981; Pfeffer, 1992)[1]

According to this approach, organizational politics is labeled neither as a positive nor as a negative, but as a neutral description of reality. This is the approach followed in this volume.

As already stated at the outset, organizational politics characterizes a large variety of power-based, self-serving activities. Such activities are deliberately intended to obtain power or to exercise it in favor of certain interests and goals of the actor who does them. Organizational actors in this context may be individuals, groups, or organizations behaving in a political way to maximize their own benefits by this mode of behavior.

There is no doubt that the use of power is widespread in organizational reality, and is routinely employed by individuals participating in the organization (such as managers, professionals, and rank-and-file employees); it is also applied by different groups of which organizations are composed (such as work teams, departments, and divisions), as well as by organizations and super-organizations (such as corporations and nation-states), through the activities of their leaders. The exercise of power involves, first and foremost, a process of bartering for the concrete or symbolic resources in which the buyers and sellers supposedly do not have equal power. These are the social exchanges that are made as a result of the mutual but not equal dependency between the participants. Therefore, these kinds of exchanges are usually quite aggressive, as they are conducted through the application of pressures, inducements, threats, penalties and rewards, persuasion and coercion. From a scientific point of view, these kinds of exchange relations reflect the political aspect of organizational life.

However, organizational politics has another side—the subjective side, which represents the way that members of a given organization perceive some specific intentions and actions of their supervisors, their colleagues or their subordinates as political modes of behavior. Since it concerns actions and interactions that do not correspond to the established rules of behavior, organizational politics reflects, at least from this viewpoint, an irregular phenomenon, one which deviates from the social norms of organizations, as they are expressed in formal rules and procedures. Therefore, for many people, the idea of politics in organizations is perceived as nothing but a manifestation of deviant, harmful, and divisive behavior.[2]

Some scholars have adopted this popular approach, and they describe organizational politics as a form of purely selfish behavior, which serves only those actors who take part in it for their own benefit. This kind of behavior, then, is informal and unauthorized by the organization or by its management.[3] Thus, a precise expression of this approach can be found in the definition given by Henry Mintzberg in his book on power and politics:

> Politics refers to individual or group behavior that is informal, ostensibly parochial, typically divisive, and above all, in the technical sense, illegitimate—sanctioned neither by formal authority, accepted ideology, nor certified expertise (though it may exploit any one of them).[4]

In light of this approach to organizational politics, it is not surprising to find that people tend to deny publicly the existence of this phenomenon in their workplaces, and to "sweep it under the carpet," or at least to underrate its importance in organizational reality and the influence it has on the processes that occur in it on a daily basis. In spite of that, as we will discover in this chapter, this phenomenon attracts a great deal of attention to people who take an active part in all kinds of organizations. Indeed, research findings support the conclusion that "talk about politics is common in the workplace."[5]

According to the *attribution theory*, people tend to search for a justifying explanation of the events that they experience, in order to understand their causes and consequences. When knowledge or common sense does not provide reasonably acceptable answers, people tend to explain those experiences by such things as fate, luck, superior powers, and a sign from heaven. In a similar way they tend to explain various acts, of their own and mainly of others, as being influenced by personal qualities over which they apparently have no control, such as selfishness, wickedness, jealousy, ambition, and the like. This is how the inconsistency of certain actions and behavior patterns of individuals that are not aligned with, and even contradict their own beliefs and opinions, is seemingly resolved by them.

Hence, *perceived politics* reflects the tendencies of people to see certain types of behavior as having political characteristics, which aim to serve their initiators at the expense of others. For example, those in a hurry to climb up the managerial ladder are seen by some of their colleagues as ruthless, underhanded power seekers whose only ambition is to get quick promotion. And many employees of organizations have reservations about those who compete for positions in workshop committees and in trade unions, treating them as low-class functionaries, and showing a cynical attitude in response to their words and actions.

The importance of perceived politics derives from two main reasons. First, it shows us the essential nature of politics as a social phenomenon that is widespread in organizational reality. Secondly, as sociology claims, people behave according to their subjective reality, the one that is perceived and interpreted in their conscious minds, and not according to objective reality, irrespective of how it is expressed. In order to understand this aspect of organizational politics we have to deal with three main questions: (1) what are the organizational situations that encourage members of an organization to see certain behavior of others as political behavior? (2) what are those behavioral characteristics that are perceived by members of the organization as political? And (3) what are the consequences that members of the organization ascribe to political behavior? This chapter deals with these questions.

Situations Perceived as Political

Various studies in this field indicate that organizations do have situations in which individual and group patterns of behavior are liable to be interpreted as political, whereas other organizational situations are not likely to be interpreted as such by members of the organization. The question is, under what conditions are situations perceived as political or not political. In a very general sense, there are three situations in which there is a widespread tendency of organization members to interpret the behavior of other actors as political: (a) situations of uncertainty; (b) situations of ambiguity; (c) situations of confrontation. These three situations are perceived as threats that organizational actors have to cope with in unconventional ways, namely through deviations from normative patterns of behavior and the adoption of exceptional actions of a political nature.[6] Such unusual situations as these are characterized by a shortage of proper informative knowledge that the actors need in order to act effectively and efficiently. Furthermore, in these situations, actors are required to act under conditions of vague or deficient information about the rules of suitable behavior expected from them. Therefore, such situations are, to a great extent, risky situations in which actors are liable to adopt unacceptable modes of behavior in order to enlarge their range of feasible options and improve their flexibility. These modes of behavior are then perceived by other members of the organization as political behavior patterns.

Typical examples of such situations can be seen in various kinds of organizational changes. Change situations are generally characterized by a great deal of uncertainty and ambiguity, and contain a high risk of confrontation between employers and employees and between superiors and subordinates. The fear of change, the lack of reliable information, and the conflicting interests among the various stakeholders in the organization arouse a sense of discomfort, dread, and deprivation. These feelings are shared by both inside workers of the organization and outside actors dependent upon it (e.g., suppliers). Such feelings usually intensify in organizations in which the management does not allow workers and the junior managers to share in their motives for change, in its objectives and its expected process. In such conditions it is not surprising to find that members of the organization attribute political motives to the management and interpret its conduct as having a political character, with the intention of doing harm to their positions in the organization.

Research findings have shown that certain procedures taken in an organization are often perceived as having more of a political nature than others. These are, for example, procedures that require careful consideration by the senior position-holders in an organization. Similarly, procedures that are associated with the evaluation of performance appraisal of workers, interpersonal relationships between superiors and subordinates, and relations between subunits in an organization—are likely to be interpreted as contaminated by political motives. Researchers point to a series of organizational procedures that are more likely than others to be perceived by members of an organization as procedures that are susceptible to organizational politics.[7]

The list of such procedures includes promotion and mobility of workers in the organization, recruitment and absorption of new workers, the granting of salary and benefits, budgeting and funding, allocation of installations and equipment, delegation of authority, coordination between units, setting of employment regulations and human resource management policy, disciplinary penalties, performance appraisal, and dealing with complaints and contractual disputes.

These findings indicate that the organizational procedure perceived as the most political is the one associated with the evaluation of the workers and managers in an organization, namely, decisions concerning promotion and mobility in the organization. It is a reasonable assumption that actions that may affect the status of people in organizations cause a high degree of trepidation. Since in many organizations such procedures are conducted under a cloak of secrecy, they constitute a source of uncertainty, mostly accompanied by guesses, rumors, leaks, and denials. In those circumstances people tend to ascribe to senior members in charge of the processes of promotion a tendency towards arbitrariness and favoritism, motives linked to personal grudges, intentional delay in decisions, and other hidden calculations.

Universities represent one example of this kind of perceived organizational politics. The process of promoting the academic staff is based on peer evaluations. To avoid pressure by candidates for promotion and by those who support or oppose them, these processes are conducted in great secrecy. The identity of the professional referees, the contents of letters of evaluation concerning the merits of the candidates and of their professional achievements, the meetings of the review committees and the matters discussed in them, as well as the considerations for and against promotion are all kept completely secret.

Under such conditions there are more than a few academic staff members who complain about being victims of persecution, revenge, discrimination because of sex, age, or racial origin. Some of them also claim that their rebellious attitude towards senior colleagues in their departments is the motive for being discriminated against in the promotion process. Others blame their academic establishment for being antagonistic towards them in response to their radical socio-political opinions. From time to time interorganizational rumors and suspicions of this kind are given wide coverage in the media and provoke vocal response from students and public attention by elected leaders in favor of a staff member who may have been discriminated against. In such cases a political struggle ensues between supporters and opposers for the candidate in question.

By the same token, there is also a clear tendency to attribute political characteristics to organizational procedures that deal with the distribution of resources. This interpretation is likely to be strengthened in those situations where the allocation is an outcome of negotiations between supervisors and subordinates, between employers and labor unions, between organizational subunits and between separate organizations. The cuts in budgets, the delay in payments, the postponement of investments, the cancellation of purchases tend to be interpreted as political measures applied against the weaker actors, so as to minimize their share of the organization pie.

A theoretical model, which a group of researchers have developed, claims that the tendency of the individual in an organization to attribute organizational politics to various situations is influenced by three main factors:

1. *Organizational influences.* These influences include the degree of centralization in decision making, the degree of stringent formality in procedures and organizational relationships, and the managerial seniority of those making decisions concerning the fate of the individual under consideration.

2. *Job influences*. These influences include the opportunities for future promotion, the time that has elapsed since the previous promotion to the present position, and the time that has elapsed since an official performance appraisal was made and conveyed to the employee.
3. *Personal influences*. These are the individual's characteristics that affect his or her status and rewards in the organization. Such characteristics include one's sex, ethnicity, and age, as well as one's work experience and tenure in the organization.[8]

These effects serve as predictive variables of perceived organizational politics; namely, they estimate the extent to which members of the organization are likely to attribute political intentions to their colleagues, their supervisors, and their subordinates. The common feature of these predictors is their reflection of the power of the employee under consideration. It is assumed that an employee with little personal power, who has not been successful at work, is likely to blame his or her inferior status in the organization on unfavorable decisions and actions made by other people. Therefore, such employees attribute political considerations to those who have kept them behind. In other words, people tend to attribute political intentions to those who are in charge of matters of promotion, tenure, and compensation in the organization. Thus, the higher the dependence of an employee on those decision makers, the greater the chance that he or she sees them as politicians.[9]

Similarly, individuals and groups that feel they are underprivileged in their relationships with the organizational system in which they are members tend more than others to attribute a political character to it; this is especially so with regard to the decisions connected with the careers of the organization members. Junior workers and those of a lower status in the organization, who feel dissatisfaction in their work and have little hope of future success, will tend more than senior workers to see their organization as political in character. Therefore, these people will see themselves as *political victims* of the system.

These feelings find an open and even harsh expression whenever employees of an organization are expecting layoff. Such employees often tend to attribute their bitter lot to their inferior status in the organization, which, in their view, results from being older people, women, racial minorities, temporary workers, or new immigrants. In other words, they present themselves as victims of organizational discrimination due to socio-political considerations; in fact, they seldom admit their lack of necessary talents or their poor performance, and prefer to blame the organizations and its managers for being unjust, unfair, and politically minded.

In general, civil servants tend to attribute a political tinge to the public administration that employs them, more than do workers in the private sector;[10] the tight linkage between the public administration and the political leadership of the state apparently encourages the political image of such organizations, at least in some countries. This attitude is presumably supported by the fact that performance is rather difficult to measure for the type of services that are rendered to the public by the public administration.[11]

The tendency to attribute political motives and considerations to organizations is especially widespread in the public sector where external factors such as party politics, interest groups, public figures, the media, and social movements are involved in the political game. Research studies indicate that people do attribute political motives to behavior that is perceived by them to be unjust, and label such behavior as improper.[12]

As explained above, the main claim of the political theory asserts that actors who play an active part in the organization do so for the purpose of obtaining all the resources they need, and to derive the greatest benefit from their activities within the framework of the organization. It therefore seems that organizational politics is actually perceived by people as a means—not necessarily a legitimate one—to obtain resources and to gain profits, at least in the minds of those who are taking an active part in the organizations. In short, organizational actors, of whatever kind, should be regarded as utility driven.

The statistical correlations that were found in research between the status of people in an organization and their biographical characteristics on one hand, and their tendency to attribute political characteristics to the organization on the other hand, indicate that these are actually subjective definitions of events given different interpretations in the perceptions of different people.[13] This means that everyone tends to perceive an event that is taking place in his or her surroundings in a way that corresponds to his/her perspective at that time. This perspective is influenced by one's experience in life, one's ambitions, and one's achievements in the organization.

One may conclude therefore that perceived politics is more of a psychological phenomenon than a factual one, and that it is entrenched in the mind rather than in reality. At the same time, it should be mentioned in this context that the reality called *subjective* has no less importance, and perhaps has even more importance than the reality called *objective*; this is because people usually react to signals that reach their cognition according to the way in which they are perceived, interpreted, and understood.

Types of Behavior Perceived as Political

In order to answer the second central question in connection with perceived politics—namely, what is political behavior?—let us now consider the pattern of organizational behavior of individuals, groups, and organizations perceived by their observers as political patterns of behavior.

Drori and Romm proposed to classify the various kinds of organizational behavior into three main types: (a) *official behavior* prescribed by the organization; (b) *unofficial behavior*, at the initiative of the actor who performs it; (c) *illegal behavior*, constituting transgression of state laws.[14] In their view, unofficial behavior is what characterizes organizational politics in all its variations.

As a general rule, unofficial behavior carried out in the framework of the organization tends to be interpreted by others as political behavior, whereas official behavior, or illegal behavior, is less likely to be interpreted as such. People associate organizational politics with procedures that deviate from the official rules of conduct required by the organization, but they distinguish between such actions and criminal actions, which in their view, veer away completely from the sphere of politics.[15] This distinction is interesting, because in the minds of people the concept of *organizational politics* is associated with negative actions that harm both the organization and other people.

Furthermore, participants in organizations tend to see behavior that is aimed at influencing the thoughts and actions of others as political behavior. This interpretation is an interesting one, because it shows that even though explanation and persuasion are widely accepted means of influence, the exertion of these kinds of influence over others is perceived by people as political behavior. Apparently, the way in which such influence is actually carried out is of less importance in such perceptions. This conclusion supports the scientific view affirming that the aim of power is to influence the other and to change a person's opinion or behavior, even against his or her will.

The use of various tactics in the exercise of power is also perceived by people in organizations as a clear sign of political behavior. These tactics—power plays—generally include the use of enticements, threats, pressures and penalties, deceptions, stratagems, and manipulations. In organizational reality, such conduct, which is meant to force another against his will to behave in a certain way, is likely to be interpreted as political behavior. As already said, this is because such actions often deviate from the norms of the established official behavior. These tactics tend to be interpreted as illegitimate behavior, since the organization did not authorize those adopting such behavior to do so. Those actions are perceived by others as behavior intended to obtain personal or group objectives that are not wanted by the organization, and are carried out in order to achieve results that could not have been obtained in ways acceptable to the organization.

One of the forms of behavior perceived as political is that which seems to conceal personal motives, which have no place in the proper relationships between members of an organization. People often tend to doubt the veracity of others when they believe that there is a real gap between their intentions and their actions. The concealment of motives serves mostly as a means to influence the thoughts and behavior of other people in an improper manner, namely, through misleading or defrauding them. Therefore, this kind of behavior is generally perceived as a political tactic that is hardly done in good faith. Generally, good faith is a key concept, both in the legal and the social sense, in exchange relationships between actors in a given setting. A lack of good faith is associated in the minds of people with impure intentions. Conspiracy is an example of behavior that is not based on good faith, and therefore is perceived by others as political behavior.

According to various studies,[16] the following forms of behavioral patterns reflect political tactics applied in interpersonal relationships.

Assertiveness: The behavior of an individual in an organization (especially the behavior of a manager), which displays assertiveness, decisiveness, insistence, and even aggressiveness, is likely to be interpreted as an expression of power, with which he or she can impose his or her will upon others. *Assertive behavior* is expressed by being strict about performing tasks exactly as required; by a consistent stand regarding opinions and positions in spite of external pressure; by a forceful and definite style of speech; and by focusing on the subject in question without being sidelined by other matters at the same time. The expression of such behavior relays personal power and the intention to use it whenever necessary. In certain contexts they are perceived as the expression of leadership, which is, at least potentially, a pattern of behavior perceived as having a clear political character. In some cultures, commanders and managers who show decisiveness and aggressiveness towards those subordinate to them are perceived as "tough bosses," as they are commonly called, namely, uncompromising people who cannot be softened or deflected from the path they have set for themselves.

Ingratiation: Ingratiating behavior, especially when directed at superiors and senior members of the organization, reflects a behavioral pattern that is disliked by people, and is often repugnant to them as well. This kind of behavior is frequently interpreted as an intention to gain benefits from the organization through unconventional means. In certain contexts such behavior is liable to be regarded as the intentional beguilement of another person, conducted for the purpose of persuading the target person to do things that he or she would not do otherwise. Compliments, words of praise and acclaim, repeated offers of serving the other in trivial matters of little value, and expressions of self-denigration are perceived by colleagues in organizations as ingratiating behavior that deviates from the norm; and they are therefore considered as having a political character. For example, the constant fawning of a junior worker over a senior member of an organization represents to many people an ingratiation that is politically driven. An observer can easily notice expressions of such politics everywhere in the realm of organizations. This kind of behavior is especially noticeable in military, governmental, scientific, and in medical organizations. Patronage relationships between senior and junior member are more likely to be found in these organizations than in other kinds of organizations.[17?]

Rationality: In every organization one can find certain people who usually influence other members of the organization through persuasive arguments and inferences that are intended to change their minds or their behavior. This rationalistic behavior floods the minds of influence targets with numerous factual data; with details of precedents and historical events; with the citation of court verdicts; with the presentation of quotations from technical or scientific literature; and with exhausting analyses of information items, culled from newspapers and media interpretations of all kinds. It is easy to understand that people tend to perceive such a verbal onslaught as political behavior, which overwhelms the commonsense judgment of the other persons, pushes them into a position of intellectual defense, and makes them feel a lack of confidence in themselves. This systematic pattern of behavior is far more than an attempt to persuade the other—it is an expression of mental coercion. Everyone who has had the experience of attending discussions held by the management or directorate of an organization; discussions in the Senate of an academic institution; or at the House of Representatives' assemblies could identify this pattern of political behavior performed by some of the participants. Even young students can recognize the person who repeatedly exhausts the teacher in class with these tactics of excessive rationality (a "wise guy" or "smart-aleck").

Exchange: This behavior deviates from the establish rules of most organizations, since its purpose, as perceived by people, is to obtain certain results— those that cannot be obtained through the usual means in the organization—by interpersonal or intergroup bargaining. The offers of assistance and support, backing and cover-ups, and special benefits are perceived as political behavior when they are given in exchange for a job, promotion in rank or position, for tenure or protection against dismissal. Even though such exchange relations are widespread in all organizations, they are actually perceived as being political ones, that is, relations that enable stakeholders in an organization to "take a short cut" and to "cut corners" for the sake of advancing personal or group interests. Only in exceptional cases are such exchange relations perceived as behavior that is meant to benefit the organization as a whole. The tendency of workers to demand negotiations over every organizational change, however small, in order to gain some compensation is a common example of exchange tactics. In many organizations there are people who are considered merchants, namely, people who generally bargain over instructions and guidelines in order to demand something in exchange for carrying out tasks and to "present a bill" for good performance and high achievement.

Relying on Authority: This pattern of behavior is expressed in the tendency of a member of an organization to rely on superiors, managers, and senior members whenever he or she makes demands on others, so as to have the backing and receive the support of superordinates to his or her requests. Such behavior is generally interpreted as an attempt to "hitch one's wagon to a star" with the aim of achieving the desired result. It is no wonder that this type of behavior, to some extent, threatens colleagues and subordinates in the organization, and provides one with an advantage over those who are unable to rely on the backing of senior members. It is therefore perceived as behavior of a political nature, intended to exert unfair influence on another person. Like the tactic of ingratiation, the dependence on the authority of those in power is a form of patron-protection relationship in organizations. The repeated appeal to authority appears to others as an attempt by those who do so to take refuge behind the power of people in authority, and to ensure immunity for themselves from possible resistance by their colleagues. Thus, members of an organization who frequently use this tactic are liable to face negative attitudes and even retaliation.

Coalition Formation: Coalition behavior means the grouping of various actors, generally those of the same rank and status in an organization, to take joint action against other actors. The initiative of forming a new coalition or joining an existing coalition enhances the bargaining power of actors in an organization—individual or group—against those who refuse to comply with their demands. The combination of several powers together gives the coalition the necessary strength to enforce a certain behavior upon a rival who refuses to adopt it of his own free will. Such coalitions are loose, limited, temporary partnerships by their very nature, formed for the purpose of attaining a specific outcome, so as to protect and enhance certain interests of the participants. As noted before, coalitions represent a pervasive phenomenon in organizational reality, mainly in the sphere of labor relations and interorganizational relationships. Coalitions are also formed between subordinates of a certain supervisor to oppose the latter's demands and to prevent his or her application of certain penalties. Coalitional behavior is most likely to be perceived as the political behavior of a group attempting to generate much greater power than the power of its members. Such behavior is typical of organizations in which the heads of the organizational subunits combine together in secret to become a majority in decision-making centers, also in situations in which groups join hands in order to struggle together for the sake of advancing a certain matter that conceals some hidden interest.

Bargaining: Every act of negotiation that takes place between certain employees and their supervisors, colleagues or subordinates, is likely to be interpreted as a political tactic. This interpretation applies to both individuals and groups alike. Since members of the organization are required to behave according to rules and procedures, bargaining of any kind reflects an obvious attempt to deviate from those rules and to circumvent the organization procedures. In effect, bargaining is aimed mainly at changing the existing rules and substituting new ones. But any result of negotiation is the direct outcome of power struggles, compromises, and agreements; namely, it is the outcome of a political process between stakeholders who are in state of conflict, and is not the result of a policy that was decided by the authorized governance of the organization. Therefore, whoever takes part in this kind of bargaining in an organization is perceived as someone who employs organizational politics to advance his or her interests.

Punishment: Threats of punishment (physical, economic, social or other) used by actors for the purpose of influencing other persons are perceived as an exercise of power against others in the organization for the purpose of imposing his or her will upon them. Military commanders, civil managers, and even

school teachers often constrain the behavior of their subordinates by expressing such threats of punishment, not to mention the actual infliction of penalties
of various kinds. Ordinary workers' control over resources allows them to threaten
punishment against those who refuse to comply with their requests. Expul-
sions, bans, suspension of membership in various organizational settings; withholding the supply of resources; delays in payment; the imposition of various
restrictions; the blocking of communication lines; and the flow of information
represent some examples of the sanctions intended to enforce compliance upon
people and organizations that do not accede to the demands of power holders.
Thus, various groups of workers in organizations tend to threaten punitive
measures against employers, managers, and other groups in the organization.
Such courses of action are most likely perceived as political maneuvers intended to make them raise their wages and salaries, to improve their working
conditions, to elevate their status in the organization, or to grant them special
rights. In many cases, various professional groups actually impose real sanctions, such as disrupting work processes or withholding vital information. One
may also discover that some senior members secretly threaten junior ones with
punitive measures if they do not accede to their demands for personal services
that are not legitimate in the organization, such as conducting sexual relations
with them.[18]

Thus, such patterns of behavior represent attempts to exercise interpersonal,
intergroup or interorganizational power. As such, they receive negative feedback, since they are perceived as political behavior that deviates from the
accepted norms in those situations. Any organizational behavior is tagged as
political behavior as long as people who encounter it subjectively perceive it
as such.

> It is clear that attributions about individuals are made on the basis of perceived (and not
> "objective") behavior, and that these attributions may differ considerably between actor
> and observer. This fact is particularly important when investigating supervisor/subordi-
> nate relationships, as the perceptions that the supervisor has of his or her behavior may
> differ considerably from those of the subordinates.[19]

For example, when a supervisor in an organization adopts decisive and aggressive behavior, his subordinates tend to attribute great power to him and to his
readiness to exert it against them, so as to force them to behave according to his
preference. On the other hand, a supervisor who offers inducements or expresses
threats against those under his/her authority is perceived as a boss with no real
personal authority of his own; therefore, those subordinates do not tend to
ascribe qualities of charisma, leadership, or expertise to their supervisor. Instead, this style of managerial behavior, usually attributed to people of power,
is perceived as a means of exercising dominion over less powerful subjects.
Hence, it is likely to encounter negative attitude.

As noted earlier, students of organization usually define political behavior
in objective terms subject to observable criteria. In contrast, ordinary people

tend to label organizational behavior as subjectively political according to their perceptions and judgments of other actors' intentions. Yet, there is a certain overlap between the objective definition of behavior as political and the subjective perception of that behavior as political. This correspondence does not lessen the importance of perceived politics—namely, the one that is based on social comparisons, labels, value judgments, stereotypes, and the subjective interpretation of others' intentions. The attribution of political motives allows people in an organization to come up with an explanation that makes sense to them for the irregular situations and events that they personally experience in the organization.

Consequences of Political Behavior

Research findings have shown that political behavior perceived in organizations does have various effects on those who adopt it, on those influenced by it, and also on those who observe it. It is therefore appropriate to present here some of the results that are attributed to organizational politics as perceived by those who participate in various organizations. In this case as well, it concerns subjective values and not facts. First and foremost, political behavior is perceived as that which serves the person in question. Therefore, in the eyes of researchers in this area, the main outcome of such behavior is injurious to the other participants in the organization, since they are the ones forced to pay the price of the benefit that is gained by those politicians among them.

As recalled, most of the political games in organizations are those that generally result in zero-sum, namely, the profit of one player is equal to the loss of another. Thus, people tend to think that the unjustified profit that others gain by political behavior is obtained at the expense of the benefits that conformist participants who toe the organizational line should receive in return for their contribution to the organization. It is not surprising, then, that those members of organizations show negative attitudes towards any kind of behavior that they subjectively label as "political." This kind of negative response is revealed repeatedly in research studies on this subject. [20]

The general picture that emerges in those research studies is that the political acts performed by individuals and groups brings about real damage to the organization as a whole.[21] People assume that the actions, which they perceive to be political, reflect attempts to deviate from the established rules for the purpose of attaining personal or group benefits that should not be gained otherwise. Such actions disrupt the organizational order, since members of the organization learn that there are methods to circumvent the rules of the organization and shortcuts can be used in order to promote their interests and attain their objectives, and they tend to try these methods themselves. These tendencies are tolerated as part of the inevitable politics in organizations and, with the passage of time, develop into internal norms of behavior. According to this view, politics creates competition between individuals, and between groups of participants, as well as between the subunits within the organization. Moreover, internal politics raises tensions, enhances conflicts, and radicalizes confrontations among the organization's participants. Therefore, organizational politics is perceived as a divisive force that gets in the way of regular processes, disrupts the stability and harmony of the organization, and gives the organization the negative repute of being a political entity rather than a productive system.

One of the more severe outcomes that people attribute to organizational politics is the way that the resources of an organization are distributed among its various components. According to this conception, a fair allocation of resources cannot be realized as a result of political maneuvers applied by stakeholders or by their delegates. Pressures, threats, promises, gloomy predictions, warnings of danger, and rationalizations represent some influences that are exerted upon decision makers by stakeholders or by their accomplices; these, in turn, lead to the preferential treatment of those influential actors when resources are actually allocated.

Another explanation maintains that this preferential treatment in the allocation of resources is intended to allow managers to ease the pressure put upon them; to appease those who criticize and deride them; to prevent confrontations and to pacify the organization as it were. Under such conditions, every stakeholder learns how to exercise influence on decision makers and to direct the allocation of resources in his or her favor. Thus, the entire process of budgeting in organizations is perceived by many people as a process that diverts the organization from the realization of its declared objectives, since it is an essentially unfair, power-based, and politically twisted decision-making process.[22] In the end, the budget takes better care of the stronger actors' interests at the expense of the weaker ones.

As already said more than once, politics of any kind is based on power and on its application for the advancement of interests. Therefore, one of the outcomes of political behavior in an organization is the amplification of personal and group power, at least for winners in the political game. But power is not only an objective resource of an actor. Like prestige, for instance, power may be a subjective asset of an actor through attribution by others. The latter kind is more abstract than concrete, since the actor in question may or may not have real power, as far as it is determined in tangible terms. Attributed power is usually an outcome the actor's achievement that was gained by the use of political means. Since attempts at influencing others are perceived as a form of political behavior, the more effective such attempts were in the past, the greater the power attributed in the present to that individual or group in the organization.

Organizational politics is then perceived as a circular process. On one hand, actors in an organization employ political measures when they have the necessary power to do so; on the other hand, the application of political measures intensifies the power attributed to those actors who employ such measures.

This accounts for the perceived linkage between power and politics in the minds of people; and it may explain the tendency of those who are interested in generating power to behave in a political manner, in spite of the negative image of this behavior among members of the organization.

Studies of organizational politics have revealed that participants, who consider their organization as essentially a political one, tend to develop certain feelings and attitudes deriving from this perception.[23] It is worth mentioning here some psychological results of perceived politics in organizations.

Job Insecurity: People come to the conclusion that in their organization the way to retain the job in which they are employed is to act in a political manner. They are in a state of perpetual anxiety about losing their jobs, since they think that their behavior is not sufficiently political so as to ensure their employment in the organization. In light of such concerns, they fear that their conformist behavior may be perceived by others as the behavior of individuals who cannot stand the pressures of power struggles and, therefore, will be interpreted as a personal weakness.

Involvement in work: People feel that the way in which an employee influences other employees in the organization is of greater importance than the way in which he or she performs the job. These feelings reduce the willingness of employees to invest much effort in carrying out their jobs more effectively and more efficiently than they have been doing so far. The psychological response to any perceived climate of politics in the organization tends to be expressed in indifference to the job, and disinterest with regard to its performance—in short, a sense of alienation at work.

Satisfaction at work: Workers who fulfill their functions in a mechanical manner, without psychological involvement and with no enthusiasm, and who are constantly in a state of dread regarding their job security, tend to develop feelings of work dissatisfaction. These feelings, like all the others, are also an expected result of the subjective perception that sees the organization (and the procedures that take place within it) as a political system rather than a professional one. The attribution of political motives to the organization members is likely to reduce one's satisfaction with one's job, supervisors, colleagues, and the organization as a whole. Such work dissatisfaction may frequently lead to the accusation of others in the organization with various kinds of misconduct and deviant behavior. This response may enhance one's frustration and dissatisfaction even more.

Withdrawal behavior: Those participants, who are not content with the political character of the organization as it is seen in their eyes, tend to withdraw from the organization or at least to limit their presence on its premises or reduce their participation in its activities. These withdrawal attempts include frequent absence from work, a tendency to contract various kinds of illnesses, repeated minor injuries from light accidents, requests for a long leave of absence, early retirement, and final exit out of the organization. On the psychological level, withdrawal is expressed through displays of non-identification with the organization and its objectives; in various degrees of disloyalty; in estrangement from the organization and its management; and in a lack of commitment to the organization.

One of the positive results of perceived politics that arouses discomfort is the tendency of organizations to induce changes of various kinds. Those participants in an organization who perceive their organization as being politically driven, yet do not wish to exit it, are likely to support change programs that are intended to prevent the continued politicization of the organization. In organizational reality, the so-called *performance gap*, namely the gap between the desired level of performance and the actual one, is the driving force of organizational change. An organizational change is likely to take place when members of the organization recognize that such a performance gap is too wide to be bridged by routine measures.[24] Opposition to politics in an organization and aversion to its results can stir the voices of protest, and put pressure on the authorities to induce proper organizational change; in some cases, lower level participants take the necessary initiative for starting grassroots change.

These results and similar ones demonstrate the effects of perceived politics on individuals and on their behavior in organizations. In other words, the way in which people perceive certain events and the moral meaning that they attribute to them determines their feelings, attitudes, and actions towards the organization in which they take part. Thus, the negative interpretation of organizational politics frequently creates negative responses of participants towards their jobs, their supervisors, their colleagues, and their organization. No wonder that those individuals are likely to be dissatisfied with their work. In many cases this state of mind brings about low levels of performance at work.

In a study conducted in the public sector it was found that employees that attributed a high degree of politicization to their organization, and who were dissatisfied with it, were likely to develop behavioral patterns that reflect a tendency of negligence in carrying out their jobs. These civil servants were reluctant to exit their jobs that, in their perception, were afflicted by organizational politics, because they were interested in preserving the job security and their safe source of income. Hence, those employees expressed a firm resistance to the implementation of more efficient and business-like working standards.[25] It is no wonder that the quality of service rendered to the public by such civil servants is rather poor.

It should be emphasized once again that the image of an organization as being highly political does not necessarily attest that politics actually occupies a great deal of the organization's affairs as people might think; it also does not prove that the influence of politics is actually harmful to the organization as people suspect. Furthermore, it should be also noted that people have a negative attitude towards the politicization of the organization or of their work environment due to their fears of losing control over the events in which they are participating. In the minds of ordinary people, politics is perceived as an obscure area, uncertain and uncontrollable. Following this view, politics is the world of manipulators of all kinds, and therefore increases the sense of fear among those for whom political maneuverings are unfamiliar. Such apprehensions of members and their consequences are not necessarily connected to the political games actually played in the realm of organizations.

Conclusion

Organizational politics has two sides—an objective and a subjective side. The former reflects the web of actions and interactions that have direct linkage to power and to its exercise for the purpose of realizing the interests of various stakeholders, whereas the latter refers to organizational behavior patterns of individuals and groups that bypass established rules and procedures, and are therefore perceived by others as various forms of political behavior.

In spite of the connection between objective and subjective politics, these two concepts refer to different phenomena. Some kinds of behavior that people in an organization perceive as political are not so according to scientific notion of politics; but other kinds of behavior that are political in the objective sense are not perceived as such by participants of organizations.

One of the explanations for the difference between objective and subjective organizational politics stems from the tendency of people to blame failures and attribute deficiencies to other, such as "the management" or "the authorities." This kind of projection serves to deny their own responsibility for the negative outcomes. Thus, the attributing of political motives and considerations to other people; the labeling of behavior as political; and the judgment of interpersonal and intergroup relationships as simply political maneuvers serve mainly as an excuse to justify those who are unsuccessful in an organization. Of course, in much more than just a few cases, perceived politics is a true reflection of actual politics in the organization.

This chapter has dealt with three main issues. First, the situations that encourage people in organizations to interpret the behavior of others as political; second, the behavioral characteristics that are likely to be perceived by others as political measures; and third, it has pointed to the psychological and behavioral implications that perceived politics has for individuals, groups, and the organization as a whole. We have covered some theoretical arguments and research findings representing scientific attempts to explain the tendencies of people to subjectively interpret certain behavior patterns in terms of politics; and have presented similar attempts to correlate perceptions of politics with actual acts of political nature, so as to examine the connections between objective and subjective data.

One of the assertions made in this chapter maintains that people tend to attribute political motives and considerations to the behavior of others when they themselves are in an inferior position in an organization, or when they have a feeling of disadvantage because of their racial origin, sex, and the like. They also tend to attribute patterns of political behavior to others whenever they suffer a sense of dissatisfaction in their work and in the organization, and doubt their chances of advancement and success in the future. Such tendencies indicate the effect of personal traits upon the way people perceive the environment; these tendencies are expressed in relation to perceived politics in organizations.

In general, people tend to see any attempt at influencing the mind or behavior of others in the organization as political behavior. Participants in actions and interactions in which decisions are made and resources are exchanged, tend to attribute political motives to those who seem to deviate from the rules and regulations of the organization. Informal behavior is perceived as political as long as it is in the grey zone of legitimate behavior rather than in the dark zone of illegitimate behavior. Following this state of mind, organizational behavior characterized by assertiveness, rationalization, ingratiation, bargaining, intrigue, or by manipulation is perceived as behavior of a political nature. Most of the activities that are perceived as political are associated with the individual's status, with the individual's chances of promotion, and with personal welfare. Organizational behavior is also likely to be perceived as political behavior whenever it is associated with the allocation of organizational resources to various beneficiaries.

The influence of perceived organizational politics is generally negative with regard to the individuals who judge it severely, namely, with regard to those who see it as a harmful phenomenon in organizational life. Those who consider organizational politics as a negative phenomenon are likely to develop feelings of anxiety about their job security, to feel alienation towards the organization, and be dissatisfied at work.

Many of those who are disgusted by politics in an organization tend to disengage themselves from it. Such tendencies are given practical expression in the high rate of absences, negligence at work, indifference, frequency of illness, high turnover and mobility of workers. At the same time, the perception of the organization as political may also have results that can be seen as positive. The most notable among them is the effort to introduce suitable behavioral norms and to emphasize professional standards in everything that concerns the treatment of workers, their status and their rights as employees.

The study of perceived politics shows another aspect of the political game that is conducted in organizations; and thus deepens our understanding of all that concerns the hidden mechanisms driving their activities. At present we do know that perceived politics affects the participants' mindset behavior. It is not surprising therefore that perceived politics has become an attractive topic of study nowadays for many students of organizational behavior.

Notes

1. Kramer, 2000: 47
2. Gandz & Murray, 1980.
3. Burns, 1961; Schein, 1977; Mayes & Allen, 1977; Gandz & Murray, 1980; Ferris et al., 1989.
4. Mintzberg, 1983: 172.
5. Gandz & Murray, 1980: 240.
6. Drory & Romm, 1988, 1990.
7. Gandz & Murray, 1980.
8. Ferris et al., 1989.
9. Ferris et al., 1996
10. Gandz & Murray, 1980.
11. Vigoda, 1997 (Hebrew).
12. Vigoda, 2000.
13. See, for example, Ferris et al., 1996.
14. Drory & Romm, 1988, 1990.
15. It is appropriate to note once again that even if illegal behavior, and all the more so behavior that is defined by law as criminal, is not political in itself, it is often the outcome of various political measures that have led to the crossing of legal borderlines (e. g., corruption).
16. See, for example, Kipnis & Schmidt, 1988; Brass & Burkhardt, 1993
17. Henry Mintzberg (1983) defines the patron relationship as a certain type of "political game." See the detailed account in chapter 6 of this book.
18. The United States, for example, repeatedly imposes economic and other sanctions on states such as Cuba, Iraq, Afghanistan, Libya, and North Korea, and on other states that support acts of terror.
19. Hinkins & Schriesheim, 1990: 224.
20. Gandz & Murray, 1980; Drori & Romm, 1990; Ferris et al., 1996.
21. See for example, Vigoda, 1997 (Hebrew).
22. Pettigrew, 1973.
23. Vigoda, 2000; Ferris et al., 1989, 1996.
24. Samuel & Jacobsen, 1997.
25. Vigoda, 2000.

6

Political Games

Throughout the chapters in this book, the term *political game* has been used as a generalized concept to indicate the political nature of organizational politics. In practice, this term serves to define a variety of activities and exchange relations that actors apply in trying to advance their interests in various ways, under changing circumstances, and within the framework of the organization in which they participate.

Clearly, there is no one single kind of political game. Just as in the world of sport, so, too, in the organizational world, many and varied political games are conducted at one and the same time. Therefore, there is both theoretical and practical importance in examining the different types of political games and in delineating the special characteristics of each one of them.

In order to identify appropriately the various types of political games conducted in the organizational arena, it is, of course, necessary to select some criteria for a systematic classification of the different types and to characterize each accordingly. In this chapter, two different classifications will be presented that presumably complement one another. The first classification is the one proposed by Henry Mintzberg over twenty years ago.[1] The second typology is proposed here for the first time by the present author.

Mintzberg Classification of Games

Mintzberg proposed three criteria for the classification of political games in organizations: (1) The function and status of the actors; (2) the means of influence on which they depend in the game; (3) The motivation of the actors to participate in the political game in the organization. In his view, one can distinguish between the main reasons for participation in the political game as follows: the wish to oppose the organizational authority, and to rebel against it; the wish to block acts of revolt against authority and to thwart attempts at rebellion; the wish to build a power base; the wish to overcome rivals; and the wish to influence organizational change.

This classification thus distinguishes between three main groups of political games: (a) games that are held in accordance with the legitimate systems of influence in the organization; (b) games aimed at opposing the legitimate systems of influence in the organization; and (c) games intended to bring about a replacement of the legitimate systems of influence in the organization, because of their weakness. These three groups include thirteen types of political games conducted in organizations.

1.   The Insurgency Game

This game is played by junior participants in organizations who oppose the implementation of decisions made by their superiors. The tactics employed in this game include delays in schedules, disturbances in the regular workflow, disruptions of rules and procedures, working by the book, work absence, and feedback of faulty information up the authority ladder. Such measures and similar ones are typically applied in organizations by individual participants who are generally located in the middle ranks. On the other hand, the general rank and file, who are part of the *technical core*, tend to play the insurgency game in organized groups, adopting measures such as sanctions and strikes, protests and demonstrations, sabotage of installations and products of the organization, locking the gates by force, refusal to obey orders, and even declared mutiny. One way or another, the insurgency game is meant to cancel the decisions made by the authorities and to use physical force to prevent their implementation in the organization.

2.   The Counter-Insurgency Game

This is the game of managers and executives, who defend themselves from attempts to undermine their authority and prevent them from using their legal power for the achievement of organizational objectives. In fact, this is the game that is intended to ensure the continued control of the governing authorities over the organization, over its workers, and over its activities in spite of the hostile acts of those opposing them. This political game is therefore characterized by closer supervision of subordinates and by tight control of work procedures in the organization. The managers who participate in it increase their efforts at detecting possible insurgents; they encourage tale-tellers and collaborators; they dismiss dissenters from their jobs; they banish anyone who is considered to be a threat; they formulate new rules and instructions, and severely punish any sign of disobedience. Forestalling acts such as surprise visits, protective strike, deliberate transfers of workers, and changes in position are the most widespread activities in games of this kind. This is the type of political game that uses a combination of authority and power, law and force, deterrence and punishment.

3.   The Sponsorship Game

This political game is one of series of games intended to help actors build a power base for themselves in the organization. In this game, various participants in the organization attach themselves to the holders of power and authority, so as to be taken under their protection. The game is based on the psychological contract between seniors and juniors, according to which the sponsored person (the protégé) renders various services to his sponsor (the patron), including unqualified loyalty; these services are in exchange for a certain amount of power that the patron allows him or her to have. The person who is sponsored thus enjoys the "rays of power" emanating from the patron. The greater the power of the patron, the greater is the power attributed to the person he sponsors. The sponsorship game is a typical one for middle-level managers, for junior staff members and the like, who seek the protection of key members in the higher echelons of the organization. This is also a game that is typical among scientists, scholars, and young professionals at the start of their career, who try to curry favor with their mentors.

    4.   *The Alliance Building Game*

This kind of political game takes place between actors of an equal or similar standing in the organization who are trying to build for themselves a basis of power through the support of their colleagues. Such alliances among colleagues are often formed when confronted by a certain problem that they are interested in solving for their own interests. The initiator of the alliance (individual or group) tends to forge support around him or her by means of various political measures, which partly include covert negotiations with potential partners. This game leads to the creation of an *interest group* held together by a common issue or purpose. The political alliance is typically a temporary one and it continues to hold so long as the issue on which the partnership was formed has not yet been solved to the satisfaction of the allies. In other words: this is an alliance of those willing to support each other in order to share the spoils of victory. In organizational politics, alliances such as these tend to last for a quite a long period of time in spite of changes that occur within it, because they yield benefits derived from the political power inherent in them. An alliance like this, therefore, grows or declines in the course of time, while the core group of members persists in the attempt to preserve it as a stable political setting.

    5.   *The Empire Building Game*

At the center of this type of game there usually stands a single actor in the organization who strives to bind together organizational units and professional groups under his authority. This is a political attempt to strengthen one's basis of power through expansion of the organizational territory. Since many organizations allocate resources, reward managers, and delegate authority according to the size of the organizational units that they are in charge of, the building of an empire means greater resources and more power. For this purpose, managers search for excuses and find ways to take under their supervision more subunits, organizational activities, areas of responsibility and functions that are found elsewhere within the organizational sphere. Similarly, they initiate the construction of new activities and units that do not exist in the organization. A political game such as this consists of demands of mid-level managers in organizations to change the organizational structure through the merging of units, the displacement of product lines from one place to another, the addition of managerial ranks, and the assembly of staff professionals.

6.   The Budgeting Game

Of all the political games, this is the one that is most familiar to the general public. Its aim is to increase the budgets intended for the organizational units, headed by the actors or units that they are interested in enriching. The increase in budget means the possibility of enlarging the unit, extending its operations, strengthening its standing, and granting jobs to those closely associated with it. In this kind of game, every actor (e.g., manager, representative, treasurer, and lobbyist) demands a much larger budget than is needed for the unit in order to increase as much as possible the amount of money to be allocated to it. For this purpose, the interested actors sometimes manipulate financial figures; they present imaginary development programs; they frequently complain about the relative deprivation of their units; and they bargain over the amount attached to every budgetary item.[2]

7.   The Expertise Game

This is essentially the game of the highly educated professionals in organizations (e.g., scientists, engineers, lawyers, economists, and the like), those professionals who utilize their expertise as a basis of power, exercising it for the purpose of influencing the other participants in the organization, especially the managers at the various levels. In this game, these experts try to prove the importance of their professions to the organization and to convince the different actors that mastery over the relevant knowledge demands expertise that is acquired over the course of many years of training. Therefore, they claim that they are the only ones who can contribute their unique expertise for the benefit of the organization. In other words, these professionals try to create an organizational dependency on their expertise. In response to this, line managers attempt as far as possible to break up the knowledge and skills of these professionals into a collection of simpler procedures, to document them in the format of work procedures and rules of behavior, and to train laymen to carry out these tasks without the need for long and difficult training. In this way the dependency of the organization on the abilities of professionals and their whims is reduced. At the same time, other actors, such as technicians, also attempt to create the impression that they, too, have an expertise that is exclusively theirs. For this reason they try to regularize the entry of new employees into their special area of skills, to establish their own standards of excellence, and to demand certain privileges in return for their claimed special know-how.

8.   The Lording Game

This is a "bureaucratic game" in which actors rely on rules and regulations in order to lord over those who need their services. This political game is typical of line workers who do not have real authority, and who are domineering towards citizens, clients, and other persons who are entitled to be served, towards novices and apprentices in the organization, as well as towards people in other units. This is a form of showing superiority to anyone who is on a lower level than them, however temporarily. Such actors justify their patronizing behavior and omission by strict obedience to every item in the regulations or code book of the organization, as well as by the need to receive affirmation from the senior authorities in the organization, and by repeated demands for all sorts of documents. Such patterns of behavior provide those rank and file clerks with some power that they can exercise against those in need of them; and by this means they try to realize their ambitions in the organization (such as promotion, salary increase, and improved working conditions). Moreover, a considerable number of them employ these methods for obtaining special benefits from their clients outside the organization such as exemptions, discounts, favors, and extra benefits. In some cases such benefits cross the line of law, turning into various bribes.

9.   *The Line versus Staff Game*

This is a distinctly political game in which line managers struggle to maintain their authority and to make decisions in the organization as opposed to members of the professional staff who try to take over their positions. This is a struggle between power based on a position in the hierarchy of authority and power derived from professional authority. The line managers strive to maintain for themselves most of the possibilities for action, while the members of the professional staff try to limit the range of option open to the decision makers. For this purpose they make tendentious use of the data available to them, formulate rules and procedures that limit the freedom of choice and influence the policymaking of the senior managers in the organization in directions that suit their objectives. They tend to initiate organizational changes and to support their implementation on the basis of their professional claims, because these increase their professional authority and grant them power over those targeted by the changes. Professional staff members "wave the flag" of efficiency in order to advance their objectives, whereas the line managers entrench themselves behind the wall of responsibility in order to repulse the advances of the professional staff members. In case of failure, each of them finds ways to put the blame on the other side by utilizing information and manipulating people to prove their apparent integrity. In a game of this sort there is an ongoing confrontation between knowledge (acquired through higher education) and experience (acquired through long-term work)—a confrontation that reflects differences in education, age, and seniority in the organization.

10.   *The Rival Camps Game*

This game reflects a situation in the organization in which the actors who hold power are divided into two opposing camps, each struggling to overcome the other over a certain issue. Both rival camps may represent two different organizational units (for example, the production division vs. the marketing division); they may take the form of a struggle between two leaders and their supporters (for example, between the CEO and the Chairman of the Board of Directors); and they might group themselves into rival camps in confrontation over a specific organizational issue (such as organizational change or privatization). Usually, such struggles end in the partial victory of one camp, which temporarily calms the struggle and conceals the conflict under the surface until the next clash between the two sides arises.

11. The Strategic Candidates' Game

This political game is seen in the attempts made by the major actors in an organization to bring about the acceptance of decisions that are of strategic implication for the organization. These are the decisions that have an influence on the organization as a whole, and are meant to pave the way that it will follow in the future. Such decisions are thus intended to create far-reaching changes in the organization and to cause a real turnaround in its functioning. Actors who initiate a strategic change in an organization are likely to be the leaders of the change, to establish themselves in some key positions, and to generate considerable power in the organization. Therefore, it is no wonder that these actors conduct an ongoing political competition with their counter-partners in an attempt to design the organizational strategy. The political aspect of this game is expressed in the measures that these contenders apply to persuade the stakeholders that their initiative suits their objectives and interests. Thus they attempt to enlist wider support for their plans and to raise favorable public opinion for their ideas among the participants of the organization.

12. The Whistle Blowing Game

This short and special game takes place whenever one of the lower participants in the organization obtains an item of secret information that indicates, in his or her opinion, that certain things are being done in the organization that do not conform to the regulations or that they violate the acceptable social norms in it; among them are acts of favoritism, corruption, illegal use of budgets, concealment or papering over organization failures, or a suspicious organizational change. The possessor of the information sees it right to give warning about these damaging actions to those who might prevent them. For fear of losing one's position in the organization and of criticism by one's colleagues, such information is often transmitted secretly to an outsider who has power and is independent of the organization and its leadership such as a reporter, a politician, a lawyer, a police officer, and the like. An anonymous letter, an unidentified phone call, a copy of an incriminating document, or disclosure of the names of suspected senior members in the organization are often used to transmit the incriminating information. As a result, an investigation is likely to be conducted. From there, the information will most likely be leaked to the mass media, leading to a witch-hunt and the pointing of an accusing finger at scapegoats. It is worth noting that in some of these cases the organization finds ways to get rid of these tale-bearers—who presumably give a bad name to the organization and expose its shortcomings in public—by means of penalties such as social blacklisting, repealing of authority, denigrations, pressures, and threats. Many whistle blowers ultimately lose their jobs, and are forced to leave their hometowns to protect themselves and their families for fear of persecution.

13.   The Young Turks Game

This game is the most difficult and dangerous of them all. It is the attempt to turn the organization around and to replace its leadership. The actors who participate in this revolutionary game tend to present themselves as reformers and their ideas as organizational reforms; their declared goal is to make a radical rectification of the organization and its mode of functioning. However, concealed underneath the ideological cloak is an intention to depose the head of the organization and his associates, to cancel their authority, and to remove them from positions of influence in the organization. In more than a few cases, this game implies rebellion, with the aim of creating a revolution in the organization. Therefore, the players who participate in this political game take a gamble from which there is no retreat, because its outcome might be fateful for those on the losing side in the game.

According to Mintzberg, then, this classification includes the majority of political games that are conducted in organizations of different types. Yet, even if this series of types does not exhaust the phenomenon of organizational politics in all its many and varied forms, it certainly exemplifies the wide range of self-serving activities conceptualized by the term *political game* taking place in the organizational scene.

Typology of Political Games

In spite of the important contribution of the Mintzberg's systematic classification of political games into the different types, the present author offers an alternative classification in this chapter. Thus, different types of political games in organizations that are in line with the conceptual and theoretical framework of this volume will now be portrayed. The classification proposed here is that of a typological scheme based on two main dimensions: (a) the players who take an active part in the political game; (b) the power bases that the players depend upon in order to win the game. The combination of these two dimensions creates nine prototypes of political games.

There is a theoretical and practical importance in identifying the nature of every type of game and in interpreting its main character. As will be clarified in this chapter, not all the political games can be immediately discerned and decoded. This is because political games in organizations differ in their degree of visibility. Some take place near the surface, whereas others lie more deeply hidden beneath the surface. With this comment borne in mind, let us look at the first dimension of the proposed typology, namely, the players of the political game.

The Players

As we have seen in earlier chapters, organizational politics is conducted in organizations among the individuals participating in them, including executives and managers, workers and members, volunteers, inmates, and patients. Moreover, there are those outside players such as investors, clients, suppliers, contractors, supporters, voters, and donors, who also take part in the political game.[3]

In most organizations the political game is also played between the various human groups that compose them; these are professional groups, ethnic groups, genderized groups, as well as other groups. These groups struggle to advance their own interests by their combined effort, usually through some elected representatives who are officially identified by various names and titles. Frequently, these groups constitute only a part of larger groups with similar interests: those national and even global groups that are active outside the organization, such as trade unions, professional associations, or social and political movements.[4]

The view of organizations as political arenas is not limited only to political games that are played within them. In those political arenas, interorganizational games are also widely played. The players are different organizations of various kinds such as business corporations, government and municipal agencies, not-for-profit institutions, voluntary organizations, political party organizations, and international organizations. These large-scale and strong actors transfer the various political games to wider and more distant areas outside the sphere of a single organization, namely to a national or an international arena, and even to worldwide areas of activity.[5]

Power Bases

Every actor who is interested in influencing the thoughts, feelings, or activities of others is required to exert power against the object of influence. As recalled, power is judged by the ability of an actor to cause another actor to behave in a way he would not have behaved of his own free will. Influence is therefore judged according to the extent to which that actor has succeeded in causing the desired change in the other actor.[6]

For the purpose of constructing a typology of political games, and drawing upon Etzioni's classification described in the last chapter,[7] we shall herewith classify the power bases into three main kinds: (a) the coercive basis; (b) the economic basis; and (c) the normative basis. The exercise of power by means of physical force is displayed in practice through the use of various kinds of coercion, including expression of threats and infliction of penalties. The exercise of power by economic means is by offering various inducements—mostly financial and material ones. The exercise of power by normative means is by the tendentious use of intellectual, religious, moral, and emotional appeals of all kinds. In practice, this power is applied by the manipulation of symbols that concretize such abstract ideas.

The broad classification of each of these criteria—players and means—into three levels creates a typology that consists of nine types of political games in organizations. Each one constitutes a prototype that represents several varieties of the same type of game taking place in organizational reality. Such varieties are the direct outcome of certain differences between the actual players or between the specific means used in one game or another; for example, interpersonal relationships between superiors and subordinates are usually not similar to the interpersonal relationships between equal colleagues in the same organization; and the expression of threat against one person has a different effect from the actual use of physical force upon another person.

It should be noted here that typology, as with every conceptual or theoretical construct, portrays the character of a certain phenomenon with a rather broad brush, outlining only some of the main features that characterize it. As such, it inevitably presents a more simplified picture of the phenomenon, since it could not otherwise describe the complex reality. However, in spite of such simplification, typology makes it possible to define a given phenomenon and to portray its main modes of behavior. Hence, typologies go one step further than general definitions of concepts by providing more detailed accounts of their internal variations.

The scientific value of a typology depends on whether it helps us to understand the underlying factors that generate behavioral patterns of one kind or another. Typology also helps to predict the influence of various behavioral patterns on the actors themselves and on others. Thus, typology is an efficient analytical tool for purposes of defining and diagnosing a complex and multi-faceted phenomenon by means of a minimal number of dimensions.

The typology of political games, as proposed here, defines the phenomenon of organizational politics by means of two dimensions; it characterizes nine different types of political games widely played in organizations of all kinds. Table 6.1 presents these types.

Table 6.1
Political Games in Organizations, by Players and Means of Power

Means Players	Penalties	Benefits	Symbols
Individuals	*Submission Games*	*Seduction Games*	*Persuasion Games*
Groups	*Confrontation Games*	*Bargaining Games*	*Coalition Games*
Organizations	*Subjugation Games*	*Collaboration Games*	*Unification Games*

As table 6.1 shows, there is a wide variety of intra-organizational and interorganizational situations in which different types of political struggles are likely to occur. These political relationships differ from one another not only in the type of players that participate in them, and not only in the means of power exercised in them. Every political game that is conducted in organizational reality has additional characteristics that set it apart from the other types of games—characteristics that will be briefly discussed now.

1.   *The Submission Game*

This game is widely found in all kinds of organizations and even outside them. This is in effect a type of battle in which every participant tries to overcome his rival in order to force him to submit. Therefore, it is a game that can be called a head-on collision between two or more hawks. In the world of sports, boxing matches and wrestling are outstanding examples of games of this type. Numerous fisticuffs between boys that frequently take place in thousands of schools also exemplify this type of struggle. More and more, such fights are accompanied by physical violence, ending in states of humiliation. Moreover, since school students tend now to carry knives and similar weapons, fistfights are likely to end in injury or even in death—either intentionally or accidentally.

In interpersonal relations in workplaces, this type of power game undergoes a certain process of refinement in which the physical violence is replaced by verbal violence; thus, open or implied threats, insulting remarks, repelling body language, castigation and incitement, humiliation and similar behavior are often used by rivals for the purpose of arriving at a clear-cut victory of one side over the other.

In the relationships between superiors and subordinates, the attempts at subjugation, if they are made, generally include deterrent threats of punishment such as the deprivation of rights and freedoms. In certain disciplinary organizations such as prisons, the imposition of physical punishment against recalcitrant prisoners and rebels is quite a routine matter both among as well as in the interpersonal relations between the prisoners themselves.

2.   *The Seduction Game*

This type of game serves as a significant incentive for work, in labor relations between employers and employees, and in the relations between superiors and subordinates. The results of games such as this find expression, on the one hand, in work productivity, in the carrying out of difficult or dangerous tasks, and in conforming to the objectives and timetables; on the other hand, in the levels of income and prestige of the actors. The individuals that take part in this type of game gain material benefits above and beyond those granted to all the other participants of the same standing in the organization. Seduction games are often conducted also between colleagues of similar organizational standing who need personal services that they are not entitled to get as part of their job or authority in the organization.

This is, therefore, a game that can be described as a "prize-winning game." Professional tennis competitions, for example, are a well-known example of this type of game, so widespread in the world of competitive sports. In these games and also those conducted in work organizations, the prizes are not only medals or certificates of honor but also actual monetary grants that are the main source of livelihood of the actors. However, the inducement offered to one player in exchange for complying with the demands of another player is not only economic. Favoritism, receipt of classified information, insertion of false records in corporation documents, and sexual bribes are only some of the non-economic baits that serve as a means of influence in such games. However, since some of these inducements are illegitimate and even illegal, games of this type are often concealed; sometimes, however, they are discovered, the players brought to court and given severe sentences. Yet, many others enjoy such improper benefits for long periods of time without being discovered. This kind of politics is widespread in various organizations, especially in Third World states, where the organizational culture regards bribes as part of the game, namely, a necessity that cannot be condemned. It is no wonder, then, that in some countries nowadays bribery is still offered and accepted not only by lower participants but also, and mainly, by the most senior officers in the government, in the military, as well as in business.

3.   *The Persuasion Game*

This type of game represents political measures taken by a supervisor, a colleague, or a subordinate in order to influence another person to adopt certain beliefs or attitudes. Such political measures include intensive use of claims, arguments, and explanations, and assertions of an intellectual, ideological, or religious nature. This kind of game may be described as the "preaching game," which has always served spiritual leaders, priests, demagogues, politicians, propagandists, and opinion leaders of all sorts. Many individuals in organizations, not necessarily their leaders, often adopt this type of interpersonal politics towards others in the organization and those outside it to gain influence. Such influence attempts make systematic use of various symbols that intend to enhance feelings of fear or pride so as to be more effective.

The persuasion game is based on the assumption that one can influence the behavior of others without using force, by means of a sustained and focused attack on one's set of beliefs, cognitions, and emotions. In popular language, the expression "brainwash" has become well rooted as a term for such attempts at influence and for their outcome. Persuasive communication, which is a means of influence in games of this type, includes the use of inflaming speeches or provocative writings with emphatic use of significant metaphors for the listener; the repeated use of the same verbal and body expressions; the emphasis of certain slogans both written and oral; rhetorical questions and tendentious illustrations through various verbal or pictorial insinuations. As a result, the person to be influenced is pressured, dragged or pushed into a mental corner until he or she apparently becomes persuaded and responds favorably to the demands of the manipulator.

4.   The Confrontation Game

Games of this type are characteristic of conflict situations between two different groups. The confrontation game is characterized by a frontal clash in which each group tries to overcome its rival. In the world of sports, American football is the outstanding example of intergroup confrontation games that involve a large amount of physical force. So, too, are games such as soccer, basketball, handball, and similar games that entail abundant instances of collisions, grappling, falls, and bodily injuries on both sides.

In the organizational reality as well, the intergroup confrontations are generally forceful in nature and are often accompanied by a considerable degree of physical and verbal violence, even by the use of firearms by one group against the other. A group of players in political games such as these are struggling for their livelihood, for their quality of working life, and for their economic security. They are not satisfied, therefore, with symbolic victory cups. They demand an increase in their share of the organizational pie, they claim more rights and opportunities, they wish to be partners in the decisions that influence their future, and they strive to gain positions of leadership and to occupy key jobs in organizations.

The struggles of women's groups, minority groups, and immigrant groups are prominent examples in our times of repeated frontal clashes taking place in public institutions, business corporations, political parties, social movements, and also in international organizations. Sanctions, strikes, sabotage, destruction of property, and bodily attacks are part of the menu of penalties inflicted by these groups on their rivals as part of the intergroup confrontation games in organizations.

5.   The Bargaining Game

This type is typical in our times of professional groups that try to snap up large chunks of the "organizational spoils," mostly at the expense of other working groups in the same organizations.[8] In spite of the mutual sanctions that these players adopt against each other from time to time, the main characteristic of players of this type is to conduct negotiations between the representatives of employers and employees regarding the improvement of salary and working conditions. This is therefore a game that may be compared to bargaining in the market.

In games of this type there are no fixed prices, because both the goods and the payment are the result of negotiation. The achievement of every group participating in this political game lies in its bargaining position as opposed to the bargaining position of the other groups, and is dependent on the amount of power it has as compared to that of its rival. In this game pre-planned presentation of exaggerated claims, maneuvers, deceptions, pretense, disclosures and denials, seeming advances and retreats, hypothetical offers and the like are used by the participants. The most probable result of this bargaining game is some kind of compromise between the players, with each side boasting of a clear victory over its rival.

6.   The Coalition Game

This kind of political behavior is perhaps the most typical of intergroup relationships in organizations. Different groups of stakeholders within the organization and outside it, who are interested in influencing the decision-making processes and to have them end in resolutions that are preferable to them, join together to increase their power vis-à-vis the decision makers and to strengthen their influence over them; that is to say: they coalesce together in a coalition.

A coalition does not resemble a partnership between individuals or a permanent alliance between groups and organizations. It is a temporary joint force that is focused on a certain issue so as to advance a common interest. The coalition game is characterized by the tying and loosening of political bonds between different interest groups in accordance with changing needs and circumstances. This is a common political game, for example, between the representatives of several trade unions confronting their common employer, or between factions that represent different political parties in the parliament or in the government. It is also typical of subunits in organizations that compete with other subunits over their share of the budget, as can be seen in military organizations, for example. This is an obvious political game that may be summed up by the popular saying: "All together but each one to oneself." This means that every group takes care of its own interests by means of a temporarily shared struggle side by side with groups that have their own interests. The moment the desired result is achieved, the justification for the coalition no longer exists, and therefore this partnership is dissolved and broken down into its former constituents that may later form other coalitions, possibly opposing ones.

7.   The Subjugation Game

This game represents a type of power struggle for control between organizations with the purpose of obtaining a monopoly over a certain market: exclusive control of the suppliers of critical resources to the organization; the seizing of control positions in hostile organizations or the takeover the ownership of competing organizations. This game represents a typical mode of interorganizational politics taking place in the world of organizations; it may be observed among institutional, business, political, and military institutions. It is kind of a game that is conducted for the purpose of subduing rival organizations.

In contrast with other political measures applied in inter-organizational relationships, subjugation games are characterized by the intentional and systematic application of coercive power through economic, legal, political, and military means. These are struggles to the bitter end, pursuing the attainment of total victory over the rival organizations. The uncompromising power struggle that is conducted by the United States agency for drug warfare against the drug cartel in South America is an outstanding example of the subjugation game. It is not an uncommon strategy for business corporations to conduct some complicated courses of action against their competitors, pushing them to the verge of bankruptcy, for the purpose of taking them over despite their resistance.

8.   The Collaboration Game

This prototype includes a series of various kinds of interorganizational collaboration agreements. The number of collaboration agreements has been continuously increasing in today's realm of organizations of all kinds. Among them are the collaboration agreements between organizations that compete in the business world as well as between rival organizations in the world of politics. The main idea that guides these types of collaboration games is well expressed by the proverb: "If you can't beat them, join them." This is clearly a political measure that links independent competing organizations by means such as a shared initiative or the shared development of an innovative product; agreement to collaborate on a specifically defined subject, such as the exchange of secret intelligence; agreement on mutual assistance such as aid to victims of natural disasters or wars; or arrangements for the supply of essential resources such as water, food and medicine at times of crisis.

In political games such as these, multi-organizational networks are created that contain several organizations collaborating together in one field of endeavor, in spite of their being competitors or even rivals in other fields at the same time. This type of interorganizational relations demonstrates the paramount importance of interests in organizational operations; it also demonstrates the great complexity of the organization's relationships with the outside environment; and it indicates the mutual intrusion across organizational borders in our times. Such collaboration games are often conducted over lengthy periods of time, as long as the players that participate in them gain mutual benefit from them; that is, as long as the benefits that are weighed against the costs and dangers inherent in interorganizational collaboration are satisfactory for the participants. International networks of police organizations that are fighting terrorism today exemplify this type of interorganizational game.

9.   The Unification Game

This prototype is different both from the subjugation game and from the collaboration game in being much more comprehensive, deep, and far-reaching. This game represents complex political measures that lead towards the uniting, consolidating, and merging of two or more organizations into one entity. Mega mergers between giant defense industries in the United States and in Europe; mergers between news and entertainment corporations; and consolidations of multiple trade unions into super-unions represent some examples of such unification. Probably the largest and most complicated unification endeavor of our times is the European Union.

The inevitable result of unification games is the increasing power of the organizations that are combined within them. In mega mergers of giant corporations, the result is the unprecedented power that they have to influence economic, political, and cultural affairs all over the world. The unification game is based on the assumption that real cooperation between certain organizations can last for a long time only if those organizations possess the same basic ideas and share some common views. That is to say, mutual interests are a necessary condition but not a sufficient one for the persistence of interorganizational mergers and unions. In order to create a common organizational setting, there is need for a shared cultural infrastructure. This pre-condition may account for the reluctance and caution of the European Union in accepting new members from the previous Soviet Bloc as well as a Muslim country such as Turkey. Therefore, the unification game is a slow, complex, long-drawn game that is often subject to comprehensive and profound organizational changes. This is a large-scale political game in which the players strive for the attainment of much greater power and influence than they have separately.

Visibility of Political Games

The different types of political games differ from each other by the degree of their outward visibility. That is to say, every political game may be conducted openly, above the surface; such a game allows for its identification and for tracing its course of development directly and immediately. However, every political game is also liable to be conducted in a covert manner, under the surface; such a game conceals its existence and hides its course of development from the eyes and ears of people interested in following it, for instance, government inspectors or news reporters. Therefore, we can identify any political game in the organizational arena as either an *overt game* or a *covert game*, depending on whether the game is visible or not.

Since we are dealing with politics and not with sports, the games that are described above tend to be conducted in the shade and behind the curtain. As it is explained in the chapter on perceived politics, political behavior in organizations is sometimes necessary, at other times useful, but for most of the time it is not perceived as legitimate behavior. Therefore, political games are generally disliked by the public in general and do not receive much applause from those watching them. Even the actors who participate in them tend to apologize for their participation in them rather than tending to boast of them in public. This is due to the negative stigma attached to the phenomenon called politics in Western culture.

It is not surprising, therefore, that organizational actors using politics, such as managers, actually hide their intentions and deny any behavior of a political nature. In many instances, they act surreptitiously and hint at the purpose of their actions in a tacit manner, such as offering inducements to another person without explicitly requesting anything in exchange.

Various political games remain obscure not only because of the negative attitude towards them. They are conducted under a cover of secrecy as covert games for pertinent reasons as well. First, the road to victory in politics is strewn with deceptive tricks and ploys, and with guile that surprises the opponent and disrupts his or her progress. Second, early exposure of the plans of action will allow the other to prepare his/her defenses in advance. Third, aggressive political behavior involves an unnecessary investment of resources that results in a decrease of power for the player. Fourth, public admission of taking part in a political game invites unwanted pressure from stakeholders inside and outside the organization. Fifth, the exposure of political measures is liable to justify retribution and encourage acts of revenge by the losers in the game or by their supporters.

In view of these considerations and similar ones, it is understandable why the real process of intergroup and interorganization negotiations often takes place behind the scenes; in many instances, secret agents and intermediaries do this job, while the main players totally deny the very existence of such negotiations. Similarly, one may comprehend the apparent contradiction between the declarations of political players and the actions attributed to them. Political activities of this kind include, for instance, the hostile takeover of a competing organization; the creation of a business cartel; the discrimination of candidates and employees for sectarian reasons (origin, sex, and religion); as well as the prevention of vital information from clients and partners.

There are political actors who pretend that they are acting for the good of the organization, when they are actually taking an active part in an underhanded political game; for example, a senior manager who takes a junior worker along with him on a business trip under the official guise of working needs (seduction game); or an appointed official who redefines some job position and thus denudes it of most of its authority under the official guise of efficiency (subjugation game). Many examples of this kind can be found in other types of political games that take place in military organizations, medical institutions, universities, colleges, and cultural institutions.

A study on combat units in military forces exemplifies the tendency to conceal games of a political nature, especially those of doubtful legitimacy in the organization.[9] This study shows that among the soldiers of field units, humiliation ceremonies and violent rituals had been held for years with the purpose of forcing the soldiers of the unit to comply with the social norms of behavior of that unit and its unofficial social leaders. Since these patterns of behavior create a "climate of dread" in those field units and harm the soldiers' motivation to fight on the battlefield, they are carefully concealed from the eyes and ears of the officers, the higher military authorities, the soldiers' parents, and the media. In the words of the researcher: "this violent activity is wrapped in a bubble of silence."

And so, from the political viewpoint, secret games have an advantage over open games. At the same time, a certain degree of openness in most of the activities of the various participants is necessary to ensure proper management, efficiency, and moral rectitude. Therefore, it is very difficult to conceal dealings, to disguise activities, and to hide behavior in organizational life. The systems of supervision and control of the organization are meant to prevent improper behavior and to expose any attempt to conceal it.

Thus, the participants in every organization are exposed to ongoing surveillance of their behavior. This surveillance is made possible by the use of human, technological, and administrative means. The hierarchy of authority in an organization also serves as the system of control. Most organizations today conduct some kind of surveillance of those who enter their gates and work within their premises. Organizations install security systems to protect themselves from intruders and thieves, and from professional eavesdroppers. Such systems include professional security officers using sophisticated devices, which are in charge of detecting prohibited activities. Moreover, there are organizational procedures that require recording and documentation of activities, decisions, events and resources. These means make it possible today to locate and reconstruct any anomaly or deviation that takes place in the organization. Political activities are thus involved in risk-taking, especially when they are seemingly conducted in the open, in a way that is visible to observation by others.

However, the desire to accumulate power in an organization, the wish to exert influence, and the temptation to increase the amount of benefits encourage the continued existence of political games in spite of the real difficulties and risks that they entail. It is reasonable to assume, then, that political games will be conducted in all organizations in the foreseeable future as well.[10] Organizational reality always consists of political games, in the same way that physical reality consists of shadows near real objects. Politics, like shadows, reflect the less conspicuous side of reality. They are shady since they often take place behind curtains and underneath the surface. Their concealment and denial make them not only dim but also somewhat virtual. Ironically, the better they are hidden, the more they are effective in bringing to their players further and better benefits. Nevertheless, these ubiquitous overt games are not likely to disappear from interpersonal, intergroup, and interorganizational relationships.

Conclusion

The concept of the "political game," which runs through this entire volume from beginning to end, implies a whole range of organized activity that is based on power and exerts influence for the purpose of gaining benefits, usually at the expense of other people. This chapter has classified and examined a variety of political games that are frequently conducted in different types of organizations.

In this chapter two methods of classification of political games have been presented and discussed: one proposed by Henry Mintzberg, and the other proposed by the present author. Each one of these classifications is based on two or three criteria by which different games can be differentiated. The purpose of the distinction between the various types of games is to explain the conditions that prompt them to take place, the patterns of behavior that characterize them, and the expected results for the players participating in them.

The classification developed by Mintzberg is based on the three following criteria: the status of the players in the organization, the means of influence on which the players depend, and the motives for their participation in the political game. On the basis of these criteria, three major types of political games are identified: games that conform to the authorized and established regime of the organization; games that are motivated by opposition to the established regime and the desire to undermine it; and games that lead to the displacement of the existing regime in the organization and the take-over of control by other hands. A more detailed division on the basis of Mintzberg's method produces a variety of thirteen types of political games in organizations. Each of these types is described in brief in the present chapter.

The method of classification developed by Samuel is based on two main criteria: (a) the type of players participating in the political game: individuals, groups, or organizations; (b) the power bases on which the players depend in order to achieve the desired results, namely, the physical force basis, the economic basis, and the ideological basis. These bases of power are expressed through the infliction of penalties, promise of benefits, and the manipulation of symbols, respectively. In this way, a typology of nine types of political games in organizations is identified. Each of these prototypes is described in this chapter. The term "prototype" in this context indicates the fact that for each type of political game there exists several varieties in organizational reality; it is thus necessary to portray a more detailed and precise characterization to further differentiate between the many games.

A third criterion, the degree of visibility of the political game, refers to the fact that each of the political games is liable to be conducted openly in the form of an overt game or secretly in the form of a covert game. The chapter discusses the organizational conditions and the personal motives that encourage the conduct of covert games rather than overt ones.

This discussion points out the advantages of the covert games and the countermeasures that organizations adopt and governments activate in order to expose them in public. Finally, it is asserted here that in spite of the difficulties and risks involved in political games, these games are well rooted in organizational reality and are not expected to disappear in the near future. Therefore, organizational politics remains an integral aspect of organizational life, in the overt as well as covert form of games, whether one likes it or not.

Notes

1.   Mintzberg, 1983. The way in which Mintzberg's classification is presented in this chapter reflects my understanding and interpretation of his ideas.

2. The subject of budgeting represents a defined political issue that is included in the political agenda of every organization. Therefore, it is doubtful if this subject actually represents a separate type of political game. The subject of budgeting is discussed in detail in chapter 4.

3. The relations of mutual influence between the individuals have been described and analyzed in chapter 7, "Interpersonal Politics."

4. The nature of the political games that are conducted between these groups are described and analyzed in chapter 8, "Intergroup Politics."

5. Chapter 9 in this book deals with interorganizational politics, and it describes in detail the political struggles that occur at this level.

6. In chapter 1 of this book the various power bases possessed by individuals, groups, and organizations are described in detail. A description is also given of the ways and means by which, on these bases, it would be possible to wield the different levers of influence.

7. Etzioni, 1975.

8. The reference is mainly to those well-established professional groups whose livelihood and economic security is generally assured: air pilots, doctors, engineers, academics, and the like.

9. Samia, 2004 (Hebrew).

10. Thompson & McHugh, 1995.

7

Interpersonal Politics

Levels of Political Action

Political action of different kinds is conducted in organizational reality on three main levels. The first level is that of relationships between individuals in the organization and between them and people outside the organization such as clients or suppliers. This is the organizational level at which *interpersonal politics* takes place. It includes relationships between office holders having defined functions in the organization who need to interact as part of their jobs (e.g., supervisors and subordinates); it also includes interpersonal relationships that are neither prescribed nor formal, but nonetheless affected by the fact that the interacting individuals do have specific jobs and certain positions in the organization (e.g., seniors and juniors).

The second level is that of relationships that are conducted between the various professional groups in the organization (such as engineers and technicians), between subunits in the organization (such as production and maintenance), or between the different social sectors represented in the organization (such as men and women). These relationships reflect the second political level in organizational life, designated here as *intergroup politics*.

The third level is that of relationships conducted both overtly and covertly between organizations having some kind of link, such as a common market. At this level of relationships, politics is not conducted between individuals or groups that belong to a given organization, but between different organizations. Thus, relationships of this kind usually take place in the environment that surrounds the organizations involved. This higher level of relationships will be treated later as the level of *interorganizational politics*.

In organizational research, each one of those levels represents a different plane of the organizational reality; it therefore requires a different level of analysis of the political phenomenon. At the interpersonal level, the individual is at the center of scientific scrutiny. The underlying assumption is that organizations constitute aggregates of people in which various functionaries act in conjunction and cooperation in order to carry out common tasks assigned to them. However, the system of interpersonal relationships in an organization inevitably consists of opposing interests, competition, and power struggles over desired benefits.[1]

At the intergroup level, human groups in general and working groups in particular are the focus of political analysis. Such groups maintain ongoing relationships that are characterized by belligerent negotiations aimed at the attainment of organizational resources.[2] Scholars who study politics at the interorganizational level focus mainly on competitions and power struggles between different organizations. From a political viewpoint, interorganizational relations display mutual attempts of organizations to establish their standing and improve their bargaining vis-à-vis their counter partners.[3]

Seen this way, each level reflects a system of mutual relationships between actors that is meant to obtain the maximal utility that can be derived through political means; that is, through the deliberate exercise of power, whether overt or covert, in order to influence the behavior of another actor. The difference between these levels lies in the distinction between the actors—individuals, groups, or organizations—and not in their objectives or their political methods. Most of the political games that organizational actors play at the interpersonal, the intergroup, or the interorganizational levels have certain similarities. Yet, each of them has unique features that distinguish them from the others. Therefore, it is appropriate to discuss each of them separately. This chapter will deal with interpersonal politics, and the following two chapters are devoted to the analysis of higher levels of organizational politics.

The Job as Political Leverage

Every organization is composed of a collection of many building blocks that are joined together in different ways into a pattern of organizational units at different levels: sections, departments, divisions, branches, and the like. The basic building blocks from which organizations are constructed are the organizational jobs. Every job or position is composed of some interrelated assignments that form a whole unit. Thus, a given job is so patterned that it enables a single worker to carry it out completely in a cyclical manner. Job description includes a specification of the authority that comes with it, and a definition of required relationships with relevant partners (e.g., supervisors, subordinates, and peers); it also determines the allocation of resources (e.g., budget, manpower, equipment) that the organization provides the job occupant or the office holder.[4]

The control over the resources that can be utilized due to the job function serves as a solid foundation for the application of political measures in interpersonal relationships between individuals. For example, anyone having served in the military of any country, knows the power of the quartermaster in charge of many kinds of equipment items that soldiers and officers constantly need during their period of service. It is no wonder then that many quartermasters of military units make use of their access to these necessary resources to conduct concealed interpersonal bargaining with their "clients." In return for preferable supply of necessary items, they expect, and sometimes explicitly demand, special privileges such as after-duty time off, exemption from night-watch duties, or maintenance tasks at the campground.

Treasurers and paymasters in organizations sometimes conduct various kinds of political behavior. It is safe to argue that the financial people in every organization and at every level enjoy privileges and benefits that other job-holders of parallel rank are unable to obtain. The obvious example for this is the privileged position of certain staff professionals, most of them economists and accountants, in the Treasury department. In some places these civil servants enjoy the status and fringe benefits of a general manager, even though they have only a few subordinates working for them, if any at all.

Besides some rudimentary jobs and rank-and-file functions, most of the job descriptions leave considerable leeway for the people manning the job as to how to do their work properly. Within the limits of such discretion, everyone is able to express his or her own will, talents, and personality traits. It goes without saying that the scope for autonomy is wider in senior positions than in junior ones. Similar jobs are also frequently performed differently by different workers. This tendency is noticeable in most organizations, especially with regard to managerial positions, in which job definitions are rather wide, loose, and somewhat vague.

The range of possible leeway for a job-holder in an organization thus serves as *political leverage* in one's relationships with other participants—supervisors, subordinates, and peers. This leverage is often realized by the exercise of power, such as inducements, threats, or penalties, against other actors; these sanctions are used as part of one's attempt to advance the interests of the organizational unit to which he or she belongs, and to respond to its needs beyond what is possible to obtain regularly in the organization and through its established modes of operation. It is reasonable to assume that the use of power derived from the job function is quite prevalent among organizational actors, especially when they try to get for themselves extra benefits that exceed the legitimate emoluments to which they are entitled in return for their work.[5]

To exemplify the dimensions of this phenomenon, it is worth presenting a short citation of an annual report made by an officer in charge of wages and industrial relations in the Treasury Department with regard to civil servants.

A minimal estimation of the range of salary irregularities in the public sector hovers between one billion and two billion [dollars]. What these groups have done is sometimes contrary to law. The unbridled self-indulgence in some of these groups is at its height. This is neither right neither proper. The society must get rid of this phenomenon. 40% of the groups under surveillance carried out irregularities in salary or pension payments. 57% of them that did so in 1997, and did so again in 1998.... Nearly every sphere examined [by the Treasury Department] they found salary irregularities. This indicated disrespect for the law, for civil government and for proper management. The main offenders were the elected managers and directors who could not withstand the demands of their subordinates and granted them salaries that were contrary to the law.[66]

The holders of senior positions in the public sector (e.g., central and local government, state-owned enterprises) organizations easily get to know how to obtain excess rights that are not officially included in the conditions that pertain to their positions. The press repeatedly exposes to the public the names of senior officers in the public sector who have arranged for themselves various benefits through measures of a political nature, which rest on personal use of the power invested in these positions.

One of the most widespread phenomena in this sphere is the tendency to obtain preferential guest reception provisions reserved for VIPs. Among the variety of such benefits it is worth mentioning here the travels abroad, seemingly in an official capacity, at the expense of the taxpayer's money; first-class flight tickets and luxury suites in prestigious hotels; private transportation, personal security services, and delivery messengers; the curtailment of the waiting period for obtaining various services, private medical services; and the exemption from various payments such as customs dues. All these as well as other excess rights are enjoyed by those privileged persons by virtue of their positions and mainly due to their personal power accrued from those positions. It is no wonder then that senior functionaries everywhere tend to exercise the inherent power of their positions, mostly covertly, although a few of them do not hesitate to impose their power, not their authority, in an unconcealed and even blunt manner.

This political use of power is frequently done with the help of an *inner circle*. This circle includes a host of assistants, secretaries, bureau chiefs, personal consultants, security guards, drivers, and domestic attendants surrounding those seniors. In this way, senior officials can avoid taking responsibility for the actions of their proxies and deny their personal involvement in receiving benefits with public pretense of innocence, claiming that they themselves "did not even know" about the receipt of such benefits.

The possibility of circumventing rules and procedures, to demand excessive benefits, to gain priority over others, and to enjoy various exemptions are not, of course, exploited by all privileged officers and not even by most of them. At least some of these privileges are within the "gray area" between what is allowed and what is prohibited, on the borderlines of standard practice. However, the opportunities of senior executives to exploit their positions for their own benefit enable them to abuse their power. These structural conditions of high-rank positions in organizations turn out to be a sort of trap into which more than a few people have fallen; among them were public representatives, senior officials, military commanders, business executives, and even honorable judges.

As already said, even when senior officials attempt to increase their personal advantage, they generally act within the gray area of rules and procedures. It is just in this undefined area that the concrete political aspect of these measures is revealed. The senior position-holders and those who assist them agree about the deal that is being fabricated; they dissemble their movements as much as possible; they take care to find a justification for their actions retroactively; they refrain from explicit and documented promises that might betray the spoils they have taken; and they employ the assistance of "loyalists" for their needs. Within the framework of such measures, these people prearrange their voting behavior in the decision-making processes in which they participate, they support the election of their close associates to important positions, approve budget allocations and grant loans; and in general they secretly help each other. In light of such manipulations it is no wonder that a popular proverb says: "You scratch my back and I'll scratch yours."

Senior positions and certain key jobs unintentionally contain built-in temptations for their holders to transgress the law in their pursuit of special benefits. Repeated actions of this kind are a betrayal of trust: acquiring something by deception, taking bribes, disruption of due processes, and abuse of the power of the position. A variety of criminal actions of this kind carried out by persons of privilege can be found in abundance in all organizations throughout the world. Such malpractices and their like reflect the dark side of organizational politics and reveal the "ugly face" of organizational reality.

Although the plague of corruption spreads beyond the sphere of political behavior and criminality, it should be noted that corrupt behavior may be the result of complex and convoluted measures aimed to transfer bribes illegally to one another, mostly at the expense of the public purse. These measures include false agreements and fabricated contracts with suppliers and contractors outside the organization, simulated accounts in banks, payments for work that was not done, and shady wheeling and dealing of all kinds. Such activities compel those making them to conduct interpersonal relationships based on strong mutual interests, on common trust, and on a powerful "balance of fear," which would deter their associates from public revelation of the deals that were being fabricated between them.

Another ongoing pattern of behavior that has long been the dark side of the relationships between senior and junior employees in organizations, mainly between men and women, is *sexual harassment*. It is worth explaining here and now that sexual harassment of any kind reflects first and foremost a specific pattern of interpersonal politics in modern organizations. Attempts at sexual exploitation represent aggressive behavior as a means of exerting personal force so that senior position-holders can gain control over more junior ones. In many cases, sexual harassment is employed by supervisors who are not satisfied with the authority they acquire by virtue of their positions; therefore, they use it as a means to express superiority and to display dominance over their subordinates.

The sense of power felt by senior employees tacitly implies the temptation to demand from others their submission to bodily contacts of one kind or another against their will. The tendency towards sexual harassment has been widespread for many years in all kinds of organizations. This kind of behavior includes suggestions to have sexual relationships, the touching of private parts of the other person's body, the use of terms with sexual implications, and even attempts at sexual coercion of various kinds. Military organizations and similar ones have been, and in some countries they still are, notorious in this respect until just a short time ago.[7]

As with all uses of force, these cases, also the persuasion and pressure, are accompanied by explicit or implied promises of reward for compliance, and even with threats to impose penalties in response to resistance. The ability of the senior official to constrain the freedom of choice of his or her subordinate and to stipulate his/her behavior towards the subordinate on relationships of this kind creates a state of personal dominance versus submission between them.

In order to establish intimate relationships on this basis, senior employees need to use measures of a political nature in their interpersonal relations with others. Such actions include the initiation of joint trips on assignment, overtime work, business meetings outside the organization quarters, joint luncheons or dinners, granting of personal gifts, and the like. Senior executives, commanders, and politicians get assistance from various aides, secretaries, security guards and the like in such matters, who strive to create the suitable conditions for privacy and seclusion, and to camouflage them as desired.

The most famous example in the twentieth century, but also the most controversial one in the world in this connection, was the sexual affair of United States President Bill Clinton with a young White House intern called Monica Lewinsky. The controversy surrounding this affair went as far as a Senate trial hearing to impeach the president. The political interpersonal aspect of this affair was expressed in the charge sheet that accused the president of exploiting his position, fabricating evidence, and pressuring others to give false testimony. Since the Senate trial was essentially a political procedure, the president was acquitted of those charges. Although this intimate relationship apparently was neither a sexual attack nor sexual harassment in the technical sense, it exemplifies the superiority of a middle-aged, married man and a father to a teenage daughter at that time, holding the highest possible position on earth, over a young unknown woman, barely holding a minor job at the White House. It is difficult to imagine how a subordinate like her could possibly resist the request of the president to engage in such an affair.

In Israel, on the other hand, an enlisted female soldier appealed to the Supreme Court against a Brigadier-General, demanding that he be denied promotion to the rank of General and a high level position in the army, claiming that he had had sexual relations with her when he was her superior officer. The court approved her appeal, and regarded the behavior of Brigadier-General as "a base and immoral behavior that should not be tolerated in any organization in which there is a superordinates-subordinates type of relationship." By this ruling the Supreme Court supported the social norm that negates the "exploitation of status, authority, influence, or superiority, in order to obtain sexual benefits."[8] In short, sexual harassment in its various forms is a political matter since it has to do with power and dominance rather that with intimacy and sex per se.

The other side of sexual coercion is expressed by the behavior patterns of some junior employees towards more powerful and senior ones in the organization. This kind of behavior is intended to offer sexual bribes in order to obtain extra benefits and rights from the senior members. There is no need to emphasize that this does not refer to ingenuous romantic ties formed between people who are by chance of a different status in an organization; it is rather calculated and intentional political behavior, using sexual bait for utilitarian purposes. The systematic use of sexual enticements serves various security organizations in order to reveal secret information, to recruit agents and informers, to betray and capture wanted people, and even to eliminate enemies. In everyday organizational life, however, sex, like money, is used by men and women as political means aimed at influencing others to do things that they would not otherwise do in their position.

Social positions in general and organizational positions in particular serve as the social basis on which individuals holding those positions typically act and interact in certain ways. Yet, at the same time, they also provide fertile grounds for the development of *functional conflict* between the various job participants within the organization and outside it. Among the various factors that encourage functional conflict between participants, we should first consider vague job descriptions; second, contradictory demands of the job performers; third, organizational changes that occur in the course of time; fourth, overlapping in authority of the various position-holders; fifth, loose internal mechanisms of coordination that prevent effective control of participants' activities within the organization.[9]

Since such inter-positional conflicts make it difficult for actors to perform properly and prevent them from obtaining the maximum utility from their positions, they generally tend to settle them in any possible way. These methods often involve the exercise of power as a means of settling disputes and solving inter-positional problems within the organizational setting. The solution to inter-positional conflicts certainly could and should be found in proper job descriptions; in clear policies, regulations, and procedures; in authoritative managerial decisions; and in the ways in which employees are trained for their jobs in the organization. However, there are sufficient indications that the formal set-up of organizations does not satisfy the needs of all the organizational actors. Therefore, there always is a tendency for functional conflicts and political struggles to be settled, if at all, by means of the power that those actors actually possess.

In addition, in every organization there are also interpersonal conflicts that arise from dissimilar interests of the participants. Opposing viewpoints and attitudinal disagreements frequently lead to confrontations between job participants in organizations. Consequently, opponents get involved in interpersonal struggles of a political nature that are intended to impose certain views and opinions on their rivals.

> Organizational politics arise when people think differently and want to act differently. This diversity creates a tension that must be resolved through political means. As we have already seen, there are many ways in which this can be done: autocratically ("We'll do it this way"); bureaucratically (We're supposed to do it this way"); or democratically ("How shall we do it?"). In each case the choice between alternative paths of action usually hinges on the power relations between actors involved.[10]

A careful examination of such cases reveals another aspect of interpersonal politics in organizations. Position-holders acting as appointees in an organization strive to ensure that their relationships with those subordinate to them will be conducted according to their wishes. Whenever disagreements appear and clashes ensue between the views of the superordinates and their subordinates as to the proper way to conduct matters, an inter-positional conflict develops. Supervisors try to settle this conflict in various ways. These supervisors redefine their subordinates' tasks, their areas of responsibility and their authority limits. In other cases they come to a common agreement over the proper patterns of behavior. Alternatively, they agree to grant greater freedom of action to the junior staff, which means the *empowerment* of lower-level employees.

Nevertheless, in many cases the apparent settling of a conflict is forced upon the subordinates by means of suspension of benefits and the imposition of penalties, namely the activation of power towards the actors involved in the matter. In such cases, the more senior ones impose their authority on the junior ones to prevent friction, disputes, and confrontations that disrupt order and are detrimental to work. Job participants, despite their junior status, will soon display a tendency to use the power at their disposal and take retaliatory actions that will cause harm to their superiors and to other senior members in the organization who, in their view, are hostile to them.

Subordinates who play power games against their supervisors display signs of disobedience, show disloyal behavior, and withhold important information from their superiors. They also tend to express criticisms and complaints about their supervisors' decisions and actions. In many cases, these workers tend to mobilize the support of their colleagues and create a hostile coalition against those in authority over them. Moreover, it sometimes occurs that the subordinates try to bring about the removal from office of their superiors through systematic leaks, slander and denunciations, the spreading of rumors and gossip. Such patterns of behavior escalate the conflict between superordinates and their subordinates. Therefore, it sometimes becomes necessary for the top management to intervene in order to settle the dispute and to avoid the harmful results of an unsettled conflict.

Even in the absence of a distinct conflict between supervisors and subordinates, political behavior is likely to be plentifully applied by employees against their superiors. This kind of conduct is intended to gain influence over the overall amount of benefits they receive from the organization. In general, workers who adopt various methods of political influence with their superiors, such as flattery, bargaining, or even aggressive behavior towards them, do gain higher performance appraisal. This in turn results in salary increases beyond those of subordinates who do not deal in interpersonal politics.[11]

Even colleagues who are immersed in inter-positional conflict adopt a variety of political measures intended to settle the conflict in the way they desire. These power struggles are liable to be decided in favor of the stronger at the expense of the weaker. In other words, power determines the outcome of the conflict. Therefore, in such struggles, there is a general tendency to seek allies and form a coalition with them in order to widen the basis of their power and increase their chances of winning. Such coalitions transfer interpersonal politics to the level of intergroup politics, which will be dealt with in the next chapter.

It should be clarified here that conflicts on a positional basis or on a personal basis do not focus only on resources and material benefits. The competition over seniority, status, and esteem, recognition of expertise, self-respect, and freedom of action lead to power struggles. These conflicts represent a considerable part of interpersonal politics in organizations. As we shall see later on, the importance of values, beliefs, feelings, and symbols are no less important than salary, property, or economic benefits as far as politics is concerned. All of these are part of the *organizational pie* of which each person wants to have a large slice.

Location as a Political Basis

The location of every participant in an organization—whether physical, functional or social—affects the degree of his or her organizational power, regardless of the power that comes from one's personal resources (such as expertise). The term *physical location* in this context means the real distance from the established location of a certain actor to the main headquarters—namely, the location of the organizational leadership. *Functional location* in this regard, means the location in which a person who performs a certain job is integrated into the organization workflow. This workflow links the various actors to a network of organizational communications through which official messages are transmitted, that is, instructions and guidelines, feedback data concerning performance, problems, and mishaps. The term *social location* reflects the location of each individual in the social network of the organization's participants. This communication network includes the transfer of interpersonal messages, generally informal ones; it contains updates and assessments of various developments in the organization that are not approved by the organization authorities (e.g., expected layoffs); it also contains a variety of communications passed along between peers and friends, such as gossip and jokes.

As we learn from the findings of various studies, the organizational location of every actor in each of these three spheres constitutes a source for the accrual of personal power and a basis for interpersonal politics within the organization and outside it.[12] The location thus determines the degree of proximity of the individual to the decision-making centers; it affects the extent of his/her control over the flow of information in the organization; and it also influences the degree of functional dependency of others in the work and activities that he or she performs. In other words, the location in the organizational space defines the degree of *centrality* of each individual in the hierarchical, functional, and social network.[13]

Organizational location facilitates or constrains attempts to form a network of interpersonal connections between a given actor and his or her superiors, subordinates, peers, and other actors outside the organization. The level of an actor's *organizational propinquity* to senior members, to decision makers and to other people of influence is realized through his or her accessibility to the power centers of the organization. Such access enables that actor to maintain ongoing interactions with persons of importance in the organization and even to create close interpersonal relationships with them.

Location thus explains the power of junior employees who work close to the organization's top management (such as assistants, secretaries, or bureau chiefs) even over their seniors in status and function. Occasionally, seniors have no choice but to persuade a *gatekeeper* of this kind to allow them personal access ("urgent" and even "immediate") to the Chief Executive Officer of an organization or to one of the Vice Presidents. Such attempts tend to develop into actual bargaining, not necessarily of the direct and explicit kind, between the senior and the junior member over the required payment of a "transit fee." It is unnecessary to stress that such interpersonal transactions do not resemble economic deals. There is no precise definition of the goods to be exchanged, neither is there a clear agreement on the nature and the rate of exchange, nor is there any explicit condition made between givers and takers.

Therefore, it is more correct to see this kind of interpersonal activity between senior and junior members as a relationship of mutual debt obligation; that is, a similar obligation created by gift interchanges in society. This exchange of favors accounts for the common custom of people inside and outside organizations to grant the secretaries and assistants of high-ranking officials and executives, various "symbolic" gifts of a personal nature (e.g., perfumes, jewelry, decorative objects, and fashionable accessories). It is reasonable to assume therefore that they expect to receive preferential treatment from those gatekeepers whenever they need time and attention of the organization leaders concerning their requests.

The organizational location also determines the access of various actors to the important sources of information regarding what is going on inside the organization. In the age of information in which we live today, information serves as a vital resource that has a diversity of uses—for example, to give and receive certain personal benefits.

Therefore, information is an important basis of power for those actors that are engaged in today's organizations in one way or another. Thus, access to information concerning decision-making processes, or to the persons who prepare this information, is an essential resource that many would aspire to have. It is no wonder then, that one's ability to retrieve such information constitutes a power basis that enables one to apply political measures against his or her counter-partners.

Through acts such as the denial of information, systematic leaks, distortion, concealment or exposure of information sources, both junior and senior participants can negotiate with those who are in need of information over the kind of payoff requested for it. Promotion, delegation of authority, and the granting of privileges are only some of the benefits given and taken in exchange for information. Moreover, in every organization there is a buildup of classified information, some being of a highly sensitive nature that is not available to most members of the organization, certainly not to external actors who are interested in obtaining it at the desired time. The greater the need for secret information of this kind, the higher the price, and so is the likelihood of interpersonal politics concerning information.

The organizational location of any person in the organization in general, and his proximity to the *technical core* in particular, determines the degree to which he or she serves as an essential input to the production processes of the organization's output. The more a certain actor is functionally essential to an organization, the greater the corresponding degree of dependency by other participants on his work. Therefore, those who are located at the important nodal points in the workflow are more essential for the organization's products and services. For example, the supervisor in the control room generally possesses much greater power than his or her colleagues stationed at more marginal points in the production processes, such as workers engaged in packaging the finished product at the end of the assembly line. An employee who interacts with many partners in the course of performing his/her work is likely to obtain much more information than an employee who works in a more isolated position with fewer interactions. Hence, the former occupies a more central position in the workflow of the organization as well as in the organizational communication network; consequently, other participants become dependent upon him to a much greater degree than the latter.[14]

Let us make it clear here that a participant's *functional centrality*, as determined by his or her organizational location, is not necessarily connected with the administrative seniority or the professional expertise of that participant. Even relatively junior employees, such as quality controllers or welfare agents, can be centrally positioned in the production flow or in the process of rendering services to clients.

As already explained above, the power of one actor (A) over another actor (B) is proportional to the dependence of B on A. This power encourages its possessor to apply political measures against others for the purpose of increasing the utility he or she can obtain through interpersonal relationships. Research studies on this subject show that those who have a central location in the functional or social network of an organization succeed in gaining promotion,[15] in salary increases,[16] and in other benefits exceeding those of their colleagues in that organization. The centrality of the actor in the organizational communication networks is likely to enable him or her at the very least to bend certain decisions in favor of the interests that he or she represents.[17]

In spite of the importance of centrality as a basis for personal power and a means for exerting influence, in every organization there are people whose power derives specifically from their position at the perimeter rather than at the center of the organization. In most cases, those participants serve as *linchpins* between the organization and its *task environment*; that is, suppliers, clients, investors, government agencies, and so forth. Purchasers and acquisition representatives, recruiters of new personnel, sales agents and marketers, spokesmen and public relations experts represent just a few examples of such employees working at the periphery of the organization.

These participants are in charge of importing the necessary inputs required by the organization for its functional needs (manpower, capital, technology, raw materials); and they also have to assist the organization to export its outputs (goods or services) to the various targeted markets. However, their power in the organization and their ability to influence the people and processes within it derive mainly from their capacity to lower the level of organizational uncertainty in the spheres of which they are in charge.

It should be noted that the main existential problem that every organization has to cope with at all times is the problem of uncertainty. This problem originates first and foremost in the external environment in which the organization functions. *Organizational uncertainty* is usually an outcome of the changes and the unexpected events that take place in the external environment of the organization. In addition, uncertainty is also determined by the complexity of the surrounding environment as displayed by the demographic and socioeconomic heterogeneity of the population. Furthermore, uncertainty results from instability of the internal environment, for instance, in situations of repeated labor quarrels, high rate of turnover, downsizing, economic crisis, and the like.

The practical implication of uncertainty is shortage of the necessary information for rational decision making. Thus, organizations subject to a high level of uncertainty are likely to encounter problems of adaptation to their changing environment; and they have to face difficulties in finding suitable solutions to the new conditions with which they have to cope. Organization members located on its borderlines represent the human interface between the organization and its surroundings and they are expected, then, to assist in coping with this uncertainty. Whatever their functions might be, they bring in vital information from the outer environment, identify trends and developments, warn about expected dangers, and supply the necessary inputs for decision making. Moreover, they create a complex network of mutual relationships with people and organizations in the external environment, thus serving as *boundary spanners*. All these constitute important resources for the organization, and they therefore become bases of power for those participants in their organizations. Through such means these boundary spanners contribute to the decrease of organizational uncertainty, and this contribution enables them to influence the decision makers to act in line with their preferences.[18]

The more vital the information that these peripheral people possess or can obtain from external sources for the organization, the greater their potential influence on key decision makers. Moreover, their ability to connect those working within the organization with those working in other organizations, allows them to make claims for personal benefits as well as to receive them in return for such liaison services. It is no wonder then that many of these actors learn to use their power for interpersonal politics. This kind of politics includes the exchange of personal favors, abuse of connections with outsider stakeholders for personal benefits, and trade of information for self-interest. Tendentious use of pleas, favoritism, pulling of strings outside the organization, and reliance on connections, are only a few of the means employed by these actors as coins of exchange for purposes of interpersonal politics.

The findings of a research study conducted in the United States on this subject support the structural approach in general, and the *dependence theory* in particular. This theoretical perspective accounts for the differences in power of individuals in organizations. The study shows that the location of an employee in the networks of organizational communication, in the workflow, and in social ties, is related to the degree of his influence over other individuals in the organization. Each of these networks constitutes a separate source of power and influence. The study supports the hypothesis that boundary positions are as important as the network central ones as far as power and influence are concerned.[19]

The Social Basis of Personal Influence

Organizations are not collection of isolated individuals making decisions and taking action in splendid solitude. They are, above all, social settings in which people interact with their colleagues. We are influenced by what our colleagues are saying and doing— the effect of social proof—and we are swayed by the things others do to get us to like them and feel good about them. We are also influenced by the emotions that are created and used in social settings.[20]

A person who is interested in verifying the rectitude of the opinions, feelings, and behavior that he maintains in certain social circumstances, has to examine their validity by means of proper standards. Usually, tested and acceptable means for these needs are available as tools of measurement and calculation. However, in social life in general, and in organizational life in particular, there are many situations in which it is impossible to examine and estimate objectively the "rightness" of a feeling, of a decision, or of a way of behavior. In such cases, people search for some kind of *social proof* by which they can measure the correctness of the choice they made.

So-called social proof is expressed by unanimity, conventions, commonly shared beliefs, and in behavioral patterns that resemble those adopted by others. The tendency of the individual in such situations is to "follow the crowd," namely, to behave as others do. The need to receive social assurance encourages people to fall in line with others and to demonstrate their social conformity.

For this reason, individuals who are interested in influencing others strive to create a social atmosphere of agreement with their opinions and actions in order to develop the tendency to follow in their footsteps. An individual who adopts a belief or behavior that is shared by a certain social group reciprocates for his acceptance as a member in it by conforming to the norms and expectations of his or her fellow members.[21] In this way, the social exchange that takes place in a group or in an organization is used for political purposes by opinion leaders, executives, public representatives, and officials of various kinds. Repeated presentation of ideas as though they were established facts and the justification of certain actions as representing a deep-rooted tradition are parts of such political efforts; the alternative is the use of political tactics of interpersonal influence such as personal flattery. In these ways, actors in organizations can also personally influence decision makers to act in their favor and for their benefit.

People also exercise personal power in interpersonal relationships in order to gain certain benefits that they cannot otherwise receive from their counterpartners. Research studies show that people tend to respond to the wishes of other people they know and like or to those to whom they are attracted, whatever the reasons might be. This fact sometimes serves to obtain the compliance of the other to one's demands.[22] As Jeffrey Pfeffer explains: "Liking is important in interpersonal influence, because it invokes the reciprocity rule."[23] People therefore tend to conciliate the person they are fond of and are prepared to fulfill his wishes. In this way they requite that person for the good feeling that he grants them by virtue of the affection or love they feel towards him, and avoid the unpleasant dissonance between their feelings and their behavior.

Affection, sympathy, love, attraction, and suchlike feelings towards the other stem from various factors such as similar personal features, attractive outward appearance, and mutual favors at work, exchange of compliments, and flattery. These factors serve as means to influence the opinions, feelings, and behavior of people by those who wish and are prepared to use them as "a spade to dig with"; namely, to use them to obtain material or social benefits. Political behavior in such cases derives from the intention of the actor to influence the other and to cause him to behave in a desirable manner. In most cases like these, politics is used as a means of manipulation of one kind or another.

One of the political uses of this type is the use of flattery. The piling on of compliments especially when done in public contributes to the satisfaction of most people and arouses in them feelings of affection towards those who compliment them. This kind of behavior enables some individuals to obtain influence over other ones through interpersonal relationships between them. Some executives, managers, commanders, and supervisors in organizations often employ this kind of interpersonal influence. For that purpose they habitually display a warm, humane, and sympathetic attitude mainly towards their subordinates. These are the "nice persons" who avoid the use of force or intimidation. Organizational participants behave politically by the repeated accentuation of similarity in some personal characteristics (e.g., origin, gender, age, religion, skin color, education, and profession) for the exertion of influence over their partners. Such a mode of behavior arouses feelings of common identity, and strengthens the emotions of affection and sympathy.[24]

Interpersonal politics in organizations also leads to the attainment of influence by the use of direct manipulation of emotions. The expression of emotions towards the other or their concealment enables one to arouse corresponding emotional responses. Through the expression of affection or love one can arouse interpersonal attraction, encourage the desire for interpersonal intimacy, strengthen positive feelings, and cause emotional satisfaction. On the other hand, an expression of hostility, arrogance, and negative emotions (such as contempt, resentment, hatred or revulsion) creates negative responses from the other, and promotes interpersonal estrangement. Just as parents (and teachers) usually express emotions in order to make their children obey their will, so from time to time do senior participants in organizations, who intentionally display positive or negative emotions towards their subordinates for the same purpose.

The calculated and systematic use of emotional display or concealment—the so-called "stick and carrot" method—reflects an intentional exercise of power in order to achieve the desired results. This systematic use represents the tactics of influence in interpersonal politics, which demands appropriate skill in the use of *emotional manipulation*. There are countless attestations that the display of emotions is widely used as an instrument rather than merely as spontaneous expression. Emotional manipulation of this kind serves individuals who wish to obtain some extra benefits by way of interpersonal politics. This is another example of self-serving behavior in organizations by which participants attempt to increase their share of personal benefit.

A well-known tactic of interpersonal influence through emotional manipulation is pestering; namely, the tiresome and annoying tones that play on emotional chords by means of repeated requests accompanied by lengthy and complicated explanations and arguments. The nagger does not desist until the other agrees to his demands. Pestering as a means of intentional and systematic influence is meant to wear down the other, to cause tension and mental discomfort, to make him sway between feelings of sympathy and disgust, and to encourage him to find a way out of this pressure by relinquishing opinions and standings. This "battle of attrition" is therefore expected to cause the other to comply with the demands of the nagger only so that he or she can escape from this oppressive nuisance. Thus, it is a form of *mental harassment* rather than a physical one, as discussed above.

Styles of Interpersonal Influence

As stated earlier, interpersonal influence is the intended change that one person causes in another. Thus, interpersonal politics is essentially the change of a person's emotions, attitudes, and behavior patterns by someone else. Research studies on this topic show that individual actors in organizations, whether they act as superiors or as subordinates, adopt a variety of methods to influence others for self-serving purposes.

One of the ways to identify the method of influence adopted by people in various social circumstances is to ask them to describe how they are trying to influence others. Using statistical analyses, scholars have been able to diagnose several types of interpersonal influence; they also developed some quantitative methods to measure such patterns of influence that are used by various actors in organizations.[25]

Generally speaking, interpersonal influence is based on various methods of assertiveness, rationalization, and manipulation. Individuals acting in organizations in a political manner for the attainment of their desired aims, tend to employ a variety of influence styles. A *style of influence* means the repeated use of a certain combination of interpersonal methods of influence employed simultaneously. The four styles of influence that follow have been diagnosed as typical styles. They therefore represent alternative modes of interpersonal politics.

a. The Gunslinger: An interpersonal style of influence that is characterized by extreme aggression and accompanied by persistent bargaining. Individuals interested in influencing others in this way usually insist on certain changes, urging the person to be influenced to accede to their requests, threatening to impose penalties in response to refusal, and offering rewards in exchange for compliance with their demands. This is a brazen, aggressive, uncompromising style of influence through which the gunslinger imposes his or her preference upon the other and forces him to behave in a certain manner against the other's will.

b. The Tactician: An interpersonal style of influence characterized by an emphatic use of rationalization and by a moderate degree of pressure in order to obtain the required results. This style of influence includes a systematic attempt to persuade the other person to make a decision or to behave in a certain manner by presenting factual information that justifies the demand, the use of logical reasons in order to explain the need for the required change. This tactic is heavily loaded with arguments and discussions.

c. The Flatterer: An interpersonal style of influence characterized by the use of conspicuous expressions of affection, flattery and esteem towards the person to be influenced. This style includes the use of methods that can be termed "making an impression," namely, creating the appearance of goodwill and cooperation, a show of pretended humility and apology for demanding change from the other person.

d. The Observer: An interpersonal style of influence characterized by adopting a stance of observing from the sidelines, avoiding any direct influence over the other person. In other words, this is a nonpolitical style of behavior by actors in an organization who claim that they have no personal goals that would justify the use of power and the exertion of influence over others, at least not in a direct and open fashion.[26]

People who take an active part in organizations tend to behave towards their colleagues, superiors, and subordinates in a set *political style*. This perseverance has advantages in being aimed systematically and consistently at achieving the desired results through the exertion of influence over others. People who maintain work relationships are able to identify the kind of style that characterizes every actor, and in the course of time they discover its degree of success. As a result, there might be a tendency to placate those "politicians" and to respond to their demands in order to avoid confrontations. Nevertheless, the various styles of influence are not usually accepted with equanimity. For every style there is also a kind of price tag, which finds expression in the organization. For example, supervisors who file periodic performance appraisals of their subordinates are likely to condemn such political behavior in their reviews. The price tag is also shown by the feelings of tension and psychological pressure of colleagues who are interacting with that individual as part of their job and in their avoidance of his or her companionship.

As said before, the political behavior at the interpersonal level of relationships assists workers and managers to fulfill a wide range of personal needs and to advance their personal interests. Interpersonal politics, with all its advantages and disadvantages, is not an end in itself, but a means to obtain personal objectives. There are people who take advantage of this instrument quite regularly, and it becomes a style of conduct that is typical for them in the organization. On the other hand, there are a number of people who adopt political measures, including the exercise of power and attempts at influence, only in situations in which the ordinary routes seem to be blocked. We should not deny the fact, however, that not everyone in organizations gets into politics sooner or later. There are always some—though not too many—participants who persistently refrain from interpersonal politics, regardless of what this approach might cost them.

Interpersonal politics is an inseparable part of the overall actions and interactions that are conducted by individuals in organizations. People are likely to join in political games taking place in all organizations for various reasons, whether continuously or intermittently, willingly or by force of circumstances. When those people act as players participating in a political game, they employ methods of political action and adopt styles of influence centered upon various power bases that suit their resources and support their objectives.[27] As described in the previous chapter, these political games may be seductive, aggressive, or persuasive in their nature.

Conclusion

The political game in organizations of all kinds is conducted first and foremost on the level of interpersonal relations; that is to say, on the level of relationships involving individual participants within the organization as well as those who are in contact with them on the outside. Interpersonal politics is the result of the personal desires of people taking part in the activities of the organization to gain benefits, rewards, and rights above and beyond those that the organization grants them. The political measures that are adopted by the various actors, both senior and junior, are based on their personal power in the organization.

In many cases, personal power is accumulated through the jobs of their members. Positions and offices allow their holders to acquire various amounts of authority, and they place in their hands the resources that others desire to have. These advantages give them the opportunity to negotiate their way in the organization so as to increase their personal utility even more. Thus, senior position-holders in the organizational apex are placed in convenient positions to accumulate power and to exercise it much more than junior position-holders.

The political uses of power in organizations are displayed by acts that exploit the advantages of an office or a position for gaining exceptional personal benefits. Such benefits are realized in the form of priority and preferential treatment, special comforts, sexual exploitation of junior members, and evasion of responsibility for irregular actions. Irregular behavior often includes illegal acts, such as embezzlement and bribery of one kind or another.

These phenomena and similar ones occur repeatedly in organizations, both public and private, for a number of reasons. One, there are too many temptations in the typical setting of any organization; two, privileged people learn to walk a "tightrope" that separates what is administratively legitimate or illegitimate, between pure motives and corruption, between what is permitted and forbidden; three, the senior ranks of the organization allow them to mask their activities and to avoid incriminating evidence. It is no wonder, therefore, that many senior members, including those of public fame and high standing, are exposed to their shame and are held to account for giving way to their impulses and desires.

Even junior employees in organizations generate personal power for themselves through the jobs they perform, and through their location in the production processes of the organization's goods and services to clients. They also gain power by virtue of their functional position in the communication network of the organization, and by virtue of their social centrality in the web of interpersonal relationships. Location therefore constitutes the basis for exchanging benefits among members of the organization and for the holding of preferred bargaining stands. Hence, both the type of job and its location in the organizational space enable them to increase the personal utility that they may derive from the organization.

In addition, individual participants in various organizations also take advantage of social weaknesses. The human need to depend on social consensus in order to cope with ambiguity and uncertainty leads people to search for guidance. Under such circumstances, interested actors tend to apply measures that create the illusion of agreement over an issue and thus influence the opinion and behavior of others.

Some participants in organizations exploit, for their own benefit, the general desire of people to gain social recognition and esteem. Thus, "politicians" display expressions of flattery, heaping of compliments, shows of concern, offers of help, declarations of loyalty, and similar behavior to their superiors and peers. By so doing, they ensure for themselves greater proximity to decision centers and they increase their chances of influence over the decision makers.

The manipulation of another person's emotions is an additional political means adopted by people in an organization in order to influence others and to gain a positive response to their wishes. The display or concealment of emotions, whether true or pretended, and the systematic use of emotions towards others, serve as efficient game devices for purposes of interpersonal influence; they also assist in obtaining compliance and receiving various benefits. The use of coercion, deception, excessive rationalization, and pretense, are forms of political behavior that individuals apply against others for selfish reasons and for their own benefit.

Interpersonal politics is therefore a common phenomenon that pervades in all organizations, in all their sectors and layers. This type of politics may be observed in the relationships between superiors and subordinates; it is also a part of the relationships between peers and between representatives of subunits in organizations. Interpersonal politics takes place between the members of the organization and individuals situated in various positions outside it as well. These political relationships are based on the power of individuals and the dependence of others upon them. They are characterized by negotiations, bargaining, exchange of resources, and the giving and taking of benefits. Such political acts are intended to amplify the participants' amount of power and to increase their personal utility. Research evidence indicates that behavior of a political nature is liable to produce greater personal utility for those individuals who adopt such behavior than that obtained by people who refrain from doing so.

Notes

1.   Katz & Kahn, 1978; Weick, 1979.
2.   Bacharach & Lawler, 1980; Pfeffer, 1981.
3.   Mintzberg, 1983.
4.   Sociology distinguishes between a business function (job) such as that of the marketing manager or storeroom keeper, and a social function (role) such as that of a parent or a marriage partner. See clarification and discussion in the book by Biddle & Thomas, 1966.
5.   Mitchell et al, 1998.
6.   Quoted from Haaretz 22 February 2000 (Hebrew).
7.   Krochmal, 2000.
8.   Quoted from *Haaretz* (Hebrew). This case is by no means unusual these days. Similar court verdicts concerning sexual harassments in organizations may be found in various Western democratic countries.
9.   Kahn et al., 1964.
10. Morgan, 1986: 148.
11. Kipnis & Schmidt, 1988.
12. Pfeffer, 1992.
13. Ibarra & Andrews, 1993.
14. Pfeffer, 1992.
15. Brass, 1984.
16. Pfeffer & Konrad, 1991.
17. Pettigrew, 1973.
18. Daft, 2004.
19. Brass, 1984.
21. Pfeffer, 1992: 207.
22. Cialdini, 1988.
23. Pfeffer, 1992: 213.
24. Pfeffer, 1992.
25. Kipnis & Schmidt, 1983; Brass & Burkhardt, 1993.
26. Schmidt & Kipnis, 1987; Kipnis & Schmidt, 1988.
27. See chapter 6 on types of political games.

8

Intergroup Politics

In the previous chapter we dealt with the power bases of individuals holding different positions and performing various jobs in organizations, as well as with the political uses they make of this power in their interpersonal relationships for the gain of more and better benefits. This chapter addresses the phenomenon of intergroup politics, namely, the ways in which various groups of people accumulate power and exercise it against other groups in organizations. The ongoing competition between groups over their share of the *organizational pie* is well described by Bacharach and Lawler, as follows:

> All organizations are networks of interest groups, whether professional groupings, work groups, or other divisions. In turn, organizational politics involve the efforts of interest groups to influence decisions that affect their positions in the organization. In each political struggle, interest groups must decide whether to pursue their political goals in isolation from other interest groups or to form a coalition of interest groups in their pursuit of a common goal.[1]

The choice between isolated confrontations of interest groups competing and struggling against one another, and their combination into transitional coalition of groups, is influenced by several intra-organizational and extra-organizational factors. Two of these are worth considering in the present context:

a. The degree of compatibility among the objectives of those groups. Social groups that cling to dogmatic beliefs on the moral level will find it difficult to reach agreement on common objectives with groups that have contrary views. Religious sects, revolutionary groups, and selective fraternities are examples of uncompromising ideological-based associations; thus, most of them are compelled to conduct their political struggles without the help of allies or the support of coalitional partners.

b. The type of political game that is conducted in a certain time and place. This factor influences, to a great degree, the tendency of actors participating in the political game to cluster together into coalitions. When a struggle is waged over the right to a certain benefit, such as a monetary award or a sports medal, the players have no choice except to compete among themselves, because the reward is not something that is divisible. However, when it is possible in some way to divide the spoils among the competitors, there is a growing tendency of some of the stakeholders to struggle jointly against other competitors to increase the chances of the coalition to win the desired gain and divide it among its members. The chances of forming a coalition are very high in political games in which it is possible to increase the "treasure" or improve its quality by means of a common struggle.[2]

Intergroup politics in organizations are daily realized in overt and covert struggles between groups that are conducted in various spheres of activity. One sphere where such politics flourish is that of labor relations between employers and employees. Another sphere of politics is in the relationships between different social sectors of employees (e.g., men vs. women). A third area may be seen in the relationships between competing professional groups, for example, engineers versus technicians. Intergroup politics is an integral part of the relationships between different divisions and departments that make the organization.

Just as with individual organizational actors, the various social groupings carry out the tasks assigned to them and behave, as prescribed by the organization, according to the rules and procedures. However, at the same time they perform actions that serve their own particular needs, and adopt political measures that are aimed at increasing their power in order to improve their standing and increase the range of privileges. Thus, those *political shadows* that go together with the prescribed activities of individuals also go alongside the activities performed by the various professional and social groups.[3]

Struggles between Employers and Employees

Most organizations nowadays experience cycles of labor disputes, which bring about a great deal of politics among employers and employees everywhere. The long-standing custom of workers to form trade unions that represent their interests have turned the continual bargaining over salaries, fringe benefits, and working conditions from a struggle of individuals to a struggle of organized groups—namely, taking this conflict of interests to the level of intergroup politics.[4]

Until a few years ago, the greater majority of salaried workers in many countries around the world was organized in trade unions, and was represented in their work places by workers' committees. These committees were recognized by employers as the authorized representatives of the employees. Their job was to obtain suitable pay, fringe benefits, a safe work environment as well as job security for their members. These rights and benefits are usually obtained through negotiations between the workers' representatives and the representatives of the employers, and are set down in collective agreements.[5] It should be noted here that, in spite of the number changes that took place during the last century, this system of labor relations still exists and trade unions have not vanished in many countries throughout the world.

However, labor relations in the organizational reality are far from being ideal. In many cases these relations are accompanied by aggressive power struggles, thus creating a balance of mutual deterrence between the two sides. The claims of workers for improved conditions, for better fringe benefits, and for wider range of rights have been traditionally met with adamant refusal by the employers, who take all kinds of measures to lower the labor costs in their organizations.

This attitude of the employers is typical today not only in business organizations, but in nonprofit service organizations as well. The government, which is in many places the largest employer in the economy, generally opposes the demands of the trade unions in accordance with its policy to spare the taxpayer money and to maintain a balanced budgetary policy. The workers, on the other hand, are concerned primarily with themselves and their revenues. Therefore, one can analyze labor relations in terms of a political game between players who try to overcome the rival they contend against: to give little and gain much.

Whenever an actual dispute breaks out between the representatives of the workers and those of the employers a typical political process is liable to develop. It is generally conducted on two parallel levels—the overt level and the covert level. On the overt level, the rivals mutually exert a series of public pressures; these include biased notifications to the press, initiated interviews in the media, the use of protest placards, and the enlisting of support from various celebrities and opinion leaders (politicians, eminent and religious figures, artists, scholars, and the like).

At a later stage the parties go on to the officially declared state of *labor dispute*. At this stage the employers take legal measures through the judicial system (i.e., labor courts, arbitration, and the Supreme Court) in order to prevent the employees from disrupting regular work schedules and paralyzing organizational activities. If these measures do not lead to a settlement of the dispute in a satisfactory manner for both sides, a mutual escalation of the dispute can be expected. In this process forceful means of coercion are likely to be applied by both parties. The workers tend to conduct noisy and even violent demonstrations; to lay siege to the organizations; to block the flow of necessary inputs (raw materials) or outputs (goods and services); to sabotage the operation of various pieces of equipment (such as generators); to wreck the property of the organization, such as office furniture and appliances; to keep away outside workers and sub-contractors from the organization premises by physical force; to interfere with the traffic flow used by the organization (roads, train tracks, seaports, and airports); to reject the decisions of judges and to cause contempt of court; to barricade themselves in the factory yard; as well as additional strong-arm tactics.

Representatives of the workers do not hesitate to exercise their power against their disobedient colleagues, and they do not refrain from applying punitive measures against them such as social ostracism, excommunication, and expulsion from the union. At various times in the history of labor relations, strikebreakers have been punished by violent physical means: beating, injury, threats to harm their families, and even by killing them. In our times it is the practice to treat workers suspected of breaking the strike as traitors, collaborators, opportunists, and dissenters. Workers' committees do not hesitate to counteract by imposing measures such as monetary fines, withholding personal or legal assistance, public denunciation on the notice boards of the organization and similar punitive measures.

The representatives of the employers do not sit idly by during the labor dispute. They resort to legal means; they make deductions from the workers' salaries for the hours spent in meetings, demonstrations, sanctions, and strikes, and they sometimes even delay the payment of wages to all the employees; they claim compensation from the trade unions for damages caused them; they threaten to hold a "defensive strike" against the employees, and in several cases they have even locked the gates and shut down activities. There are also some employers who send suspension letters or notices of dismissal to the representatives of the workers. In difficult and drawn-out labor disputes that have occurred in the past, employers have withheld payment of salaries from their workers for many months and wore them down until their economic distress made them yield. In various countries, a number of cases occurred in which employers sent in platoons of "mercenaries" and private guards who acted with violence and attacked the strikers severely in their own homes. There is no doubt that much blood has been spilled in the history of labor relations ever since the industrial revolution.

It should be clarified at this point that the political game that is conducted between employers and employees is not confined only to the unsettled matters between them. As contemporary work organizations grow greater and become more varied and complex, the assemblage of stakeholders who are involved in them and the increasing number of players participating in this kind of political game grows, too. In many organizations there are several workers' committees, representing different interest groups, in the same workplace. Thus, schoolteachers at various levels have separate unions; technicians and engineers are represented each by their own leaders; and even in some places doctors and nurses are unionized, all separately represented. The unions' local leaders of all trades and professions struggle with their common employers to advance the particular interests of their constituencies.

Since each of these occupational groups is struggling to increase its share of the organizational pie, a conflict of interest prevails among them most of the time. The underlying assumption of these competitors is that labor relations are a zero-sum game; namely, that every gain of one group of workers necessarily reduces the gain of the other groups participating in this game. Hence, in many organizations there is an ongoing competition that is taking place underneath the surface over the division of the *organizational spoils* among the various groups of employees. The spoils in this context include wages and salaries, fringe benefits, incentives and bonuses, promotions, pension plans, and unique group privileges.

By the nature of things, different occupational groups are not of equal power. The relative power of every one of those groups is determined by the quantity and quality of resources that are at its disposal. The strength of a group power is also determined by the degree to which its members are essential in carrying out the production of goods and services of the organization. A close scrutiny of the political struggles in the field of labor relations reveals the following phenomenon: The stronger groups claim many more benefits for themselves than are granted to other groups. This tendency is displayed by the demand to "differentiate" between them and the other groups in the organization with regard to income and benefits. On the other hand, the weaker groups demand that income gaps be closed and that their working conditions be improved to the level of other groups; namely, to institute equalization between them and the stronger groups.

Such politics reflects a continuing struggle between two different ideologies, each of them claiming to suggest the proper solution for socioeconomic justice at the workplace. The first one, the *ideology of equity*, advocates the granting of suitable recompense for the professional talents, high education, and rare skills of certain workers that exceed those of others. The other outlook, the *ideology of equality* advocates analogous conditions of income and benefits for workers of all types, so as to avoid the deprivation of low-skill workers. Thus, doctors, engineers, scientists struggle for so-called equitable income in their favor. At the same time, laborers, drivers and messengers, handymen, junior clerks, shop assistants, and those with similar vocations struggle to narrow these gaps in income in their favor. Both of these groups complain of *relative deprivation* in comparison with other workers, and demand *distributive justice* of the resources of the organization in return for their contribution.

In spite of the conflict of interest that prevails among competing occupational groups, from time to time the workers realize the advantages of cooperation between them, and they join forces in a common struggle against their employers. Needless to specify, such an alignment of forces increases the power of the employees and improves their bargaining stand. Therefore, they usually form a coalition of several stakeholders in which every group has an interest of its own. Those coalitions are temporary by nature and are meant to solve a specific problem that threatens all the different occupational groups; for example, privatizing of a public organization; significant downsizing of a business organization; relocation of an organization's facilities and installations; and an across-the-board cut in the income or benefits of all employees in the organization.

Turnaround programs that plan to induce broad and deep change in an organization represent a clear example of situations interpreted as states of emergency for employees. These situations justify the formation of multigroup coalitions against the management and the owners, because of the danger to the organizational pie as a whole. In other words, the political struggle in such situations is not on the division of spoils, but on its availability for allocation to the entire body of employees. These professional groups are not only struggling together against their employers, they also enlist working groups in other organizations of the same kind to support them in their struggle. Since the mid-twentieth century, workers employed in state-owned monopolies in the United Kingdom, France, and other countries in Europe and elsewhere have been struggling against the privatization plans of their government. This kind of political game presents a concrete example of this kind of multigroup coalition joining forces against their "common enemy"—the public administration of their countries.

For example, the employees of the national Electricity Company of Israel have shown for many years a stubborn resistance to the planned reform in the electricity industry. The reform was intended to allow private electricity producers to be connected to the national grid. The various ranks of workers in the Electricity Company have joined hands in order to defeat these plans.

> What would actually happen if any company could produce electricity and supply it directly to the customers (through the general delivery grid)? The monopoly workers would "discover" that it is possible to produce electricity with greater efficiency and lower cost, and would be forced to enter into competition with other producers. Competition means to make greater effort and to forgo monopolistic profits; it means the cutback of inflated mechanisms and convoluted work processes; it means that the monopoly would find it hard to pay its 200 senior members a [monthly] salary of 31,000 shekels or more, and every worker an average salary that was nearly three times the standard average in the country. Even the [free] distribution of electricity to its members at the cost of 100 million shekels a year would be endangered.[6]

This case is far from being unique in the public sector of various countries. Privatization is still being perceived by civil servants all over the world as the most serious threat to their job security, income, tenure, pension, and other privileges.

The cooperation in one political struggle does not prevent the continuation of the rivalry and competition among the coalition partners on other matters concerning labor relations. Employees of governmental agencies, municipalities and local administration, the education and health systems, state universities, and defense industries tend to affiliate themselves with separate trade unions. These occupational groups are generally represented by elected leaders who do not hesitate to combat each other, amplifying their power by gaining the support of other stakeholders outside the organization (clients, suppliers, contractors) against their rivals within the organization.

In politics of this kind, every group of players tries to prove that it is leading the struggle against the employers, and it takes upon itself the credit for the achievements of the struggle. Moreover, each group of players blames the other groups for weakness or fear of an over-determined opposition with the employer, and it asserts that were it not for the weakness of the partner groups, the victory in the struggle could have been much greater. In order to prevent such accusations, each vocational group tends to adopt a more aggressive policy towards the employer than the policy of its fellow groups in the organization. Under such conditions, the political game develops into a complex and forceful multigroup game in which the most radical player sets the parameters of the game.

It is worth noting that politics conducted among the various professions and vocations in the organization, has an additional aspect, namely, competition over recognition of the special expertise of each of these groups. Exclusive expertise can serve as a valuable basis of power in an organization. Its recognition allows the various members of the profession to acquire special authority; for example, the right of signature for engineering plans and technical designs which is the reserved right of engineers only; the authority to disqualify certain sub-standard materials and products which is the reserved right of quality assurance specialists; or the authority to prescribe medications and treatments which is the exclusive prerogative of doctors. Expertise provides employees with a better bargaining stand from where they can demand special privileges. In many workplaces such privileges include paid participation in professional conferences, unique bonuses for special skills, extended insurance policies, improved retirement plans, access to restricted zones and to classified material, and the like.

The Struggle for Gender Equality

The continual struggle of women to gain equal pay, equal promotion to higher ranks and senior positions, equal authority in commensurate positions, and equality in working conditions have paved the way to one of the most significant revolutions in the work culture of the Western world. This is a persistent and forceful struggle that women conduct in many kinds of contemporary organizations. This struggle is backed and supported by various lobbies and a variety of voluntary associations that have an interest in the advancement of minority groups in society and the economy. Success in these struggles proceeds at a slow pace, but it paves the way to additional gains in gender equality. The experience of women in various organizations to improve their situation and enhance their standing is an inseparable part of a systematic series of broad, comprehensive struggles that may be defined as *gender politics*.

According to one theoretical approach,[7] two main strategies characterize the political struggle between the sexes that has been taking place in organizations. These strategies are designated as the *exclusion strategy* and the *inclusion strategy*. The former is the inherited legacy of the men in organizations while the latter is the reaction of the women. Men fill administrative positions in the organization, especially the senior ones in the organizational leadership; therefore, men try to hinder women from taking an active part in the organization in those key positions of power and benefits. One of the trends that illustrates this strategy is the entry of retired senior military officers into leading positions, mainly in governmental agencies and in similar organizations. These newly civilian executives surround themselves with former military men to serve as their deputies, administrators, bureau chiefs, assistants, and consultants.

To preserve their exclusive control over these preferential positions, such men use a "professional language," so to speak, that is familiar only to them, and through which they conduct a type of interpersonal communication that "strangers would not understand." Hence, outsiders are unable to participate in these circles of power. This kind of communication promotes work relationships between people of a similar social level, who share common life experiences and professional background, and who make use of identical symbols and images to convey basic ideas. This type of communication is supposedly expected to be trustworthy, exact, clear, and useful; it therefore saves precious time for managers and protects them from unnecessary and troublesome misunderstandings.

According to that viewpoint, women are not a natural part of this confederated band. Such men tend to label women as incomprehensible and uncomfortable associates, unpredictable and non-adjustable partners. The alien nature of women seemingly arouses communication problems that encumber administrative teamwork and create inter-functional friction and interpersonal tension among the managers. In this way, men justify the need to exclude women from top administrative positions in the organization and to deny them the organizational power that derives from such senior offices.

In fact, both administrative and professional senior positions demand a relatively high degree of loyalty to the organization and great devotion to work. Hence, many women find it difficult to carry out *total jobs* of this kind, which require uninterrupted full-time work and an investment of many working hours above those normally needed in junior positions. However, a more thorough examination of the situation shows that in today's realm of work several efficient solutions have been developed for problems of this kind. One solution, for example, is partial performance of job duties at home (i.e., teleworking); another is flexible working hours (i.e., flexi time); and the use of computerized communication from remote places (i.e., intranetworking) presents an additional solution. All these enable women to perform senior positions in full, even when they are mothers of toddlers.

In the era of globalization, executives and senior officers are required to do a considerable amount of frequent traveling to distant places for business purposes. Thus, senior members in various organizations are compelled to be absent from their offices and their homes several times a year to participate in intensive discussions, trade fairs, study programs and workshops, professional conferences, and various kinds of business negotiations. In contrast to men, whose frequent and extended absences from home are understandable, many women find that this style of working life makes it difficult for them to fill such senior positions. The main difficulty arises from their family commitments (as wives and mothers), which impedes their promotion to higher organizational ranks. These and similar demands will of course give men a real advantage in the competition between the two sexes over positions of prestige that offer power and wealth.[8]

From an examination of hi-tech organizations it is clear that women can fit in very well even in senior professional positions of this kind, in spite of the difficulties mentioned above. However, their contribution as senior members of the organization is made possible if it provides them with some supporting services such as child care and home maintenance during their working hours inside and outside its premises. In our times, younger and highly educated women prefer a professional career to traditional family life. Yet most employing organizations have not taken suitable steps to cope with the unique problems of dual career families in general and working mothers in particular. On the other hand, the trend of career women, at the expense of raising a family, does not encompass the majority of women even in many Western countries, especially among the more conservative sectors of the population.

In light of this masculine perspective, it is not surprising to find that a greater number of women employed in the public sector are relegated to the lowest ranks and only a small minority is situated in the upper ranks. Compared with women, less than a half of the men employed in the public sector are in the lower ranks, and approximately one-tenth of them are situated in the upper ranks. A committee for the application of reforms in the public sector and for the advancement of women in Israel, for example, drew the following conclusion: "It is sad and distressing to see that since the law was amended there is only a reduction in the representation of women in the senior ranks. In the present state of affairs nothing will change even in twenty years' time. Only a change in the law and in government policy will bring about any change".[9] These gaps between men and women in rank, salary and functions apparently are typical for many Western democracies, showing that even if female workers in the public sector have more seniority and are more highly educated than their male colleagues, they have not managed to jump the hurdle of senior ranking.

A similar picture of obstruction for women is characteristic of the defense sector: the military, the police force and the various security, and secret services. Until a short time ago, the unquestioned assumption was that most of the senior command positions in these organizations were meant solely for men. This normative approach, which is held by the men who determine and promote policy in these organizations, affirms that in order to man battle positions and similarly dangerous field positions, there is need for personal abilities (such as physical capability, courage, and leadership) at levels that are far beyond those with which most women are endowed. Therefore, it has been the practice to allocate only non-operational positions to the women employed in such organizations. By their nature, these positions lack the challenge and glory of operational jobs such as combat ones. Women were therefore assigned to jobs such as secretaries, telephone operators, paramedics, graphic designers, and the like. These positions are essentially service tasks that support the organizational core manned by men only. This policy preemptively obstructed women from being trained to become fighter pilots and navigators, sailors and divers, paratroopers, patrollers and sharpshooters, etc. In addition, they were also being denied promotion in rank, in authority and the fringe benefits of such positions.[10]

Today many combat and command positions in the United States, Canada, Great Britain, some European countries, as well as in a few other military organizations in the Western hemisphere, are open to women. However, the number of women who reach the most senior ranks and top positions in those organizations is still very small indeed. There is sufficient basis for the assumption that the process of women's full integration into the combat and command positions will be a slow one and will take quite a few more years due to subjective and objective difficulties. Apparently, there are still a significant number of senior officers who disagree with this policy and even oppose its implementation in the army, the police force, and in the intelligence services; they will therefore take overt or covert measures to encumber the advancement of women to the senior staff positions in their organizations. Thus, notwithstanding the improvement in status and income of women, the *glass ceiling* is still blocking their advancement to top positions.

In the course of the years that have passed since the movement for the advancement of women began its organized activities for the sake of equality and women's rights, this struggle has gradually permeated various kinds of organizations. The so-called *feminist revolution* impinged on, first and foremost, those organizations that belong to the public sector; among them were governmental agencies, local authorities, the courts of law, institutes of higher education, public health services, and security and law enforcement organizations. Even though intergroup politics of this kind in these organizations is not necessarily violent, it is definitely a power-based, coercive type struggle. This means that women take a series of tactical measures intended to force the various governmental authorities to adopt rules and regulations that will bring about a change in the balance of power between men and women in the organizations in which both sexes are employed.

The concept of *affirmative action* that is taking an increased hold in many organizations in the United States—and to a lesser degree in other countries—expresses this goal precisely. The practical implication of affirmative action is the explicit and systematic preference of people identified with underprivileged racial, religious, ethnic, and similar groups over others that are identified with privileged social groups. This preference is meant to be exercised wherever demand exceeds supply in the organization, namely, whenever the number of candidates exceeds the number of vacant positions. Based on the principle of affirmative action, women make claims to be preferred over men in the attainment of senior positions, promotion, tenure, participation in training programs, and the like, as well as to be entitled to special benefits that organizations grant to their favored employees. Thus, in practice, the law of affirmative action is essentially a coercive policy, because it forces employers to attach a greater importance to ascribed features of workers, such as sex or skin color, than to their acquired achievements, such as education or professional experience. In this sense, it represents an outstanding example of intergroup politics in the realm of organizations. It is no wonder then that women as well as other minorities adopt it as a political strategy for self-advancement.

Another way that women attempt to improve their employment status in organizations may be called the *precedents method*. This method is based on the submission of legal appeals against employers demanding recognition of the right of women to enjoy equal treatment with that being enjoyed by men in the organization. Any appeal of this kind represents the personal case of a specific woman, and is meant to create a legal precedent for other women to follow. In this way, every verdict in favor of the person appealing will provide the basis for the right of women to compete for positions that were previously the sole prerogative of men. In this way, as slow as it might be, public recognition is gradually being won for the rights of women to compete for preferential positions under equal conditions to those of men.

The obligation of governmental agencies, local authorities, universities, and other public institutions to appoint an "advisor on the status of women" represents an additional mechanism meant to assist women in their political struggle for equal opportunity. The main activities of such advisors are detection and prevention of discrimination against women. The women who fill this kind of position are expected to locate procedures that practically prevent or deter women from competing for high-ranking positions, promotion, and the attainment of benefits that are available for men in the organization. They should initiate intra-organizational procedures that will ensure equal rights to women in salary and advancement; warn the heads of organizations about cases in which there is a suspicion of partiality, disadvantage or discrimination; and deal with complaints about sexual harassment, assault, or intimidation of women by male colleagues in general and senior ones in particular.

The advisor for the status of women is also required to initiate ceremonial events to improve the image of working women in the organization; set-up training programs in order to raise the professional quality of the women in the organizations; and strengthen their bargaining power in the labor market. They are thus responsible for protecting women against the arbitrary actions of managers and commanders as well as defending their rights according to law. The fact that these advisors are directly subordinate to the heads of the organizations increases their ability to exert influence upon them on behalf of the women.

However, the degree of their success differs from one organization to another, and depends on the support and cooperation they receive from top management and elected representatives such as ministers and mayors. Thus, this is a political position in which its incumbent does a political job to advance the particular interests of a group of stakeholders.

As said earlier, in every system of exchange relationships, whether economic or social, the degree of power held by an individual or a group is inversed to the degree of his or her dependence upon others. The dependence of women on the male-dominated establishment encouraged them to develop several kinds of secondary organizations. The main goals of those organizations are to serve the needs of working women, to help them when difficulties arise and to be concerned for their welfare. Voluntary organizations of this kind serve only women in need; and they include health services, shelters for battered women and girls in distress, institutes for education and professional training, day care centers for the children of working women, organizations for legal and economic consultation, organizations for self help, and the like. These organizations assist needy women to improve their vocational abilities, to develop self-awareness and self-esteem, and to provide them with better tools in their struggle to alleviate their living conditions.

Besides the direct service of such women's organizations to their clientele, their main advantage lies in their ability to amplify the power of women in general, to strengthen their bargaining position and to increase their capacity to compete with the male sector. These organizations go beyond the intra-organizational activities of women against men, and intrude into the sphere of work organizations that employ both sexes; yet, at the same time they serve as support networks for those women who struggle over their employment, their status, their income, and their rights in the workplace.

The struggle of women for equal opportunity is an intergroup struggle, even when it concerns individual women in specific organizations. There is no doubt that this intergroup politics has considerable success in various spheres of life, and will gradually culminate in a state of equal rights. Under the influence of the feminist movement and its ideas, women in most of the progressive countries have developed a strong sense of self-awareness that has encouraged them to participate in political struggles to improve their image and to strengthen their position.

Just as women have done, so various minorities (e.g., labor migrants) demand their share of the organizational spoils: employment, income, promotion, benefits, rights, and job security. They exert pressure on public representatives, on courts of law, on the media, and on the employers to advance their interests and better their relative situation in the labor market in general and in the public sector in particular. Hence, more and more countries find themselves in the midst of political struggles of underprivileged groups against their governments, against major employers, and against multinational corporations.

Quite frequently, these struggles take the form of violent clashes between demonstrators and the police force.

Contests between Organizational Subunits

One of the advantages of organizations over individuals is built on their *functional differentiation*, that is, on the structural division of labor between the organization's subunits. This division of labor determines the sphere of activities, the authority and responsibility of each section, department, division, branch, and the like. According to this division of labor the management of the organization allocates the necessary resources to each subunit so that it can carry out its assigned tasks. These inputs include physical, economic, technological, and human resources. However, due to their complexity and fluidity, organizations can hardly delineate clear-cut borderlines between their subunits. In spite of the repeated attempts of subunits to define their "territories" precisely and to have exclusive control over them, they do intrude upon each other's territory. Consequently, subunits of all kinds encounter frictions and confrontations with other ones most of the time.[11]

Confrontations of this kind tend to develop into political struggles between subunits within the organization. Each organizational subunit employs forceful means and adopts political measures to overcome its rival in the organization. By the nature of things, the competition between organizational subunits is over the division of the organizational pie; thus, every subunit attempts to gain more and better resources from the reservoir of the entire organization. Since this reservoir does not suffice for the needs of all the organization's components, the competing subunits take part involuntarily in a political game. As said earlier, this is a zero-sum game in which every gain by one actor means a loss by another actor. Therefore, the total gains in this game are equal to its total losses. Subsidiary units in organizations and corporations frequently strive to increase their influence over strategic decisions; they aspire to show the way for the organization to act in the directions they prefer; and they make efforts to establish for them a senior position in the organization complex. Andrew Pettigrew, who studied decision-making processes in organizations, sums this up in the following manner:

> It is the involvement of sub-units in such demand-and-support-generating processes within the decision-making processes of the organization that constitutes the political dimension. Political behavior is defined as behavior by individuals, or, in collective terms, by sub-unit, within the organization that makes a claim against resource-sharing system of the organization.[12]

In order to be victorious in these games, each subunit strives to amplify its relative power in the organization. For this reason, the subunits try to give prominence to the importance of their contribution to the organization's endeavors and its achievements. Each organizational subunit attempts to claim credit for the attainments and successes, even when these are the direct result of

the efforts by the entire organization and even if they are due to external circumstances.

For example, the marketing division of business organizations will invest
efforts to show its unique contribution to overall organizational performance.
Accordingly, it will claim to have an important standing in the organization as
a result of its marketing efforts. For this purpose it will find corroboration
through the publication of quantitative data that apparently support its claims
and justify its crucial importance, such as sales records, market analysis, consumer surveys, and the like. The research and development division in the
same organization is likely to attribute the success to its own efforts in the
research and development of new, innovative products that allegedly brought
about a significant rise in sales. In the same way, all the other branches of the
organizations, such as the finance division and the production division,
will also attempt to persuade the top management that they have made a
unique contribution to the positive business outcome. It goes without saying
that poor organizational performance is always the result of the other subunits'
deficiencies.

In these conditions of intra-organizational competition, it is not surprising
to realize that various organizational subunits, especially the major ones, endeavor to be entitled to determine the nature of goods and services that the
organization produces for the environment—at least to have a say about them.
The marketing division of an industrial firm, for example, will insist on providing the consumer products of the organization with a pleasing exterior, an
attractive packaging, and a design that is congenial for the user. This marketing
approach is more saliently expressed in the cosmetics and perfume industry, in
which a significant part of the price is a direct result of the appearance of the
products. The production division will probably emphasize aspects related to
the durability, reliability, safety, and efficiency of the organization's products.
This approach is evident in the home electrical appliances industry, and is the
approach that generally characterizes the products intended for industrial use
in agriculture, defense, medicine, and the like. The research and development
division will struggle over the design of innovative products that are sophisticated and unique, at the "forefront of advanced technology." This approach is
typical for hardware and software products in the field of computers, electronic
media, airlines, and biotechnology.

Subunits want to influence the strategic decisions because they strive to
emphasize their importance in the organization and to enhance their status in
comparison with other units. These political struggles represent continual inter-unit competition over a position of dominance in the organization as whole.
This competition sheds light on the power struggles that prevail between subunits in all kinds of organizations. Such struggles prevail, for example, between governmental ministries, military corps, intelligence agencies, university departments, and between the various branches of police forces. Those and

similar contests are an integral part of intergroup politics in organizations.

Political struggles of this kind display the structural and functional conflicts that develop between organizational subunits in the course of time; and they continue to be conducted despite the unavoidable changeovers of those who head such units—ministers, managers, commanders, supervisors, or scientists. In many organizations these kinds of struggles are inherent in the organizational culture, and their histories are the subject matter of *political discourse* for long periods of time. It is true that inter-unit politics is an agitating factor in organizations but at the same time it serves as an important spur for organizational change and innovation.

According to the *resource dependence theory*, the performance of an organization is determined to a great extent by its ability to obtain the necessary resources for its regular functioning as well as to carry out its assignments and to achieve its objectives. Organizations need capital first and foremost; but they have no less a need for manpower, raw materials, technology, information, and energy. These are essential resources without which organizations will not produce their outputs to the environment. However, every organization is in need of certain inputs defined as *critical resources* for its proper operation and thus for its survival.[13] Therefore, the power of organizational subunits lies to a great extent in their ability to import those critical resources for the organization. Accordingly, subunits generate power in the organization proportionate to their recruitment of critical resources. Their power enables them to influence decision-making processes in such matters as budgets, investments, and programs, as well as to have a say in the allocation of monetary benefits to various stakeholders.[14]

In the pioneer research conducted on this subject about thirty years ago on twelve industrial organizations in the United States, it was found that in nearly all the organizations, the department of marketing and sales was regarded as having far the greatest intra-organizational power; whereas the department of research and development was considered as having much less power.[15] Nearly thirty years later, the evaluation has changed. Research evidence indicates that departments that deal with applied research and development mainly in high-tech organizations enjoy today the greatest power as compared to other departments.[16] This finding reflects the comprehensive changes that have occurred in the past decades in organizational reality; thus, it appears that technological innovation has seized a decisive position in the commercial competition between organizations.

Since money is a most important resource in all organizations, the subunits that manage to raise money from the external environment—from sources such as sales, contributions, loans, taxes, bonds, or grants—succeed in obtaining large slices of the organization's budget. This phenomenon has been revealed in several studies that examined the ways in which the budgets of American universities have been divided.[17]

University departments that excel in the field of Life Sciences collect considerable sums for their universities through enormous research grants that are transferred by various research funds to the scholars belonging to these departments. On the other hand, professional schools (e.g., law, medicine, business) acquire large contributions to their universities; but these sums of money usually come from business corporations, capitalist tycoons, and wealthy philanthropists. Unlike many scientific departments that have plenty of researchers but only a few students, the professional schools have an abundance of students and a minority of researchers. The scientific departments therefore earn distinction and prestige for the scientific achievements of their researchers, while the schools earn publicity and public esteem for their graduates who attain senior positions in the best private and public organizations.

In a similar way, hospital departments that do recruit the best surgeons in their areas of specialization have higher priority in the acquisition of updated medical equipment, in the construction of modern operating theaters, and in the allocation of support staff. Famous surgeons like these attract contributions and grants from external sources: philanthropists, foundations, associations, the government and the local municipality. These funds are meant to strengthen and develop those specific departments, but they also enhance the fame and prestige of the hospital as a whole at the same time.

In addition to organizational subunits' access to critical resources, their ability to cope with factors of strategic significance also constitutes an important element in determining their status in the organization. Thus, the higher the status of a subunit within the organization, the higher is its potential to influence other subunits. Factors of strategic importance are, among others, the ability of the subunits to lessen the external uncertainties that threaten the organization as a whole, as well as their centrality in the production processes of the organization's outputs, and their special expertise in the organizational setup.[18] Research findings have confirmed these relationships, and indicate that the power of subunits in a given organizational context is indeed a direct result of their strategic abilities.[19] It is quite common for the power of subunits to be realized in practice through the inter-unit politics in all kinds of organizations.

The preference for subunits that are considered strong because of their success is not accepted in all organizations. In fact, the claim to grant them privileges that are not granted to other subunits is liable to encounter opposition. Therefore, these subunits apply various political tactics to achieve their objectives. Such inter-unit politics includes threats to split the organization; they form coalitions to bring about acceptance of certain decisions; they exert direct pressure on decision makers (directors, executives, and the like); they withhold internal services within the organization; they refrain from cooperation with others; they initiate changes in the regulations and procedures of the organization; and they obtain secret support from outside actors who have influence over the organization (stockholders, suppliers, clients, public figures, journalists). It is a matter of fact that the heads of the other subunits and their members are forced to resist such political measures and to prevent, or at least reduce, the allocation of resources that might deprive them in the division of the organizational benefits.

As said earlier, every successful organizational subunit claims the right to a sizable portion from the organizational plate; therefore, it struggles to obtain a "suitable reward" in return for its efforts, whether in budget, buildings, equipment, manpower or special rewards for its personnel. Moreover, these subunits often act in political ways to ensure adequate representation in the main decision centers of the organization, in key positions within its top management, and in the process of its resource allocations.

The political game played between the various units in commercial organizations is radicalized in corporations where every major subunit, such as a division, is managed as a *profit center*. These divisions enjoy a wide range of autonomy within the corporation, and their performance is mainly assessed according to business parameters, such as sales volume, market share, or profits. An organization structured in a *multi-divisional form* assigns to every division its specific basket of products; it defines the markets within which it is supposed to do business; and it grants each division the necessary resources for producing its outputs. Each division receives the necessary resources for producing its outputs. As a result, there is a significant decrease in the interdependence between the various subunits of the organization, and their mutual couplings are quite loose.

Under these conditions, those divisions that operate as semi-independent mini-organizations within the corporation compete continuously for dominance. In this competition each major subunit attempts to influence the strategic decision-making processes of the entire corporation. The claims of these divisions to obtain positions of influence are based on the proportionate contribution of the divisions towards solving the problems of the larger organization, mainly in its relationship with the external environment. Such contributions by the divisions affect, directly or indirectly, the organization's survival as a whole. The more the success of the organization or the corporation depends on the success of a certain division, the greater is the power of that division within the organization. It is not unusual to find that internal competition between divisions and other large subunits is no less intense than the competition conducted between corporations that do not have the same ownership.

One of the political tactics to obtain a position of influence is to ensure that the general manager of the division will be granted the title of Vice President, which gives him or her right to be a member of the corporation's top management and even a member of the Board of Directors. In this way, division managers represent the interests of their units and try to channel strategic decisions in the direction favorable to their divisions. In order to increase their degree of independence, these divisions struggle to get wider scope of authority within the corporation. This authority gives them more control over the resources that they consider to be critical for them. However, an increase of their influence over the top decision makers in the corporation may require them to join hands in a coalition of divisions, despite the conflict of interest and power struggles that prevail among them.

As can be expected, the formation of coalitions and oppositions of this kind intensifies the political struggle among the divisions and subunits in organizations; and it most likely escalates the political means that each coalition applies against opponents. At the same time, the common interest of all stakeholders to maintain the organization as a single entity allows for such political games to be conducted at the top levels without endangering the unity of the organization.

Another aspect of the political game between groups is revealed in the mutual relationship between the so-called line and staff personnel in organizations.[20] A somewhat inherent conflict of interests exists between these two types of hierarchies, based on the differences between the authority of the line employees and that of the professional staff personnel. Since the line managers are in charge of the actual carrying out of the organizational assignments and the production of its goods, they are granted managerial authority that enables them to make the required decisions. On the other hand, the various professional experts are active in the organization by virtue of their professional authority; their expertise thus enables them to collect and process data, to submit evaluation reports, to issue professional guidelines, to assess the efficiency of layouts and procedures, and to propose proper improvements.

The staff personnel tend to extend their authority and to trespass into "management territory." This tendency is realized by the formulation of binding guidelines, rules of conduct, and work regulations. Furthermore, staff personnel disseminate top down instructions approved by the Chief Executive Officer to the line workers. Line managers take various measures to prevent staff personnel from intruding into their sphere of responsibility and to keep them out of their territory. Such opposing tendencies had already been observed in research studies forty years earlier.[21] They most likely create tensions between line and staff subunits that sometimes develop into open confrontations, such as the budgeting versus the manufacturing units. These conflicts of interest are typical to both current work processes as well as to various decision-making processes.

By the nature of things, each of the opposing sides tries to make use of the resources at its disposal (manpower, money, experience, know-how, and the support of senior members) to improve its bargaining position. Thus, whenever the organization has to deal with disputes between members of the line units and those of the staff units regarding the correct way to solve the problem at hand, an argument arises between the managerial personnel and the professional personnel. Since arguments of this type conceal an underlying conflict of interest and power struggle, they are accompanied by a *hidden agenda*, namely the undercurrent objectives of these political actors that go beyond the matter under discussion. This is another example of the political shadows that go together with the seemingly functional behavior of individuals and groups in organizations.

The staff units, such as the department of information systems, are capable of disturbing the smooth workings of the organization as a whole and disrupting its activities by withholding intra-organizational support services; these are vital services for the line units that produce the goods of the organization. This capability, which is essentially structural, provides the staff units in the organization with real power, even though managers of staff units do not have equal weight as compared with managers of line units in making strategic decisions that are connected with the organization's goals.[22] In certain circumstances, this power is liable to be expressed in practice by the way in which they channel the resources at their disposal, and in the quality of the services they render to the line units. And indeed, studies show that political considerations are of high importance in the exchange relationships between the staff and line units.[23]

A well-known and outstanding example for political struggles between line and staff units is exposed to public view every year in the annual round of confrontations over the division of the state budget that takes place between the Treasury and the various governmental offices. The Treasury department, manned by a team of economists and financial experts, tries to dictate the activities of the governmental agencies and to determine for them the services they will supply to the public during the fiscal year. On the other side, the ministers and the heads of various agencies (e.g., the education and health systems, the military, and the police force) struggle to obtain maximal resources in order to realize government policy and to finance the activities they have set out for themselves.

In the course of these confrontations, each side strives to obtain the support of the head of the nation-state (i.e., the prime minister or the president); to mobilize the support of members of Parliament or the Senate; to influence public opinion through the mass media; and to seek endorsement from the opinion leaders, prominent intellectuals, first-rate experts, ex-military commanders, and other celebrities. The contentious argument that is conducted among the professional experts for long weeks and months suddenly comes to an end—always at the last moment of the budgetary year—in marathon and exhausting negotiations among the politicians, in some places even in the presence of TV cameras. As expected, the national budget is approved at the end of every fiscal year, and, of course, all cabinet ministers and heads of political parties declare victory in this political struggle.

It should be recognized that the budgeting process in every public or private organization, civil as well as military, is a clear case of internal intergroup politics. This political game is played year after year, based on the same premises, according to the same "rules of the game," although the players change from time to time. The political nature of the budgeting process in organizations is an outcome of both the goals of the participants and the methods they use to realize them. That is, they strive to maximize their own resources and their relative power by means of various tactics such as manipulation, intimidation, disinformation, and the use of promises and threats.

The official endorsement of the budget is only the beginning of the internal bargaining between subunits. The staff that is in charge of budgeting frequently tries later on to introduce certain required amendments. Therefore, during the working year they tend to delay or prevent the flow of funds intended for financing certain projects, based on administrative reasons. This type of interference in work processes includes various measures used to cut, to postpone, or to halt the expenditures of certain subunits, even though they were initially approved in the budget. One of the most popular devices used by Treasury staff for those purposes is setting up various committees such as steering committees, planning committees, inspection committees, and the like.

Since the budgeting process is essentially a power-based struggle between the units that allocate budgets and those that receive budgets, the relative power of each line unit as compared with the power of every staff unit affects the total budget as well as its composition in each case. To a great extent this power also influences the way in which funds are transferred after the budget has been approved.

Another kind of competition between line and staff personnel also takes place in many organizations nowadays. This competition focuses on personal privileges and benefits that members of each group of employees are entitled to receive. One example is the competition between the academic and administrative staffs in colleges and universities; similarly, combat and support units in military organizations compete over differential benefits; and production workers compete against maintenance staff in industrial firms. This kind of competition reflects intergroup politics in which every group desires to maximize its profits at the expense of the rival group. In spite of the professional cooperation that prevails between these units, crews, and individuals in the course of the workflow, their functional interdependence is the source of power struggles and, hence, of intergroup political games.

Finally, most organizations include within them at least three occupational groups of employees: managerial, professional, and "rank and file." Every type of employee develops in time its own organizational sub-culture that does not fit in with those of the other ones. In fact, there is constant tension between these cultures, since they are based on different perspectives and serve as a value standard that justifies the separate interests of the professional bodies.[24] Since these occupational groups are spread out among the different organizational units, they intensify the internal conflicts even more; and this increases their tendency to solve problems among themselves within the organization through political means. Like the struggle of women and other minorities, this intergroup politics takes place not only between organizational units, but also within the major subunits that compose the entire organization. In this case, too, the stronger occupational groups make the effort to widen the gap in quantity and quality of benefits between themselves and their competitors, whereas the weaker groups attempt to close this gap as much as possible towards the goal of equal utility for all.

Conclusion

The view of organizations as political arenas leads to the analysis of the relationships between their groups and subunits as competitive and combative processes. These political struggles by various groups are intended to influence the division of organizational resources so as to ensure their privileges and to grant them more benefits. Such political games are aimed at the utilization of resources for the amplification of the players' power and for the improvement of their status in the organization. In short, this is the very essence of intergroup politics that is often conducted in every organization. The various groups make use of a variety of political strategies and tactics, including coercive means, for such purposes. This chapter has dealt with three types of intergroup political struggles that are widespread in organizations: the struggle between employers and employees, between men and women, and between organizational subunits including line and staff conflicts.

The political game—known as *labor relations*—is conducted in organizations in a cyclic manner as a result of collective agreements between employers and their employees. These agreements are the outcome of tough negotiations over pay and fringe benefits on one hand and over working conditions and the rules of conduct on the other hand. Each party to the bargain tries to gain the most and pay the least. Therefore, peaceful negotiations between representatives of employers and employees quickly turn into power clashes that are characterized by mutual strikes, verbal aggression, property sabotage, and even physical violence. As a general rule, the clientele serves as the hostage of such confrontations, and in effect pays the price of the political struggle between employees and employers.

The employer-employee political game is often much more complex, because it includes a number of occupational groups who fight among themselves over the share that each gets of the "organization's spoils." Such political struggles are typical of large organizations such as governmental agencies, defense industries, public services, and state-owned enterprises. Several occupational groups are employed in these organizations, such as engineers, technicians, professionals, clerks, unskilled workers, and the like. The stronger professional groups (e.g., doctors, scientists, pilots, and engineers) demand for themselves some extra rights and benefits that are unique and excessive as compared to the other employees. On the other hand, the weaker vocational groups (e.g., production workers, maintenance personnel, rank and file clerks) fight for the sake of equal opportunities and for fair returns for their work.

In these struggles workers mobilize all the resources at their disposal to force the employers to increase their share in the basket of benefits. Therefore, labor conflicts often go beyond the limits of organizational dispute and develop into public struggles over public opinion, and the support of opinion leaders in society at large. In addition to the material aspect of such labor struggles, they are intended to serve as leverage for improving the bargaining position of various occupational groups, and to amplify their power vis-à-vis their counter-partners.

Most of the organizations of our times employ women in considerable numbers that are constantly increasing. However, most of the women who participate in the workforce are employed in jobs of inferior status, with fewer rights and poor salaries as compared to the employed men. Moreover, even highly educated and professionally trained women find it hard to compete with men over senior positions in both public and private organizations. This *glass ceiling*, which women come up against in their efforts to advance through the ranks of the organization, demonstrates the disadvantage they have in comparison with their male colleagues. Even women who actually hold full-time senior administrative positions encounter discrimination in income and in fringe benefits as compared with men.

Although the discrimination against women in opportunities, salaries, benefits, and promotion to senior positions has been decreasing nowadays, nonetheless, it still exists in more than just a few organizations. This kind of discrimination, whether deliberate or merely unintended, continues to serve as a fertile soil for the growth of gender-centered politics in organizations. Thus, women still have to fight for equal opportunity, equal rights to those granted to men, personal respect, humane treatment, and suitable reward for their contribution. The political struggle that is conducted at various levels and in a variety of ways and means, characterizes the organizational reality of today, and it is far from ending. Sociology describes it as a confrontation between two contradictory trends, *exclusion* and *inclusion*, that is, between the tendency of men to keep women away from power centers in organizations and the effort of women to constitute an equal and inseparable part of any organization.

This struggle for equality between the sexes is now being transferred to the sphere of minorities of all kinds who suffer from relative deprivation in various organizations, especially in work organizations that employ them in sub-standard conditions as compared with the majority of social groups. The minorities are also organized into interest groups and combine into multi-group coalitions with the aim of furthering their cause.

Organizational subunits (e.g., divisions) tend to be engaged in intergroup politics within their parent organizations, such as business corporations. Inter-unit competition over power and influence is essentially a structural one, since it acts as a direct result of organizational work divisions. This competition reflects the interests of various organizational units—interests that derive from the function, size, location, and composition of each one of them.

The primary assumption of the members of these units maintains that their managers do all that is possible to increase the proportionate share of the unit in the resources at the disposal of the organization, even at the expense of other units. To do this the unit heads have to increase their power, improve their bargaining positions, and influence strategic decision processes related to the planning and appropriation of resources. Therefore, the various organizational subunits participate in an ongoing political game, year after year. For that purpose they employ different political means and carry out political maneuvers. Such means include the formation of coalitions, exertion of pressures, justification of certain expenditures, endorsement of specific changes in the organization, and so forth.

Every large and complex organization is, in fact, a mosaic of a variety of subunits, of line and staff groups, of assemblies organized around some inputs and those organized around some outputs. The relative power of each of these units is based on the resources it possesses, on its centrality in the production and supply processes of the organizational products, and on its ability to assist the organization to cope with the pressures of the external environment. This power is the driving force of the inter-unit political struggles over primacy in the organization, with the aim of gaining the greatest utility possible for the units, for their managers, and for their members. It accounts for many of the political games that are played in various forms between groups and subunits in the realm of organizations.

Notes

1. Bacharach & Lawler, 1980.
2. Chapter 6 in the book deals with various types of political games.
3. For an explanation of the theory of political shadows, see the introductory chapter of this book.
4. Some of the labor relations in various countries are conducted as continuous political struggles between nationwide professional unions and various associations of employers, namely, on the level of interorganizational politics.
5. During the past decade this trend has changed because of the ongoing proliferation of individual labor agreements in many private organizations. The present trend is influenced by the establishment of branches of multi-national organizations, especially those of technological and high-tech organizations originating in the United States, such as IBM, Motorola, Intel, and the like.
6. Abraham Tal, Haaretz, 8 November 1999 (in Hebrew).
7. Kanter, 1977; Savage & Witz, 1992.
8. Kanter, 1977.
9. Haaretz, 16 November 1999 (in Hebrew).
10. On January 3, 2000, the Knesset plenum (i. e., the Israeli parliment) voted in the law for gender equality between men and women soldiers in the IDF. The law states that: "(a) Every woman soldier has the same rights as men soldiers to fill any position in the armed forces; (b) It will not be regarded as a violation of the right of a woman

soldier to fill a position if this is necessitated by the nature and character of the position; (c) A woman soldier who serves voluntarily in one of the positions determined by the Minister of Defense and confirmed by the Knesset Defense and Foreign Affairs Committee is to be treated in the same way as a man soldier."
11. Daft, 2004; Goldner, 1970.
12. Pettigrew, 1973: 17.
13. Yuchtman & Seashore, 1967.
14. Pfeffer, 1981.
15. Perrow, 1970.
16. Harpaz & Meshoulam, 1997.
17. See for example: Pfeffer & Moore, 1980; Hackman, 1985.
18. Hickson et al., 1971.
19. Cohen & Lachman, 1988.
20. The organizational term "line" includes the functions in the organization that deal with the production processes of its goods and services for the surrounding environment. "Staff" implies all the positions held by the various experts that assist the line managers in the gathering and analysis of the necessary information in order to make reasonable and well considered decisions (Samuel, 1996, Hebrew).
21. Dalton, 1959.
22. Sagie, 1990 (Hebrew).
23. Dagan-Nissim, 1997 (Hebrew).
24. Schien, 1996.

9

Interorganizational Politics

Every organization is embedded in a larger and more complex system identified as the *organizational environment*. In its broadest sense, organizational environment refers to the aggregation of relevant factors that exists outside the boundaries of the focal organization and, therefore, is not part of it. Those factors, however, are capable of affecting the organization structure, its composition, its functioning, and its unity. The environment of organizations consists of several layers such as the territorial, demographic, economic, technological, social, cultural, and political layers. Each one of those layers may be characterized by a set of parameters—namely, complexity, density, stability, certainty, flexibility, unity, and the like.[1]

The organizational environment creates conditions that compel organizations to cope with it in ways that will enable them to import from the environment the necessary resources for their proper functioning and to export to the environment the goods that it produces; in other words, to adapt themselves to the special conditions of their surroundings. Organization theory argues that appropriate adjustment to the environment and the changes that take place within it, is a necessary condition, although not a sufficient one, for organizational survival.

The organizational environment includes a wide range of economic, social, political, and other kinds of actors. Many of these actors, of which the environment of an organization is composed, are organizations themselves (e.g., governmental authorities). Suppliers, contractors, partners, clients, trade unions, political parties, and governmental agencies, represent some examples of such outside organizations. Every organization is thus embedded within a web of interorganizational connections—direct or indirect—with many different organizations.[2] These interorganizational connections create a state of interdependence between an organization and its environment. This interdependence naturally constrains the freedom of action of organizations and limits their ability to maneuver between the various demands addressed to them from the outside.

The concept of *dependence*, in this context, is useful for understanding how organizational decision-making processes are influenced by interested actors outside the organization. If organizations achieve their own ends by using their power to affect the behavior of other organizations, then it is possible to consider organizational decision-making as the consequence of such influences. It is more common to view organizations as self-directed, making strategic decisions and vigorously pursuing courses of action. However, the concept of dependence suggests that organizations are at least partly directed by elements in their environment. Organizations formulate their own action in response to the demands placed upon them by other organizations,[3] as well as by the constraints that limit their span of feasible alternatives.

Organizations, like people, also adopt various measures intended to lessen their dependence on other organizations. Such organizational measures represent *strategies* and tactics, which are an inseparable part of interorganizational politics. The use of political strategies in interorganizational relationships assists organizations to survive in their environment, even when it is hostile, and to establish themselves in an appropriate niche. In effect, the political resourcefulness of organizations is a major key to their long-term success.[4]

The dependence of any organization on those that surround it determines its ability to withstand the pressures of the organizational environment. The greater its dependence on other organizations, the more influenced it will be by its environment. In order to lessen their dependence on the environment, organizations take control over vital resources (capital, manpower, raw materials, technology, expertise, information), and try to use them to enforce certain patterns of behavior upon other organizations. Since a significant portion of the mutual relations between organizations are essentially exchange relationships, every organization strives to attain a state of asymmetry in these inter-organizational exchange relationships, namely, a state in which it can receive a higher remuneration than it is required to pay to the other organization.[5]

In organizational reality, most organizations are nearly always in a state of mutual dependence between them. This interdependence is a direct outcome of the competition over inputs or outputs that are conducted among various organizations within the same environmental niche; for example, organizations that produce similar goods (e.g., cars, computers) or organizations that render similar services (e.g., health, education). This represents a state of affairs in which the conduct of one organization necessarily affects the behavior of competing organizations in the same environment. Hence, this kind of influence is identified as *competitive dependence*. The most widespread example in the business world for this type of interorganizational dependence is price policy: every increase or decrease in the price of a certain product generally influences the price of the competing product in the same market.

Another mutual dependence in interorganizational relations is the so-called *symbiotic dependence*. Interorganizational cooperation leads to mutual dependence because the cooperating partners have to coordinate their steps with those of the others. Cooperation of any kind limits the range of possible actions that an organization may perform. Every organization is thus required to take into account the plans and activities of its partner organizations, and to act according to the understandings and agreements between them. An example of this kind of mutual dependence can be seen in the growing trend of business organizations to establish *joint ventures* in the spheres of technological research and development. This kind of cooperation depends on the extent to which the partners contribute their fair share to the venture, coordinate their moves that concern the joint venture with their fellow organizations, and refrain from opportunistic behavior at the expense of the others.

When one organization takes control over another organization, then a state of dependence emerges between these organizations, too. However, this kind of interorganizational dependence is not unilateral. The organization in power does depend to some extent upon the organization that it actually controls. This dependence is due to the resources that the controlled organization has at its disposal such as reputation, know-how, clientele, and the like. Moreover, in the process of takeover or merger, the organization that gains control of another becomes dependent on the willingness of the latter to cooperate with the new owners and managers and to help them to implement the necessary changes. Resistance to the new balance of power may be expensive and painful to the reorganized administration.

Although mutual dependence between organizations is an important factor for a state of conflict between them, it is not a sufficient condition for its actual emergence. It is only when this interdependence is accompanied by a shortage of vital resources that a political struggle can be expected to occur between those organizations. Therefore, in order to lessen their degree of dependence on the external environment, organizations try to vary their supply sources for the inputs they need. The availability of more than one supplier enables the organization to choose between optional sources; it also increases the organization's degree of independence; and it amplifies its relative power vis-à-vis competing organizations.[6] Organizational power is thus the key factor in the exchange relationships conducted between organizations. "The more power any organization has the more influence it has to determine the nature of the interorganizational exchange."[7]

Therefore, organizations take all kinds of steps to set up environmental conditions in which they enjoy a real advantage over competing organizations. This advantage means a situation in which one organization, or a small number of them, controls the supply of resources that are essential for many other organizations acting in the same environment. Thus, the tendency of organizations to monopolize supply chains of critical resources is displayed by their political behavior.

The way in which organizations cope with the constraints imposed on them by the external environment takes various forms that include political measures of various kinds. In this chapter we shall focus on three prevalent forms of interorganizational relations—*competition*, *partnership*, and *dominance*.

Each of these forms is based on the power of the organizations involved in these relationships, and it reflects the way in which the organizations actually exercise their power against their rivals. These interorganizational exchange relationships serve as an alternative means to obtain critical resources; to increase their economic, social, political, and cultural gains; to reinforce the stability of the organization and to improve its chances of survival. These types of relationships between organizations represent alternative modes of interorganizational politics.[8]

Competition between Organizations

A *competitive strategy* is essentially a master plan of a given organization to struggle with other organizations for the purpose of attaining a desirable outcome. As a result, an interorganizational competition is most likely to take place in a given environment. This kind of competition may be conducted at various levels at one and the same time, or focus on one issue after another consecutively. For example, organizations compete over the clientele for their products (i.e., market share); over the supply sources of their vital inputs; over obtaining recognition for them and for the legitimacy of their activities by their surrounding constituencies; over the seizure of primary positions in a certain competitive arena and over the attainment of privileges at the expense of the other competitors.

Organizations frequently compete among themselves over the attainment of a certain capital, a budget, a donation, a credit line, a specific loan, a research grant, etc. This kind of competition is essentially economic not merely a commercial one. It may easily be seen that organizations, which are not commercial firms (for example, public agencies, voluntary associations, sport and culture organizations, trade unions), engage in tough and stubborn competition to obtain such finances that are vital to their survival. Interorganizational competition of this kind may easily turn into a bitter political struggle between the competing organizations. Once such competitions escalate, they often include the use of coercive means (e.g., threats against the rival's leaders) and the application of political measures (e.g., manipulation of the supplier). Only a few decades ago, such struggles in the world of business, for example, were accompanied by the burning down of factories and the destruction of installations, by the intentional sabotage of equipment and raw materials, and by preventing the supply of goods to the markets. Even physical injury of managers and workers was not uncommon in those days. In our times, most of the struggles between competing organizations are conducted with more subtle and secretive methods.

Organizations depend upon a regular supply of similar resources, which are usually in short supply, to ensure their operation (e.g., raw materials, equipment, manpower, capital, and information); hence, they are compelled to compete among themselves for these resources. Thus, organizations offer various suppliers tempting prices and conditions of payment; they offer to sign long-term contracts; they invest in advertisement and propaganda; and above all, organizations pile up more reserves of materials, equipment, and essential manpower than they require for their current needs. These reserves are defined in organizational terms as *slack resources* that are intended for special needs and unusual circumstances, such as in times of emergency.

The economic and political power of large organizations allows them to stipulate that acquisition of these materials and services should be conditional on exclusive rights granted to them by the suppliers. Newspapers and TV channels, for example, frequently promise to publish certain "scoops" if, and only if, they get the information on an exclusive basis. The military forces of some countries acquire certain armaments from defense industries on condition that the sale of that equipment to any other client in the world is strictly forbidden. Restrictive supply contracts are quite typical for the pharmaceutical industry as well. The wealth and power of the giant corporations enables them to purchase exclusive rights to certain medical equipment, technologies, materials, and medications.

More than a few organizations do not hesitate to intimidate suppliers, agents, contractors, and transporters—covertly and even overtly—to ensure their uninterrupted access to the resources that they need. Some of them secretly encourage strikes and sanctions by workers in competing organizations. And many organizations assist in the "brain drain" of expert workers and specialists employed in competing organizations, using professional or monetary enticements. This phenomenon is characteristic, in our time, of high-tech industries in which human resource is the most vital resource of all.

A widespread phenomenon in interorganizational competition today is that of espionage of various kinds; thus, spying in the areas of national security, commercial affairs, applied research, innovative technology, credits and finances, and even in the area of individual privacy has become a big business. The availability of advanced technologies facilitates the exposure of all kinds of organizations to undercover activities that were not possible in the past. Examples of such activities may be seen in the penetration of unauthorized people into computerized databases; unauthorized listening to classified communication by means of electronic devices; remote photography of objects with amazing precision; unraveling of secret production formulae and the deciphering of coded messages; and the identification and neutralization of sophisticated security devices. Such undercover activities allow organizations today to reveal the research and development plans of their competitors for new products before they are completed; to keep track of political and business developments; to discover the competitors' sources of supply; to estimate the economic situation of the other organizations; to identify agents and collaborators; and to gather personal incriminating information against the competitors, especially of the senior position-holders in the rival organizations.

This highly valuable information is frequently used for political purposes in interorganizational competition, that is, for gaining an advantage over the competitors by underhanded means. For instance, the press, the media, and now the Internet spread unceasingly tendentious information derived from leaks, slander, defamations, fabrications, warnings, and unsubstantiated disclosures. Information of this kind is meant to influence public opinion and behavior in general and specific target audiences in particular (e.g., consumers, social movements, pressure groups, and foreign observers). In the sphere that is hidden from the public eye, the information at the disposal of organizations is used as a means for exerting pressure, for extortion, for transmitting threats, and for presenting claims and dictates to competitors. In one case, competing daily newspapers conducted mutual acts of espionage against each other. Both sued by the State in the court of law. In his verdict, the presiding judge condemned the unethical behavior of the newspaper editors while making general remarks about the press.

> The press has altered its appearance lately. It has become more centralized, more commercial, and more competitive. The competition among newspapers has eroded the ethics of them all. Ethical erosion leads, above all, to the injury of certain people and groups. Beyond this, it is also liable to injure important public interests. These are matters that seem to be well known and in no need of proof.[9]

Business corporations tend to use their power in order to remove their competitors from the market, or at least to limit their competitive ability, in various political ways, which are not always legitimate. An example of this is Microsoft, the famous computer software corporation owned and directed by Bill Gates. This company developed the operating program known as *Windows*, and saw to its installation in most of the personal computers in use throughout the world. According to observers who closely follow the developments taking place in the industrial field of software, Microsoft employed all possible means in order to control the programming market. It was only in October 1997 that the American Department of Justice decided to press charges against Microsoft, claiming that it had recently forced the hardware producers of the PC's to install in the computers its browser (Internet Explorer) as a condition for the installation of its popular operating system Windows. On December 11, 1997, the judge issued a decree prohibiting Microsoft from continuing with this policy. After a few months Microsoft began preparations to market its new operating system, Windows 98, in which its browser was embedded. In the verdict handed down in the monopoly trial that the United States administration conducted against Microsoft, the judge found this firm to be guilty on all charges and declared that it had illegally taken advantage of its monopoly to prevent other firms from developing programs that might compete with it, and forced the producers to integrate the Explorer browser within the Windows operating system. The judge ruled that Microsoft had used its power in a "bullying" manner in order to dominate the browser market. Later, the judge decreed that Microsoft should be divided into two separate business companies.[10]

It is worth noting here that Microsoft is merely one of the many giant corporations that have taken advantage of their power to oust their competitors from the market and to dominate it exclusively. The United States administration has been suing such companies and corporations since 1890 when the law of business cartels was enacted. Among the famous cases in connection with this were the legal claims that the U.S. authorities submitted against the IBM computer company, the ATT telephone company, the Standard Oil Company, the Alcoa aluminum company, and the American Tobacco Company.

In all these legal struggles and in others, some of which stretched over many years, the giant corporations being sued were forced to open the market to free and fairer competition. A few of these giant corporations were broken down into smaller companies, some were sold by the government to competing companies, while others signed on cooperative agreements with foreign companies. There is no need to specify in detail here the injury caused to the reputation of business organizations sentenced for unfair competition, which harms the customer public, and the business implications that such a negative image has for their economic success. Some experts actually believe that the verdict of condemnation against Microsoft for conducting "dirty" interorganizational politics, and the sentence that forced it to break up into two companies, could be the beginning of a process that will lead to the inevitable end of this economic empire, despite further appeals against that sentence. Meanwhile, it is still in good shape.

Cooperation between Organizations

A large number of organizations—businesses, state, political, professional, and voluntary—tend to cooperate whenever their leaders realize that interorganizational cooperation yields greater utility than interorganizational competition. Such cooperation may begin with an occasional exchange of information and may even end with the full merger between organizations into a unified corporate body.

One of the basic and widely found forms of cooperation in the organizational reality of our times is the series of mutual and continual links between organizations. The concept of *network*, in its widest sense, expresses an interwoven fabric of links among actors: individuals, social groups, various types of organizations, sovereign states, and even superpowers.[11] A continuous mutual relationship among different organizations creates a pattern of an *interorganizational network*. Such a network may be conceptualized as a sort of super-organization that is based on loose couplings between independent and mostly equal organizations.

An interorganizational network is a form of cooperation between two or more organizations, directed towards the realization of goals which each organization separately could achieve only at greater expense, or not at all. In such a case, a network can act as an organizational unity, and can make decisions as such…. A network is concerned with a set of partly dependent and partly independent organizations, which have partly conflicting and partly corresponding interests, and which arrive at forms of collective decision making and collective activities.[12]

Interorganizational networks differ in their composition, size, the quality of mutual relationships among their components, and in their patterns of activity. Such networks adopt different strategies intended to assist the organizations that comprise them in achieving their goals and to provide them with the vital resources they need in order to function effectively.

According to one theoretical approach, interorganizational networks represent a structural and behavioral pattern of activity that can be identified as *political economy*. This term indicates the fact that organizational networks focus upon two rare and vital resources: money and power.[13] These resources are to be found in the environment, but since they are usually scarce, organizations are compelled to compete in order to acquire them. The competition between organizations over capital and material assets reflects the economic side of the interorganizational network; whereas their competition over power and dominance reflects the political side of the network. Interorganizational networks thus serve as a means to obtain resources and to distribute them among the members of the network at the expense of other organizations that are not partners in the network. This partnership facilitates the political-economic struggle of organizations; it improves the bargaining position of the organizations in such struggles; and it ensures a reasonable degree of fair distribution among the participants.

The interests of the organizations that form an interorganizational network are not necessarily identical, and they may even oppose one another to some extent. Hence, these organizations occasionally adopt strategies that are aimed at changing the structure of the network and its function in order to improve their status within the network; and their goal is to increase the utility they gain from their partnership in the interorganizational network. Such attempts may, of course, cause tension among the organizations and arouse mutual suspicion between them; but at the same time they serve as a useful lever to improve positions and redesign the interorganizational arrangements in accordance with the changes that occur in the balance of power among the organizations. Therefore, while interorganizational networks attract independent organizations with some common interests to set up some form of partnership among them, they are subject to recurring changes in their composition, goal, strategy, and their power structure.

Structural and functional changes such as these occur as a result of the political use of power possessed by members of the network towards their partners. This kind of political maneuvering is usually taken in an undercover manner to avoid breaking up the interorganizational network, and to retain the advantages of that network. Therefore, the organizations that participate in such networks are careful not to take any steps that might be considered as hostile from the standpoint of the participants. Instead, participants tend to use various incentives such as strategic cooperation, economic advantages, information sharing, and technological assistance in order to keep their network alive. However, the same organizations do not hesitate to exert pressures on their partners, to present various claims, and to condition their cooperation on certain situations and their outcome. Such power pressure is, in fact, a disguised form of blackmail wrapped in rational justifications, the purpose of which is to avoid confrontations between participants in the interorganizational network. One can easily find examples of this kind of organizational behavior in coalitions between political parties; in multinational business networks; in international cooperation between police organizations and secret intelligence organizations; and in various kinds of regional cooperation.

As mentioned before, interorganizational cooperation represents a political strategy of dealing with competing organizations and with other rivals. Therefore, the main political struggle takes place between the various interorganizational networks and not within them. One of the advantages of such cooperation is the assistance given by interorganizational networks to members who need to substantiate their legitimacy and credibility in the environment. The fact that a specific organization is linked to a certain network of organizations is likely to increase its credibility among clients and suppliers, for example. Interorganizational support thus assists participant organizations to advance their interests in a more practical and efficient manner than they could have done if they had acted alone. Such support enhances their power, widens their ability to maneuver, and improves their bargaining position. In this way, networks serve as an advantage in interorganizational politics no less than in economic affairs.

It is easy to understand, therefore, the efforts made by the United States, in the wake of the terror attack that took place on its soil on September 11, 2001, to construct the widest possible international coalition. This coalition is essentially an international network that would help to eliminate the terror organizations and the states that had assisted them in harming the United States, and that would create a wide front against terror activity. As with the coalition that was formed in 1991 in the First Gulf War against Iraq, the United States, in the Second Gulf War, also tried to utilize temporary international partnership to obtain vital intelligence information, military bases for its forces, and control over the supply of vital resources to hostile countries. In addition to the practical advantages of this international network, it was meant to provide worldwide "moral leverage" to justify the projected military, economic, and political actions of the United States and its allies against the "enemies of the free world." It is unnecessary to detail here the heavy political pressures that the United States imposed on various Muslim and Arab states in order to make them join this coalition and support its purposes and measures.

Research has shown that interorganizational cooperation does provide assistance to organizations to adapt quickly and efficiently to changes that occur in the environment. These organizations can learn from the experience of their partners, imitate their methods of action that have proved to be successful, and make use of the classified information that is accessible only to the partner organizations. Such means are likely to be especially decisive in crisis situations, while changes are in the process of being carried out and remedial programs are being applied in organizations. The political aspect of the so-called *organizational learning* in this connection takes the form of coordinated policy of the network, which attempts to impose limits on the activities of organizations that are not members of that partnership.

The partners of an interorganizational network apply this kind of joint policy by practical means such as making strategic decisions, forming secret agreements among them, and sharing classified information for political purposes. Frequently, they exert combined pressure upon competitors and rivals; they take security measures against external penetration into the partnership space; they coordinate their positions vis-à-vis the general public and public opinion; and they emphasize the agreed rules of cooperative behavior among the managers and workers of the partner organizations.

One of the mechanisms that motivate coordination and cooperation among organizations in the business world is that of *interlocking directories*. Business groups, investment firms, strategic partnerships, interorganizational networks, and holding companies make an effort to staff the Boards of Directors of the organizations affiliated to them with "proper" directors, that is, with persons who will protect the interests of these stakeholders. Moreover, in order to ensure that the decisions of the various directories should suit their interests, they appoint certain persons to represent them in several directorates at the same time. It thus happens that a relatively small number of people, such as senior managers, government officials, specialists in various areas, and public figures participate in a relatively large number of directories. The loyalty of those directors obviously grants them generous remuneration, honor, and prestige, as well as considerable power. By means of this kind of interlocking directories, certain stakeholders steer the strategic decisions made by seemingly independent organizations, and influence them to take the steps that are in line with the stakeholders' interests.[14] Banks represent an outstanding example of such influential stakeholders who make sure to have their representatives on the boards of directors of various business firms in which they have vested interests.

This is, then, the political game in which a few players are capable of influencing a whole range of organizational decisions, which are supposedly disconnected and independent of each other, in such a way as to make them interdependent. For this reason, those allied directors have to be equipped with reliable and updated information that can be used by them in the various boards of directors in which they are members. Studies have actually shown that the sources of information of those directors serve as an important factor in increasing their ability to influence the strategic decisions of those business organizations in which they play an active role as members of their boards.[15]

This political mechanism enables business organizations to act in favor of those enterprises that are affiliated with them at the expense of organizations that compete with them; to regulate their supply of resources in favor of their allies; to focus their efforts on preferable clienteles; to protect prices and conditions of payment indirectly; to prevent the uncontrolled diffusion of technological know-how; and to influence, indirectly, the employment and salary policies in these organizations. Since these and like measures might violate the laws of business cartels, the various boards of directors take care to present a semblance of independence, confidentiality, and business etiquette as legally required. Therefore, the mutual influence of such an interorganizational combination is mainly the result of interpersonal ties among the directors; their accessibility to similar sources of information; their similarity of interests; and the economic and political power attributed to the stakeholders whom they, in effect, represent.

The inclusion of outside stakeholders or their representatives on the board of directors of a firm or a corporation is an accepted political procedure in the reality of business organizations, known as *cooptation*. On many occasions this measure is intended to neutralize competition, to reduce tensions, and to blunt the hostility of elements that have the power to disrupt organizational procedures; it is also intended to prevent the advancement of harmful objectives or to avoid deprivation of vital resources. The cooptation of persons such as the leaders of trade unions, the heads of voluntary organizations, the chairpersons of professional associations, of senior politicians, and the like, is meant to widen the circle of external support for the organization and its activities.

A number of such leaders are tempted into joining the decision-making centers of their rivals in order to influence them to accept decisions in favor of the organizations they represent. Their assumption is that through penetration into the higher levels of the rival organization and taking an active part in its direction they will achieve better and more efficient results than through struggle and confrontation outside the organization. From their viewpoint, this membership means conducting the interorganizational political game in the court of the rival and gaining control over its main group of players. Moreover, this membership entails personal benefits that ambitious people would be glad to obtain.

From the viewpoint of the co-opting corporation, the entrance of rival leaders into its leadership is intended to enable it to have a direct influence over the opposition and to steer their political behavior according to the objectives and interests of the organization. The assumption that lies behind this expectation is that authority involves responsibility; namely, whoever is allowed to make decisions in an organization must render account of the results. For instance, directors are personally responsible by law for all decisions of the Board of Directors in which they are members.

Under such conditions, those who have been invited to the Board of Directors of an organization are now required to weigh every matter first and foremost for the good of the organization they are managing. In this situation, it will be difficult for them to support decisions that will harm the interests of the organization, even if such decisions were to correspond with the demands and preferences of the rival organizations from which they have come. From the viewpoint of the organization in question, this consists of a political game in which the leading player of the opposing team cooperates with the team of this organization. Naturally, in a game like this a business corporation or a certain public organization will have a significant advantage over opposing organizations, and this advantage justifies the price of cooptation.

Since cooperation of this kind is essentially a political measure, the *quid pro quo* is generally given in the form of various benefits, both on the personal level and on the organizational level; for example, the grant of a generous expense allowance for those directors, and the provision of various kinds of support for their organizations.

However, the real price paid by the business organization that integrates such external stakeholders is its "exposure" before those outsiders, their intrusion into its decision-making centers, and their influence on its policies.[16] Therefore, as studies have shown, during the high-tide periods of economic progress in which capital is liquid and relatively cheap, production and service organizations tend to co-opt representatives of banks and of financial organizations to their boards of directors. On the other hand, in times of economic recession, the fears of intrusion by such elements into the management system reduces to a significant degree the mutual integration among directorates in general, and in particular between them and banks or similar institutions.[17] One way or another, cooptation is a typical act of politics, which is usually applied mainly by business organizations for the purpose of neutralizing potential and actual rivals.

A higher degree of interorganizational partnership may be seen in the cooperation of two or more organizations in the creation of *joint ventures* and in managing them. Many multi-organizational partnerships of this kind are common today in various organizational spheres. This kind of cooperation is typical for industries dealing with communications and computers, defense industries, biotechnology and pharmaceutics, space research, and environmental protection. The unique character of such cooperative ventures as compared with other partnership activities is the integration of information and funding at the disposal of those private and public organizations that are earmarked for the treatment of complex problems that have not yet been resolved. Therefore, such ventures generally focus on scientific research at the cutting edge of science, and on the development of innovative and multi-purpose technologies, but not on designing specific commercial products.

On the face of it, such joint ventures indicate the readiness of business organizations to cooperate with their competitors for the sake of advancing human knowledge. However, this kind of interorganizational cooperation is likely to take place whenever it is based on the serious economic interests of the involved parties. It should be understood that in the world today, scientific discoveries and technological developments might yield enormous financial profits for their owners. The value of patents, copyrights, and the ownership of know-how are very high in the present world economy. Nonetheless, in order to obtain such properties, organizations must cooperate with other ones in one kind of joint venture or another. This is because the giddy race in search of break-through innovations involves gigantic investments that many organizations cannot afford to make alone. A joint venture reduces the uncertainties entailed by technological research at the forefront, lowers the costs of risk capital, and shortens the period of time need for its completion. The shared utilization of information from different sources and of expertise in a variety of fields promises better results with greater efficiency.

Thus, organizations pursuing innovations are likely to take part in the political game that takes place at the interorganizational level. In this political arena, every scientific or technological achievement increases the power of the partners in these joint ventures and gives them an edge over their competitors and rivals. Obviously, the owners of new discoveries and novel products do their utmost to enjoy the fruits of their efforts, transforming them into economic profits. Moreover, such organizations exploit their success in applying political courses of action in order to obtain exceptional rights vis-à-vis their competitors, for example, tax shelters or special credit lines. They take advantage of the media in order to enhance their prestige among the public at large. They exert influence over the directors of research funds and philanthropic institutions in order to receive large grants over extended periods for their continuing activities. And they initiate professional connections with well-known experts and renowned scientific institutions in order to link themselves publicly with the scientific state of the art.

In the framework of such endeavors, organizations make practical use of their power; they offer rewards and threaten retaliatory actions, deploy their competitors and rivals, bargain and argue, reveal and conceal information according to their needs, and join hands with their partners and allies to advance their goals. This power is expressed in the exertion of pressure on the governments of various countries to grant them tax exemptions, to give them state guarantees for crediting huge sums, and to subsidize training programs for workers. It is reasonable to assume, then, that the stronger and richer the partner corporations are in such ventures, the more generous will be the state benefits that they receive.

An outstanding example of interorganizational politics of this kind can be found in the race to decipher the complete genetic code of the human race, known as the Human Genome Project. Scores of academic establishments, government research institutes, medical centers, and business firms in various countries of the Western world have been involved in this competition. After the president of the United States publicly announced the completion of the task, and with the beginning of the next stages of the project, much excitement is being generated among those participating in it. Many of them are now competing over the highest awards and prestigious honors, over research contracts and grants, and over highly paid positions. At the same time, the economic and political motives of the stakeholders behind the scenes apparently have been intensified, too. These stakeholders are both organizations and individuals. They include, for example, capitalists, entrepreneurs, and politicians, as well as academic institutions, pharmaceutical industries, banks, scientific magazines, and governmental agencies.

On the level of interorganizational relations, various partnerships are being arranged, joint ventures are being created, and contacts are being made for the sake of interorganizational cooperation. Economic competition in this promising field is in full swing, and even organizational politics is generating corresponding momentum. Without belittling the immense importance of this endeavor to improve the health of the human population, it seems that *political shadows* unavoidably accompany this endeavor. Those political shadows unveil themselves in the form of confrontations, disclosures, accusations, incitements, the spreading of tendentious information, personal dismissals, and legal claims. Even though the major part of the disagreements are basically professional, many "dark" deeds that are suspect will come to light in coming years through the mass media, and will serve competitors to influence public opinion in their favor at the expense of their rivals. The stakes of this project are too high to keep politics away from the scientific work.

The strategy of partnership in interorganizational alliances has a long history in the realm of international relations. Sovereign states have been forming international alliances for military, economic, political, and other purposes. NATO and the Warsaw Pact are good examples of military alliances that were made between states—the former among democratic and capitalist states, and the latter between totalitarian and communist states. These alliances conducted a Cold War between them from the end of the Second World War and until the collapse of the former USSR.[18] These multi-organizational alliances set up and run joint headquarters manned by representatives of their members; and each of them has an all-members council, a central governing board or command, an agreed common policy for all the members of the alliance and mutual commitments to behave according to the board's decisions.

Unlike organizational mergers, such alliances do not abolish the unique structure and character of its partners. Members of an alliance contribute their share to the general reservoir of resources necessary for this roof organization such as money, manpower, information, expertise, natural resources, equipment, etc. In return, each member of the alliance receives the alliance's protection of its sovereignty, its economy, its population, and its culture. The alliance is also supposed to guard the common interests of all its members, as did NATO in the civil war in Kosovo at the end of the twentieth century. For the first time since its establishment, after the September 11 terror attack on the United States, the NATO Council decided to include the paragraph in its signed accord, saying that an attack on one of its members is to be considered as an attack on all the members of the alliance; therefore, they would all enlist in the common battle against those who attacked the United States.

The process of globalization encourages the formation of strategic business alliances between producers, marketers, transporters, and the like, across countries. Similar trends may be observed in the sphere of labor relations, as well as between social-democratic political parties of many countries, and among nongovernmental organizations of various kinds. All of these realize the advantages that lie in the integration of their power. Such alliances are therefore meant to serve as "powerhouses" that increase the strength of the member organizations and allow them to conduct decisive and more effective political struggles.

In these cases, interorganizational politics ascends to a higher level, since it now takes place between allied forces of multiple organizations rather than between separate ones. The political game is thus more difficult and complicated, since those who participate in it are very powerful players, possessing immense resources and a greater ability to maneuver; hence, they are placed in better bargaining positions than rival organizations acting alone.

This cumulative power allows multi-organizational alliances to set for themselves more ambitious goals; to act with greater potency against their rivals; to select more radical courses of action; to invest many more resources in their struggles; and to utilize their *economies of scale*. Nevertheless, it is just because of their great power and because of the dangers involved in its exercise that rivals are caught in a deadlock, which deters them from being drawn into a frontal clash, and prevents a total warfare—either political, military, or economic. This is what occurred in the confrontation between NATO under the leadership of the United States, and the Warsaw Pact under former Soviet Russia leadership—a conflict characterized by a "balance of horror," which lasted for the last fifty years of the twentieth century.

In sum, it should be noted that the numerous organizational alliances conducting politico-economic struggles in most spheres of life represent a major trend in the present era of globalization. Such struggles heighten the degree of complexity in interorganizational relationships, due both to the large number of players participating in these world league political games as well as the significant amplification of their power. Interorganizational alliances, treaties, partnerships, networks, coalitions, consortia, and joint ventures turn the political game into a group contest, in which teams of organizations rather than single ones fight to win.

Takeover of Other Organizations

In addition to the strategies of competition and cooperation, inter-organizational politics is also rife with takeover strategies. In brief, *takeover* signifies a procedure by which one organization takes control over the assets, personnel, and activities of another organization. Whether the takeover is carried out militarily or in some other way (political, economic, cultural, legal, or any combination of these), it entails a clear-cut political act of a forceful nature, with the aim of negating the independence of the organization being controlled, and bending it to the will of the new regime. In many cases, organizational takeover is meant to abolish the target organization as an independent, defined, organizational framework. Frequently, this takeover is carried out against the will of the organization's ownership and its governance, and is therefore identified as a *hostile takeover*.[19]

One of the main drives for organizational takeover is the need of organizations to make sure that they get a regular supply of vital resources that serve as input for the production of goods and services they supply to their environment. According to the *resource dependence theory*, the shortage of necessary resources is a threat to every organization and enforces competition with other organizations in order to obtain them.[20] This competition magnifies the dangers that lurk for the organization; increases the level of uncertainty in which it is placed; raises the price it must pay for each resource (raw material, equipment, energy, manpower, capital, and land); and requires investment in the storage of current stocks and in the accumulation of reserves for a rainy day.

In order to minimize the costs and the risks involved in managing resources under such conditions, many organizations prefer to take control over the sources of supply and to incorporate suppliers with the organization as one of its components. This kind of takeover represents a strategy of *vertical integration* between clients and their suppliers. While the objectives of such a takeover may be economic, the activities involved in the process of taking over the target organization are of a political nature. A hostile takeover is an asymmetrical merger of a larger and stronger organization with a smaller and weaker one. A hostile takeover is imposed by the more powerful organization upon the target organization through the exercise of some kind of power—namely, economic, technological, political or military power. Sooner or later, the dominant organization incorporates the subordinate one and thus negates the latter's independence and its unique character.

The phenomenon of taking over by the use of physical force has been prevalent since the dawn of history, and it is still widespread today. In this way, various political entities (e.g., empires, kingdoms, states, and provinces) have vanished and have been incorporated into the population of stronger powers that have conquered them. The main reason for this kind of takeover has always been the attainment of precious resources such as fertile lands, vital underground deposits (e.g., metals or petroleum), expensive agricultural products (e.g., spices, coffee, and tea), innovative tools and appliances (e.g., ships or machines), and important transportation routes (e.g., ports, rivers or mountain passes).

In the realm of business, large corporations in various industries such as automobile, paper, steel, textile, and food used to take control over the suppliers of raw materials that were vital to them (e.g., mines, saw mills, agricultural plantations, and transportation companies), even by the use of force. Large and powerful professional unions have taken control over the press, banks, health and welfare services, which they needed in order to conduct their struggles of labor relations from a position of strength vis-à-vis the employers.[21]

Business organizations frequently attempt to dominate their competitors for the purpose of improving their bargaining position in the market. This kind of takeover, known as *horizontal integration,* usually takes the form of a merger between two or more competing organizations. Such mergers frequently turn into elimination of some organizations since they are "swallowed," in fact, by the merging competitors. Following this strategy, then, wealthy and powerful organizations apply certain complex procedures that enable them to buy out their competitors, and merge together with them into a single corporation. Needless to say, many of these acquisitions are carried out in a friendly manner through mutual agreement. However, a great many of the interorganizational mergers are carried out through political maneuverings by the merging organizations so as to force the target organizations to merge with them.

In these cases, organizational power is deliberately exercised against the target organizations, including promises and threats; the use of disinformation; deterrence of suppliers and incitement of clients; recruitment of some key managers and professionals of the target organizations; covert restriction of credit lines; industrial espionage, and secret support of hostile elements. Pressuring activities of this and similar kinds continue so long as they do not constitute a gross violation of laws and do not openly contradict international treaties and conventions. Such pressures and manipulations reveal the political nature of asymmetrical mergers, acquisitions, and takeovers that commonly take place in the world of business these days.

In recent times there has been increasing evidence that illegal organizations, active in Eastern Europe and Latin America, have managed to gain control of legitimate organizations (e.g., banks, financial institutions, newspapers and electronic networks) by means of illicit methods. Such acquisitions and takeovers are made possible through large-scale smuggling and money laundering derived from drug dealings, arms deals, and blackmail of protection dues. These acts of corruption are identified with organizations considered as "organized crime." This phenomenon itself is not a new one, of course, and has prevailed for many years in European countries and in the United States. The novelty is in its sophistication and in its scale of activity in the era of globalization.

At the beginning of the third millennium, a systematic and consistent trend has been spreading throughout the world for large corporations to merge together and to create *mega mergers*. Through this kind of strategy mergers have been made among more than a few corporations such as defense industries, the electronic media and the press, airlines, large banks, and large-scale hi-tech firms dealing with technologically innovative goods and services. In an age of globalization, these mega mergers have created giant conglomerates of immense and unprecedented power, which allows them to influence the policies of governments throughout the world. In the sphere of world trade, such as foreign investment, tax laws, tariff barriers, exchange rates, labor and wage laws, patents and inventors' rights, this kind of influence entails enormous profits for these giant conglomerates. However, the concern here is with political power of the highest degree, which results from such mega mergers. These organizational entities apparently do not restrict their potency to business affairs alone; but they tend to exercise strong and extensive leverage to affect national and international economic, social, and cultural affairs worldwide.

One of the power levers that giant corporations exercise against the governments of developing nations is the threat of withdrawing their business interests in those countries if their conditions are not met. These multinational corporations employ forceful and manipulative measures that have wide-range economic implications for the host countries that do not conform to their terms and conditions. Such measures include refraining from investment in the local economy; transfer of industrial enterprises to other countries; withdrawal of profits to foreign banks; import of cheap labor; blocking access to advanced technology and scientific knowledge; and marketing restrictions for vital goods and services. All these are political pressures exercised by giant multinationals against the local establishment in order to gain preference vis-à-vis their competitors. Moreover, because they are big, rich, and strong, these multinational corporations are capable of taking over local organizations in various countries, changing their character to suit their needs, and turning them into their own subunits. These takeovers, whether they are defined as *hostile takeovers* or as *friendly takeovers*, are growing more widespread in the global village of our time.

Local authorities therefore face a dilemma that is not at all simple: on the one hand, they harbor doubts about the control of foreign businesses over the domestic economy; on the other hand, they are afraid of the danger of economic drought as a result of an effective business boycott against the state. Developing countries in particular are in great need of foreign capital and know-how to boost their economies. Thus, they always need to import advanced technology, scientifically trained workers, investment in infrastructure, more jobs for their local population, and international trade. No wonder, then, that at least some of them have no other choice but to yield to the demands of these multinational corporations and to grant them exceptional benefits.

As may be expected, the power of giant business corporations interlinks their owners and managers into a network of important and useful interpersonal ties to the corridors of government of various countries. Such connections with senior officials help to protect the interests of those corporations accordingly. Within the framework of interpersonal relations that are woven between the wealthy and the ruling authorities, tendentious messages are transferred; opinion and positions on actual matters are expressed; and mutual personal commitments are made. In many cases these ties also lead to the exchange of material benefits; prestigious public appointments, and delegations to foreign countries; contributions to politicians' campaigns; various discounts and sponsorship of public events.

The supposed winning of a lucrative tender in construction and supply; the apparent giving of state guarantees to preferred businesses; the granting of reductions in tax dues to powerful corporations; the imposing of restrictions for the import of certain goods and services, as well as price subsidies, are all common examples of benefits that business organizations enjoy by virtue of the personal ties they have forged with the ruling authorities in the public sphere and with the affluent in the business sphere. Both sides act in their own interests no less than in those of the organizations they oversee. It is no wonder, therefore, that these relationships sometimes cross the bounds of legitimacy in the direction of bribery and favoritism, and go as far as "buying the government with money." In such cases, politics turns into corruption, so that the authority of one side and the power of the other side mix together into mutual assistance of an illegal and even of a criminal nature.

The political maneuverings of those powerful corporations and their dominance in the local economy arouse feelings of antagonism and the resistance of all kinds of nongovernmental organizations and voluntary associations such as the associations for the protection of consumers' rights; organizations for the protection of local products; organizations for the quality of the environment. These organizations mobilize themselves against the corporations, each in its own way. The mobilization of opponents frequently takes the form of protest activities such as sanctions, street demonstrations, and various strikes; blunt classified ads in newspapers; appeals to legal jurisdiction; lobbying politicians and government officials; and in certain cases even acts of violence.

Aggressive procedures of these kinds are an obstruction for the corporations under attack and disrupt their plans. Hence, some of them take retaliatory actions against their opponents that are no less powerful and even more destructive. Interorganizational confrontations such as these are liable to continue for a long time and to extract a high price from all those involved in them, even from the strongest and richest among them. Sooner or later, the rivals will have to find a way to compromise in order to attain a position in which they can conduct their affairs without hindrance. These processes involve negotiation by an overt or covert agency, by mutual recourse to arbitration, by agreed bridging measures or the signing of contracts for cooperative actions. Thus, interorganizational politics constitutes a mechanism by which organizations resolve disputes and settle conflicting interests between them. Sometimes, instead of leading to mutual compromise, interorganizational politics serves as the catalyst for the escalation of conflict between organizations. In such cases, the political activities of the rivals drag them into a frontal clash that can only end in clear victory of one side over the other side. These are costly confrontations that may destroy the parties involved in them, the winners inclusive. At the extreme, the outcome may resemble the mythological Pyrrhic victory, in which the king of ancient Epirus concluded that "one more victory like this one and we are undone."

To prevent some of these frictions or at least to blunt their sharpness, giant corporations and multinationals avoid the direct act of takeover, pursuing alternative moves by which they are able to neutralize conflict of interests. Thus, as already mentioned, the heads of business corporations adopt the political tactic of *cooptation*, which is the tactic of allowing the leaders of rival organizations to seemingly participate in the decision-making processes of the corporation. This means that those rivals are invited to join as members of the board of directors, of the council of governors, or of the steering committee. Another political tactic adopted by some corporations is the use of the so-called *industrial espionage*, which is the tactic of infiltrating trusted persons into some sensitive positions within competing organizations for the purpose of obtaining inside information. A practical control of competitors, rather than a judicial one, is an option that wealthy and powerful corporations are likely to use under certain conditions. This kind of political tactic is essentially manipulative, that is, the case in which an organization covertly applies various acts of manipulation, which significantly restrict the range of alternative courses of action that are open to the target organization. Organizations are thus able, by remote control, to navigate major decisions of their rivals according to their will.

Organizational takeovers have various forms, beginning with the influence on the strategic decisions of other organizations and ending with their physical, economic, or cultural conquest. Organizational takeover is a behavior pattern representing one type of political game that is quite common at the level of interorganizational relations. Its political nature results from several causes: firstly, because its aim is to ensure possession of the assets owned by another organization; secondly, because this is coercive behavior based on the use of power—political, economic, military, or spiritual—in order to impose the will of the owners of one organization upon another; and thirdly, because this is a manipulative kind of behavior which uses various stratagems in order to force the target organization to submit to a takeover.

Conclusion

Every organization must adjust itself to the environment in which it exists and functions. In our times, these environments are filled with many different kinds of organizations. Therefore, a great deal of the ongoing relationships between any organization and its external environment are, in fact, relationships between itself and other organizations. These relationships are characterized by the exchange of various goods and services, by friendly relations of mutual assistance, but also by struggles with competitors and rivals. Hence, some of those interorganizational relations are essentially hostile ones, expressed in the form of confrontations.

All organizations, in any environments, constantly have to cope with two main existential problems: the problem of insufficient resources, and the problem of uncertainty with regard to the environment. These problems oblige the organizations to be linked to a network of interorganizational ties, through which they may search for solutions to lessen their dependence upon the resources of the environment and the uncertainty that arises from its complexity and dynamic nature.

In order to achieve these objectives, organizations must generate economic, technological, political, or social power, which will give them an edge over other organizations in the same environment that need the same resources. This means that they are in need of organizational power that will provide them with a preferential bargaining position and a wide range of options, through which they can successfully participate in the interorganizational politics for obtaining the necessary resources.

On the basis of the power at their disposal, and in accordance with their own interests, organizations conduct various kinds of interorganizational relationships at one and the same time in different areas of activity. Three main types of interorganizational relationships—competition, cooperation, and takeover—were discussed in this chapter.

Interorganizational competition is usually concerned with the availability of resources and the products of organizations. In order to ensure a regular inflow of resources and a constant outflow of products, many organizations are not satisfied with simple economic competition based on supply and demand in the free market; hence, they have recourse to political competition based on the exercise of organizational power. The elimination of competitors from the market; manipulative relations with suppliers and clients; the enforcing of the rules of the game and required behavior patterns; the application of inducements and threats on government officials and on publicly elected figures; and the tendentious misleading of the media and public opinion are some of the courses of action that organizations take as part of interorganizational politics, in order to overcome their competitors, their rivals, and the organizations upon which they depend.

An alternative strategy to interorganizational competition is the strategy of interorganizational cooperation. Following this strategy, organizations affiliate themselves with multi-organizational networks. The partners of these networks share vital information between them; they assist each other in solving problems; they impart to other members the lessons learnt from their experience; they form coalitions coordinated in the struggle against their common rivals; and they set up cooperative joint ventures for the sake of innovative developments in applied technology. Thus, they form alliances among themselves for the purpose of protecting their vital interests against external threats. In these ways and others like them, organizations transfer the political games conducted between them to the arena in which multi-organizational groups combine forces to fight groups of competing organizations.

Another way to confront other organizations that function in the environment was described in this chapter by the term "organizational takeover." This strategy is based on the assumption that the best way for an organization to reduce uncertainty is to takeover its sources: suppliers, contractors, competitors, clients, and the like. The objective of a takeover is to impose the power of one organization on another in such a way as to negate its independence and to neutralize its oppositional ability. Conquest, elimination, acquisition by guile, control of decision centers, imposed mergers, and similar activities, represent a selection of various kinds of takeover, which powerful organizations apply against their weaker competitors and rivals. All these acts are essentially political measures, which combine the use of coercive means and manipulative tricks that are aimed to overcome rivals and competitors in the political arena where interorganizational fights take place.

Notes

1.   Samuel, 1996: 197 (Hebrew).
2.   Granovetter, 1985.
3.   Pfeffer & Salancik, 1978: 54.
4.   Katz & Kahn, 1978.
5.   Emerson, 1962, 1972; Pfeffer, 1981.
6.   See, for example, Thompson, 1967; Cook, 1977.
7.   Cook, 1977: 66.
8.   Chapter 6 describes three kinds of political games conducted among organizations: the subjugation game, the collaboration game, and the unification game.
9.   Ha'Ayin ha-Shevi'it, Special Issue, August 1998 (Hebrew).
10.   *Haaretz*, 4 April 2000 (Hebrew).
11.   Nohria & Eccles, 1992.
12.   Gils, 1984: 1074.
13.   See, for example, Benson, 1975.
14.   Burt, 1980; Mizruchi & Stearns, 1988.
15.   Haunschild & Beckman, 1998.
16.   Burt, 1980.
17.   Mizruchi & Stearns, 1988
18.   NATO still exists, and it is gradually being joined by several former members of the Warsaw Pact, such as the Baltic States.
19.   It is worth mentioning that in many cases there is a friendly takeover which accords with the wishes of the organization's owners or those that head it to transfer the responsibility over the organization into other hands, generally to save it from a crisis or to prevent its collapse. Such a takeover is carried out through purchase or merger. Numerous start-ups have been purchased by large corporations this way.
20.   Pfeffer & Salancik, 1978.
21.   The General Federation of Workers in Israel (Histadrut), for example, has been for many years in control of manufacturing factories, a bank, a daily newspaper, a large association of sports, the general health fund, and convalescence resorts.

10

Managerial Politics

Managers as Politicians

Executives—whether in business, government, education, or the church—have power and they use it. They maneuver and manipulate in order to get a job done and, in many cases, to strengthen and enhance their own position. Although they would hate the thought and deny the allegation, the fact is they are politicians. "Politics" according to one of the leading authorities in this complex and fascinating field, "is ... concerned with relationships of control or of influence." To phrase the idea differently, politics deals with human relationships of super ordination and subordination, of dominance and submission, of the governors and the governed.[1]

Theoretically, organizations are designed in such a way that managers, whatever their title might be, control them. It is the managers who make binding decisions and it is they who make the choices, while the other participants are those who realize them. It is well known that this state of affairs is made possible by the principle of the delegation of authority, namely, by granting legitimate power to the various managers in the organization. Such a delegation is made in the form of unequal distribution of power, which leads to the typical hierarchy of authority in organizations. Throughout this hierarchical management system, legitimate power in the form of authority is exercised from the top of the organization down to the bottom.[2]

Given this authority system under which the *organization machine* is supposed to work, there is in theory no place for organizational politics.[3] But the organizational reality is much more complex and dynamic. As already explained in previous chapters, power is by no means the exclusive asset of supervisors, managers, and executives in organizations. Ordinary members and other kinds of participants have various kinds of effective power. Although this power may not be of the same scale as that of managerial authority, it is no less effective in the pursuit of personal or group interests, mainly when it serves political purposes.

As long as managers become involved in power struggles with their subordinates, whether individuals or groups, they tend to exert their power in more practical and efficient ways than the organizational code prescribes. By stepping out of their formal authority, managers get caught up in political games:

tactics of intimidation, seduction, manipulation, and even deception are then likely to be used against trouble-making subordinates. This is the vertical direction of managerial politics—from the highest level to the lowest level of the organization.

Needless to say, every manager is subject to another manager who is senior to him or her in the organization. This subordination obliges all managers to obey the instructions of those appointed over them and to carry out their decisions. However, managers tend to extend the scope of their authority and responsibility to the greatest possible extent. Therefore, they attempt to influence the decision-making processes of those appointed over them so that the final resolutions will be in their favor. To the same extent they actively try to delay and change decisions that are not in line with their preferences. Such courses of action represent another direction of managerial politics—namely, the one facing upward in the managerial ladder.

Managers are generally placed at the top of organizational subunits, including those units that deal with the production of goods and those that deal with rendering internal services—that is, *line* units versus *staff* units. In everyday organizational life, line units, led by their managers, conduct an on-going competition among themselves, mainly over obtaining organizational resources. Another kind of competition may easily be detected in most organizations between line managers and their parallel senior staff officers. The managers of line divisions as well as those of staff units are likely to get into disputes on professional matters, which hide more profound struggles for power and influence. Unofficial rivalry obliges those managers to adopt a variety of political measures including claims and complaints, warnings and threats, secret deals, manipulations and intrigues of all kinds. This kind of managerial politics represents another part of organization politics taking place in the ongoing relationships among various subunits.

Executives and senior officers engage in relationships with various actors outside the organization. Such external actors include representatives of business organizations, representatives of the central and local government, newspaper reporters, opinion leaders, politicians, leaders of interest groups and social movements. These relationships are maintained for the purpose of assisting the organization to advance its interests, to protect it from the antagonism of hostile elements, and to foster its public reputation. Such relationships require a considerable degree of political wisdom to use tendentious information and propaganda; to promise various benefits and advantages; to implicitly threaten sanctions, to secretly support politicians; and to nurture personal ties with celebrities and VIPs. Maneuverings and manipulations as such reflect the external politics of organizations in which managers take part as the key players of a political game.

The notion of *managerial politics* refers to a multifaceted phenomenon consisting of a variety of political games played by managers at all levels. The targets of these political activities are sometimes subordinates; at other times, superordinates; occasionally they are peers in other subunits, and outsiders who exert influence upon the organization. As complicated as it is, and also in some respects unpleasant, managers cannot completely refrain from engaging in politics as part of their jobs in organizations. It should be noted, however, that not all managers behave in a political manner to the same extent, just as not all managers behave in a similar manner when they do not take active part in the *political game*. Yet, it is doubtful if there are managers who have never behaved politically while carrying out their managerial tasks. In other words, there are managers who engage in a lot of managerial politics and those who engage in only a little of it, but, in fact, all of them take an active part in it one way or another. Let us remember that politics is a means of survival in managerial positions, mainly in the more senior positions.

In any given organization, the character and intensity of managerial politics is closely connected with its internal culture. There are organizations in which intra-organizational politics is deeply rooted in the organization's shared values, beliefs, and social norms. In such organizations, managers, and commanders are expected to exercise power, to impose law and order, and to resolve forcefully internal conflicts. Such expectations encourage managers to play "hard politics." On the other hand, there are organizations in which there is widespread disapproval of internal politics, mainly of the coercive kind, and this is expressed by reservations held against managers who display their power and exercise it. In such organizations, then, "soft politics" is more typical than the open use of force by their senior participants. Thus, organizations differ in the level of managerial politicization that is practiced within them and the degree of tolerance of their participants for this style of managerial behavior.

For purposes of exemplification, some of the behavioral patterns typical of managers representing managerial politics are listed below.[4]

The use of consultation: There are managers who usually ask the opinion of their subordinates regarding matters concerning the activities of their unit. On the face of it, this is clearly a cooperative type of managerial behavior, and therefore many people are in favor of it. Hence, organizational consultants usually recommend that managers should behave in this way as far as possible. However, a large proportion of managers apparently make up their minds in advance on the matter in question and their decision is already taken before they discuss the matter with their subordinates. Therefore, this is merely a pretense at consultation that is intended to make the workers participate in the responsibility for the outcome without true participation in the decision-making processes. Managers who employ this tactic take care not to allow their subordinates to have a real share in the decisions, and prevent them from having the right to demand their implementation. For this reason, a manager who behaves in this way is expected to agree to a semblance of consultation with his or her subordinates—as individuals or as a group—only if it is at his/her own initiative and under conditions that are favorable to him/her, but in any case not very often.

Maneuvering ability: Managers using this tactic refrain from openly committing themselves to any specific plan of action or to a certain principle of management. Such managers, in every course they take and every statement that they make, are careful to maintain some degree of obscurity, to keep their options open, and to make changes in their policy without being considered inconsistent persons. They also take care to provide themselves with escape routes in their personal careers, so that they can transfer to other positions or organizations whenever the need arises. They are cautious not to be attached to their superiors, avoid total loyalty to one person in the organization, however senior he may be in position; and in the presence of their colleagues they stress the need to adapt to new situations. A manager of this kind is never "held in anyone's pocket," neither in the organization nor outside it.

Selective communication: There are more than a few managers who consider information an important resource and a vital source of personal power. They therefore tend to pass on information sparingly to both their subordinates, their peers, as well as to their superiors. These managers take care to share the knowledge in their possession a little at a time; to conceal any information that concerns their future plans of actions; to determine the timing for the transfer of information according to their personal judgment; and to set out for themselves a suitable agenda for communicating with their working partners—subordinates, superiors, colleagues, suppliers and clients. Such managers are sensitive about any bit of information that they think might arouse dispute, dissension, or confrontation in the organizational unit that they head, and all the more with regard to information that might cast a shadow on their status in the organization. They therefore determine who will receive the information, what kind of information will be revealed, and when it will be transferred to the recipient, everything being subject to their personal judgment and the political measures that they may have in mind.

Negative timing: From time to time all managers become involved in situations in which they are under pressure to make decisions contrary to their own views. To prevent the risks entailed by disobeying the instructions of their superiors, some managers repeatedly postpone the implementation of imposed decisions to a seemingly a better time. Those managers rationalize such delays by various excuses such as the need for planning, coordination, guidance, acquisition of the necessary means, formulating procedures, obtaining permits, and so forth. The typical message says: "The process of implementation is going forward, but at a slower pace than projected due to [this or that]." The actual timing for implementation is eventually set so late that the program has by then already died out or no longer has any value for the organization. In most cases, those managers openly endorse the importance of the idea, the wisdom of the decision, and their support for its implementation, but at the appropriate time.

Compromise agreement: The agreement of certain rivals to compromise when they become engaged in certain confrontations or when they take part in processes of negotiation, is usually perceived as a wise and welcomed behavior. However, in managerial politics, compromise is perceived by many as a sign of weakness, and even as a lack of leadership by the manager or the officer. Therefore, more than a few managers would refrain from an actual compromise and apply instead the political tactic of pretending to compromise. Those managers seemingly retreat from their initial positions on some marginal issues, and even declare their readiness to change their positions and to respond to the demands of their subordinates; but, in fact, they continue to advance with their plans through underhanded pressure and hidden attempts to exert influence on their executives. In the course of deliberations they push for a clearer definition of goals and objectives so that these will serve as a reference for the future measures they are planning to apply.

In any compromise of this sort, managers and those who are in similar positions of authority are careful to maintain their power and their image. Therefore, in seeming to compromise, their behavior is more one of pretense than a real concession on their basic positions. This pattern of behavior is widespread in negotiating processes, in interpersonal confrontations, and in coping with opposition.

Theatrical behavior: One of the tools that assist managers in influencing other people and changing their behavior is to present an appearance that suits the specific situation in which the attempt at influence is made. Managers, like theater actors, put on an external façade to suit the image they wish to project to their colleagues. Such behavior is shown in their facial expression, their tone of voice, their style of dress, and their body language. By such means they try to persuade, to encourage or intimidate, to deter, to bring closer or keep away the targets of their influence. Such effects are obtained through the means of communication and the ways they are transmitted rather than by their content. Therefore, this theatrical type of behavior has more of an emotional effect than an intellectual one, and impresses more by the wrap up of the message and less by its contents. As in the theater, managers present themselves as having a certain character that corresponds with the intentions of the producer and the expectations of the spectator. It is not surprising to hear members of the family and friends of such a manager say: "At home he or she is not like the character known at work; this person behaves like two totally different people." The difference in appearances at work and at home is sharper among senior military and police officers, governmental officials, and people of authority in the corridors of power. This kind of role-playing thus serves executives, managers, commanders, and supervisors for political purposes in the world of organizations.

Self-confidence: Among managers and officers, especially those in senior positions, there are some who maintain an outwardly calm and assured posture, even in times of crisis and emergency. They talk and behave as though they always know where they are heading and what they intend to do, even when this is not actually true, even when they feel somewhat lost. This mode of appearance inspires a sense of knowledge, experience, decisiveness, certainty, consistency, vision, and thoughtfulness. By means of a show of such self-confidence, those who see themselves as leaders encourage others to follow them without fear, trusting to the justness of their cause and convinced of the success of their endeavors. As with theatrical behavior, this kind of behavior is also a kind of pretense, with the aim of demonstrating personal control over people and events. It is a behavior that is based on power, uses power and by the same token enhances it. This style of behavior in public appearances is typical of national leaders: rulers, presidents, prime ministers, and high-ranking commanders. Thus, the pretended display of self-confidence in front of subordinates is likely to serve as an effective means of organizational politics for those in positions of power.

Maintaining distance: Those who have managerial positions try to ingratiate themselves with their subordinates to arouse in them feelings of loyalty towards their superiors and to receive from them the help and support they need to fulfill their jobs. For this purpose, some managers tend to draw closer to those under their authority and to make them feel a sense of closeness and a personal attachment to their superiors, although these are within well-defined parameters. Such managers are careful to maintain a certain social distance from their subordinates. They retain personal relationships with them, but refrain from any emotional commitment towards them. They encourage "conversations down the hall" on matters concerning work, but at the same time avoid intimate companionship or friendship. They do participate in the festive ceremonies or occasions of bereavement among their workers, but do not take part in any of their family events. In short, they try to keep a thin, concealed line of separation, yet clear and unequivocal, between themselves and their subordinates. Even when they declare an open door policy, namely, the invitation to juniors to come in and present their complaints and requests, they allow them to do so only on specific occasions and in certain circumstances; they limit the subject of the conversation; keep a protocol of the conversation; and even invite a third person to be present at such meetings. By means of minor and seemingly unimportant details they maintain their superiority and demonstrate their higher position. This is a double-edged tactic, at the same time bringing closer and keeping at a distance, bridging and separating, opening doors and closing them, participating and not participating. It clearly reflects a political kind of behavior with the aim of transmitting the message: "I am always the boss," and using it as a means of control and as an expression of power.

The common factor for such patterns of behavior among all types of managers, officers, and persons of authority is the outward appearance that characterizes them. In other words, these are patterns of manipulative behavior that outwardly present one intention straightforwardly, but in fact cover some hidden intentions. Such behavior patterns are based on power and are aimed at the advancement of personal interests. In principle, they are within the limits of legitimate managerial authority; in fact, they frequently exceed it, and sometimes deviate from it; therefore, they represent various styles of political behavior performed by managers to influence their subordinates.

Let us consider now somewhat different styles of political behavior that prevail in many organizations most of the time. This kind of managerial politics is frequently employed by managers in order to dominate organizational actors who are not under their direct control.[5]

Creating contrasts: Psychology teaches us that the way things are presented, whether they are concrete or abstract, influences the way people perceive them. For example, the way that prices for various products (houses, cars, electrical appliances) are presented to the buyer has an influence over the subjective evaluation of each product. When the most expensive products are presented at first, the prices of the other products that follow are seen as much cheaper in comparison even when the real differences are not so significant. According to this principle, managers influence discussion and decisions from the very beginning by presenting the subjects on the agenda in the order that they prefer. In fact, anyone who participates in decision-making processes learns in time that the ordering of the items on the agenda determines to a great extent the outcome of the discussions. After a decision is made on a subject that is considered complicated and controversial, the rest of the subjects on the agenda are seen as simple issues and the decisions regarding them are relatively quickly and easily accepted, even if, in fact, they concern matters of importance. Thus, by setting the agenda the chairperson manipulates the other participants to take stands that are in line with his or her order of preference.

Creating commitment: As long as people are required to take certain actions, they assess their options according to similar actions they have taken in the past. People tend to develop a psychological commitment to these actions and to adopt them once and again. By so doing, people attempt to show their coherence, consistency, and perseverance. According to research findings, such qualities are highly valued in organizations.

> These results suggest that as one progress up the organizational hierarchy, one develops a theory of leadership in which consistency and perseverance, particularly in the face of adversity, are valued. Such generalized social expectations about what constitutes effective management help to explain why many organizational leaders strive for consistency.[6]

It should be noted that quite a few managers take advantage of such social expectations of consistency as a managerial contrivance to attain influence and at the same time to win the support of others.

Creating rarity: People would like to believe that they have a free choice among various alternatives. The degree of rarity in any resource influences the value that people attribute to it. The more difficult it is to acquire the resource, so much higher does its subjective value rise, especially if other people are also interested in it. Therefore, managers act to prevent their counter-partners from obtaining resources similar to the ones they possess in the organizations, whether it is information, know-how, or authority. In this way managers deliberately create rarity and thus increase the power of attraction for their resources. This rarity enables them to influence other actors to act against their own free will merely in order to achieve their objectives. By this kind of political conduct managers generate power and gain influence, which strengthens their bargaining position in the organization.

Jeffrey Pfeffer identifies these political measures and others like them by the term "framing procedures."

> Establishing the framework within which issues will be reviewed and decided is often tantamount to determining the result. Thus, setting the context is a critical strategy for exercising power and influence...because decision and action inevitably have multiple components, which can be viewed along multiple dimensions, the ability to set the terms of the discussion is an important mechanism for influencing organizational behavior.... Decisions and activities are not begun anew each day. We need to be aware of history—the history of commitments, of past choices that set the context within which present events are evaluated, and the set of cognitive lenses that affect what we see and how we see it. Being skilled at both recognizing and using these ideas provides great leverage in getting the things that you want accomplished.[7]

Managers, officers, and persons of authority who are unaware of the advantages that lie in such framing procedures may not be fully aware that they can affect the outcomes of decision processes by framing and reframing the agenda; hence, they lack the available administrative tools that might help them to achieve their objectives and advance their interests or those whom they represent in more practical and efficient ways than the usual ones. As stated above, the question of the legitimacy of methods, such as those in the management of organizations, depends on the organizational culture, namely, the values and social norms shared by the various actors that play an active part in the organization.

It is clear that not all the political tactics that managers adopt in their relations with their subordinates can succeed in having the same degree of influence. A study on this subject has produced some interesting findings regarding the use of various influence tactics.[8] On the basis of the research literature, scholars have classified the outcome of influence for three kinds of reactions of subordinates to the demands of their superiors: (a) commitment; (b) obedience; (c) opposition. The first reaction expresses agreement of the subordinate to comply with demands due to his or her feeling of commitment to the organization or to his or her superior. The second reaction expresses the following of orders for lack of choice, so long as there is someone who oversees the implementation of the orders and supervises the behavior of the subordinate. The third reaction reflects the lack of readiness to fulfill the demands of the superior and reluctance to act in line with his or her preferences. The following is a summary of the main findings.

1.   Requests made by the superiors who use value-inspired arguments are liable to cause the commitment of the subordinates rather than obedience or opposition.
2.   Requests to consult with subordinates are likely to raise their commitment rather than their obedience or opposition.
3.   The exertion of intellectual persuasion is expected to create obedience rather than commitment or opposition of subordinates.
4.   Flattery expressed by managers in order to influence their subordinates is liable to create obedience rather than commitment or opposition.
5.   Requests by managers who use a personal tone towards their subordinates are liable to cause obedience rather than commitment or opposition.
6.   Exchange tactics are liable to cause obedience rather than commitment or opposition by subordinates.
7.   Pressure exerted on subordinates to act in accordance with the demands of their superiors is liable to cause opposition rather than obedience or commitment.
8.   Attempts to give legitimacy to the demands of superiors are liable to cause opposition or obedience rather than commitment by subordinates.
9.   The creation of a coalition against certain subordinates is expected to arouse opposition or to cause obedience rather than to create commitment towards superiors or towards the organization as a whole.

Research also shows that the combination of a few soft tactics that act upon the emotions of subordinates and on their sense of self-esteem bring better results than any other tactics. On the other hand, the combination of a few administrative tactics that have a manipulative character bring about less successful results than all other tactics that are used by managers.

In light of the negative image given to behavioral patterns of a political nature in organizations, many managers tend to deny their involvement in political games, to renounce political behavior; and they even blame other managers who try to advance their interests in such ways. But managerial politics may be found everywhere in organizations, since many managers typically utilize such behavior in one way or another to maintain their control over others and to attain their objectives. Nonetheless, it should be noted once again that not all managers and officers adopt these methods of influence towards their subordinates in the organization. However, there are those who tend to behave in this way always and everywhere, because of their true belief that "this is way to behave" for a manager or a commander who wants to succeed in his position. Whatever the reasons might be for managerial politics, it would be a mistake to deny its existence and to overlook its consequences. As Martin and Sims explain:

We live in an era of "groupiness"; we are bombarded with admonitions which insist that everyone who is participating in an enterprise should have a part in the management of it. In the light of such a trend, even the terminology used in this article—"power," "maneuver," "tactics," "techniques"—appears disturbing when set down in black and white. But in fact it is neither immoral nor cynical to recognize and describe the actual daily practices of power. After all, sweeping them under the rug—making believe that they are not actually part of the executive's activity—does not cause them to vanish. Open and honest discussion of political aspects in the administrator's job exposes these stratagems to the constructive spotlight of knowledge. They exist; therefore, we had better take a look at them and see what they are really like.[9]

Managerial Patterns

The political use of resources and the application of political skills such as those described here do not result from the personality of the manager and his personal ambitions alone. Beyond the interpersonal differences between managers, there are also interorganizational differences in their political intensity. These differences originate from the shared perceptions of organization leaders as to how the organization has to negotiate its way vis-à-vis its competitors. Organizational perception of the environment most likely affects the choice of strategies and the application of tactics, political ones among them, for the implementation of the organization strategy. It should also be taken into consideration that objective conditions of the organization environment determine, to one extent or another, the set of options that are feasible to the organization leaders in dealing with various conditions and constraints. In light of severe opposition or tough competition, for example, executives, managers, commanders, and supervisors may be compelled to behave in a political manner—both outside and inside their organization—that is, to exercise power, to manipulate, or to deceive others for their own interests.

Some forty years ago, Amitai Etzioni proposed to classify organizations according to two dimensions: the dimension of power and the dimension of commitment. The first dimension reflects the basis of power of the leaders who administer the organization. This power of the organizational heads and the other managers relies upon one of the following bases: (a) *Coercive power,* which rests on physical force possessed by the leaders (such as military weapons); (b) *Remunerative power*, which is based on control over material resources (such as money or property); and (c) *Normative power*, which rests on the ability to exploit symbols of value, social, religious or ideological ones (such as holy books, statues, or other emblems).

The second dimension expresses the orientation of the subordinates to the exercise of organizational power. Etzioni uses the concept of "involvement" to describe this orientation: "*Involvement* refers to the cathectic-evaluative orientation of an actor to an object; characterized in terms of intensity and direction...we refer to positive involvement as *commitment* and to negative involvement as *alienation*."[10] Accordingly, there are three zones of involvement:

(a) *alienative*, for high alienation; (b) *moral*, for high commitment: and (c) *calculative*, for the two moderate zones.

The combination of these two dimensions creates a typology consisting of nine types of organization. However, this typology states that of all the possible types, only three types of organizations are the most probable in organizational reality. These are the organizations in which there is congruence between the dimension of the leaders' power and the dimension of the participants' involvement. The first type represents *coercive organizations*—organizations in which the leaders use physical power and the lower participants comply for fear of punishment (e.g., prisons). The second type represents *utilitarian organizations*— organizations in which the leaders use remunerative power and the rank and file comply as long as the material rewards (e.g., wages, fringe benefits) are worth it (e.g., business firms). The third type represents *normative organizations*—organizations in which the leaders use normative power in the form of symbols and the members follow them for the attainment "a better world" in the present or the next one (e.g., churches).

Whoever has served as a soldier in any army has learned to recognize personally the rule of power and the prevailing climate of fear. Beginning with the period of initial training, even the junior officers treat the soldiers that have been just drafted harshly, and make them undergo physical stress and mental humiliation. Needless to say, the frequent use of threats, punishments, intimidations and reprisals for any act or failure that is not in accordance with the orders and commands given by the organization and by the officers is most typical of military organizations. They have a built-in culture of violence in which coercive force plays a major disciplinary role.

Generations of soldiers have spent sleepless nights in exhausting marches, in transferring tents and belongings from one place to another, in digging worthless pits and trenches, in unnecessary roll-call exercises and sanitary inspections. Ostensibly, such punishments are meant to toughen up the soldiers, to train them in unquestioned obedience, to prepare them to cope with warfare conditions of hardship. But many officers at all levels of command take advantage of these means of intimidation and punishment to enhance their power and raise their prestige, to advance their military career and receive extra benefits. The legitimate authority and personal power provides military officers with a wide leeway in the "grey zone" to take advantage of those under their command, from obtaining personal services up to sexual exploitation.

Since coercive organizations like the military, the police force, the prison houses, and others like them, deal with various forms of violence and physical force, those organizations operate in the shadow of inherent conflict between the powerful and powerless. The former identify with the organization, while the latter are hostile towards it. The superiors try to rule those under their control, while those subordinate to them or under their protection prefer to escape from such control and from the organization. The leaders are required to exercise their power to enforce discipline, while those under their control are forced to obey in order to avoid punishment.[11]

It is not surprising, therefore, that whenever managers, officers, inspectors or supervisors adopt other methods of control such as explanation, persuasion, consultation, or cooperation, it creates a state of incongruence between them and their subordinates. The latter tend to suspect that their superiors are trying to deceive them, to cause disruption among them, to soften their resolute stand, and to take advantage of their weakness, namely, to adopt a political attitude towards them that is non-coercive. Such managerial behavior seems to deviate from the authoritarian nature of interrelationships that characterize many coercive organizations. For this reason, the ongoing political game in these organizations is essentially a continuous struggle between superordinates and subordinates, in which the players in positions of power (e.g., prisoners) try to impose their will on their powerless opponents (e.g., inmates), by the use of physical force, if necessary.

Utilitarian organizations (for example business firms, banks and financial institutions, marketing and service chains, and various kinds of industrial enterprises) are based on the give-and-take considerations of their participants. In most organizations of this type, the dominating organizational culture is characterized by the pursuit of material benefits. Managers of such organizations try to influence the behavior of those subordinate to them for the good of the organization mainly by means of various economic rewards.

Since the participation of individuals in such organizations is non-compulsory, the use of coercive means and physical penalties is neither acceptable nor widely practiced, at least not in recent decades. Therefore, most of the managers of utilitarian organizations are required to invest significant effort in negotiating suitable payment to their subordinates for their contribution to the organization. It is not surprising, therefore, that any additional effort in work, whether real or pretended, requires a raise in pay. Similarly, any innovation or organizational change constitutes a motive for increased salary and additional benefits. This kind of bargaining is apparently the essence of most labor relations between employers and employees, and the main justification for trade unions.

The managers in these organizations are thus placed in a state of constant confrontation with line workers (e.g., production workers, clerks, service personnel, and salesmen), as well as with professional workers (e.g., technicians, engineers, and school teachers), on issues such as working conditions, wages and salary scales, fringe benefits, promotion systems, and pension plans. The fact is that a significant number of managers in various countries take part in the political game of this kind. In this game the price tags for every action and outcome is determined, and every gain by one actor is a loss by another actor.

Managerial politics focuses on strategies and tactics with the aim of obtaining the best results at the lowest possible cost. In such politics, competition is held not only over material resources but also over authority and autonomy, over rights and duties, and above all—over power and influence in the organization. Both parties to this political game know that the greater the power, the greater the utility.

As we have seen, control methods that are identified as political tactics are essentially manipulative ways of behaving that "reveal a bit and conceal a lot." The behavior of managers is thus often characterized as seemingly naïve, concealing their goals and intentions. In utilitarian organizations, in which the use of force is not legitimate, it is the promise of rewards and the threat of avoiding them that serve as the main means of managerial influence. Since such promises and threats may go beyond the limits of their authority, and to avoid the risk of self-implication, there are managers who make use of various tactics that hide their real intentions. So they might claim: "I promised nothing of the sort," "I never make threats," or "I have not been aware that such acts took place under my area of authority." Ploys are a special way, not necessarily negative, to influence another and make him or her do certain things that they are otherwise unlikely to do. Thus, there are quite a few managers in utilitarian organizations who resort to various ploys against their subordinates so as to advance their self-interests and to achieve their own objectives.

Normative organizations such as churches, religious sects, and underground organizations, various kinds of fraternities, voluntary associations, and political parties are mostly based on some shared beliefs. The leaders of such organizations recruit believers into their ranks and direct them to carry out various tasks for the benefit of the organization, and their own benefit, too, in the name of sacred values and ultimate goals. These values are expressed in sacred scriptures, in legal codes, in mythological stories and legends, in songs and hymns of ideological content, in prayers, and in the doctrinaire history of the founding fathers.

On the face of it, subordinate members in such organizations are prepared to accept the authority of leaders because they identify with the same values and take it upon themselves to obey the norms of behavior that are derived from them. But in fact, most of these rules are difficult to carry out continuously, demanding a considerable amount of self-denial and personal sacrifice, and are filled with prohibitions that contradict the natural human desire to enjoy life. As a result, in the course of time, many believers begin to ask questions, are seized with doubts, neglect their duties, show their grievances against the leaders, and express criticism of the way they govern the organization. Sooner or later many of the faithful dropouts of those organizations become heretical, and in certain cases turn into "apostates for spite."

It is easy to understand why the leaders of normative organizations are not satisfied with transient and limited influence over their subordinate members, as is characteristic of utility organizations; instead, they strive for complete and prolonged control over their flock. For this purpose they make use of symbols that enhance identification with the organization and its leaders such as flags, costumes, badges, titles, ceremonies, processions and rallies, statues, monuments, temples, pilgrimage sites, and various educational institutions.

To prevent the neglect of duties and desertion of the organization, those leaders (e.g., priests, rabbis, ministers, spiritual leaders, opinion leaders, gurus, and the like) do not hesitate to intimidate members of the organization by a cynical use of blessings and curses, amulets and spells, bans and interdictions. They mock the so-called heretics and libel them publicly before other believers. They proclaim against those forces of evil that try, in their view, to repudiate the absolute truth of their beliefs and show hostility towards the existence and well-being of the organizations in their charge.

Managerial politics in such organizations is mainly characterized by the systematic nurturing of feelings of disadvantage—religious, economic, ethnic, social, or political. These and similar feelings of deprivation encourage in turn the desire for revenge, yearnings for change, and dreams about a better and more just world. Therefore, these normative organizations have always succeeded in causing people to retire and close themselves up in isolated monasteries; to leave their homes and communities and to journey to far off and dangerous places to serve as missionaries and apostles; to spend the best years of their lives in underground, secret hiding places; to be recruited as fighters in guerrilla terror units, even to agree to become human bombs in order to carry out attacks that cannot be reversed. It may seem that such modes of behavior are the outcome of free will and voluntary action, but, in fact, the people who behave in this way are totally dependent upon the will of their superiors and therefore have become the playthings of the political struggles of these leaders. In such organizations, even moderate and reasonable subordinates tend to identify with the will of their superiors. The latter exercise this power for their own benefit, and for the benefit of their direct colleagues and assistants, as well as of their relatives. It should be thus recognized that even such moral leaders, who embody the value system of their organizations, have always taken good care of themselves by overt and covert means, and by political maneuverings of various sorts.

To understand the enormous power of managerial politics, one should note the huge gaps that prevail between the senior managers of organizations of all kinds and the ordinary participants. These gaps are expressed in wealth, standards of living, privileges, and benefits that they possess, not to mention power. Such gaps are evident at all periods of time and in every place in human history; hence, they indicate a general phenomenon showing that managerial politics benefits the members at the top of the organization at the expense of members at the bottom.

In spite of the differences in the objectives of various organizations, and despite the upheavals that most organizations undergo in the course of time, it may be a safe assumption that those who manage them will always know how to play the political game so as to derive the outmost utility from their control. In this respect there is no real difference between those who control the organizations by means of physical force or by virtue of material benefits, and the leaders who control by means of ideas and beliefs. All of them derive great personal utility from their bases of power and the various political uses they make of them for their own purposes.

Some recent examples of the enormous wealth accumulated by modern time dictators such as those of the Philippines, Uganda, Rumania, Panama, Iran, and Iraq were revealed to the public when they were demoted from their seats of power. Such rulers conduct an extravagant life style with lavish expenditure far beyond the wildest imagination of their mostly poor citizens.

Managerial Turnover

In general, organizational leaders invest time and energy to remain in their positions, to preserve their power, and to continue their control of the organization that they head. In spite of such efforts, the managers of organizations or organizational subunits are replaced from time to time for various reasons: promotion, transfer, demotion, dismissal, or retirement, or death.

Quite often this phenomenon of managerial changeover is neither natural nor voluntary for those who are the heads of organizations (e.g., CEOs, general managers, presidents, chairpersons), since it is imposed upon them by more powerful forces. Other executives and managers at lower positions (e.g., vice presidents, deputies, division heads, and staff directors) are no less immune from a similar changeover. This group constitutes the *strategic apex*[12] of every organization, and it represents the *dominant coalition*. While the members of this group enjoy the full privileges and benefits that the organization can grant them, they are at the same time exposed to criticism, vulnerable to attacks and manipulations, which make them susceptible to their removal from office and loss of power. Evidently, the head of an organization is the main target of all those challenging his or her leadership. Owing to the power of the organization's head, a great deal of the opponents' efforts to bring about his or her demotion is made under cover by means of political tactics. CEOs and leaders of similar organizations strike back with their own arsenal of political measures.

Given that senior officers are replaced over and over in the course of time, it is interesting to find out what kind of measures accelerate and what measures decelerate the pace of removing them from their offices. The political game that takes place in conjunction with such turnover at the top layer of an organization reflects an important and interesting aspect of managerial politics in organizations.

We can safely suggest that there is a negative connection between the organization's level of performance and the strength of its Chief Executive Officer, at least as far as business firms are concerned. Stakeholders obviously expect to get their return on investment and, therefore, tend to blame the top management for failing to do so. The return on investment, however, is not necessarily measured in financial terms alone, as in the world of business, but it is also indicated in terms of educational and scientific achievements, in health and welfare, in quality of services as well as in electoral gains.

It should be remembered that "assessing organizational effectiveness is complex and reflects the complexity of organizations as a topic of study." [13] Therefore, they are a matter of discord both among researchers and among practitioners. In one way or another, stakeholders (e.g., owners, investors, managers, workers, suppliers, and clients) learn in time to have an idea as how "their" organization is doing as compared to their expectations. But whatever the objective reasons may be for certain outcomes, the success or failure of organizations is attributed first and foremost to the head of the organization.

In most organizations there is a select group of people who represent the owners of the organization and its main stakeholders. According to law, it is the task of this body to keep track of the way the organization is run, to monitor its decisions and operations, and to approve of the allocation of resources that it has accumulated to the various beneficiaries. This body has the authority to appoint or dismiss the highest officer in the organization—the Chief Executive Officer. In the world of business, this group is identified as the Board of Directors, whereas in nonprofit organizations it is defined in terms such as the Executive Committee, the Managing Council, the Chamber, and so forth.

Stakeholders participating in an organization and investing their resources in its operations expect to yield the greatest possible utility from that organization. Therefore, an organization that encounters difficulties, losses, and other problems naturally causes these stakeholders to reconsider their further involvement in that particular organization and to withdraw their investment in it. Thus, disappointments, doubts, and fears expose the management to criticism and complaints, which create a climate of discontent.

Under such conditions, and in line with the principle of accountability, there is a tendency first and foremost to depose the CEO of the organization and to appoint someone else to replace him or her. This is the task that is required of the Board of Directors, or its equivalent. This is a very sensitive stage in which managerial politics significantly intensifies at the top of the organization.

> The choice of a new chief executive or new chief administrator, and the consequences of such a choice, could be examined more generally under the rubric of the politics of careers. However, the choice of the chief administrative officer of an organization has a significant symbolic importance, and may have more consequences for the organization's structure and decision-making. Therefore, it is worthwhile to highlight a few facts. First, the replacement and selection of chief executives is as political, if not more so, than any other promotion or demotion in the organization. Second, the choice of a new chief executive typically puts in motion a series of actions which are designed to solidify and institutionalize that executive's power; these actions also have consequences for the careers of other high level executives. [14]

When the operations of the organization run aground and its continued success is jeopardized, the balance of power between the various subunits is undermined and the relative power of their managers is altered accordingly.

The members of the organization show signs of dissatisfaction and try to influence the decision makers to improve the situation. Moreover, the relative power of the external stakeholders, who are involved in the organization and influence it, is also expected to change. The replacement of the chief administrator of the organization indicates a new balance of power in the decision centers of the organization.

"More generally, the selection and replacement of chief executives represent the interplay of power and politics in use, as these positions are symbols of control and powerful hierarchical positions in their own right".[15] It is worth mentioning that in many cases the replacement of the general manager causes the replacement of other senior managers as well; among them there may be some vice presidents, deputy general managers, senior staff directors, division's managers, and senior professionals.

Although in organizations that perform poorly, the chances that the chief of the organization will be dismissed are greater than in those that operate well, the chiefs who have generated a great amount of power are more immune to being demoted; and all the more so when the organization is functioning well, in spite of all the criticism against the chief by some hostile stakeholders. The power of the chief executive is derived from various sources, among them the personal composition of the members of the Board of Directors.

Most boards of directors are composed of representatives of their organizations (e.g., senior managers) and of representatives of outside stockholders (e.g., stockholders); in some cases there are representatives of the government and also representatives of the public at large. The power of the CEO vis-à-vis the board rests on the internal representatives and the relationships between them and the external representatives. The larger the number of the board members who are subordinates of the chief, the greater will be his or her power over that board. This power is enhanced when he or she is the one who personally appoints some senior managers as board members.

By the same token, the structure of the organization's ownership and its composition of owners determine the power of the chief administrator. Ownership that is spread out among numerous stockholders allows the head of the organization to influence board members to align with his or her preferences, because the power of each member is rather small. On the other hand, directors that represent a small number of major stockholders, such as corporations, can create a *veto bloc* against the chief administrator and prevent him from controlling the board. In private business organizations where the managers own the largest number of shares or have a relatively high percentage of the ownership, they possess organizational power beyond that power accounted for by their managerial positions per se; in fact, they have much greater influence on the Board of Directors as compared to those executives who are not owners at all.

The greater the power of these managers, the greater their ability to thwart any attempts to depose them from their positions and dismiss them from the organization. Managers like these have a better chance to survive, even when the organization is not functioning properly.[16]

> Although no incumbent has absolute power, it is well known that some CEOs are in a better position than others to forestall their removal. They may derive extraordinary influence from a variety of sources: *personal characteristics*, as in the case of a revered founder or charismatic figure; control of critical resources, such as major clients, proprietary technology, or regulatory contacts; external status or prestige; or sheer voting control.[17]

In order to construct a protective wall to guard their positions and ensure for themselves the continued reception of benefits, such senior managers need political wisdom. It should be emphasized once again that the structural basis on which the power of these managers rests—the high seniority of their position, the scope of their authority and their centrality at the pivotal points of information and decision—are necessary conditions, but certainly not sufficient ones to immunize them against removal and dismissal.

It is for these managers, then, to work hard in generating personal power; to have a stable influence on the members of the board; to gain the trust and support of the senior members that are subordinate to them; to maneuver and neutralize their rivals inside and outside the organization. At the same time, they must provide for themselves *golden parachutes*, namely, exceptional benefits at the time of their retirement, whether it is done willingly or unwillingly. This is a lengthy struggle of political survival by those who hold the reins of control, which involve overt and covert confrontations with actors who strive to gain control themselves or to transfer it to those who are close to them.

Obviously, the pressure to step down from office and the drive for change do not cease so long as the situation in the organization is unsatisfactory. Hence, it is for the chief executives of an organization that have managed to retain their positions to prove that they are capable of helping the organization to recover and to make a real improvement in its performance. One of the political tactics that chief executives tend to adopt in such situations is the "beheading" of senior managers subordinate to them. The heads of the organization thus try to appease their opponents by the demotion of some senior managers (e.g., vice presidents, deputy managers, heads of branches, and senior professionals) on the pretext that they are responsible for the organization's malfunction. In light of their seniority and close association with the head of the organization, these senior administrators become, in fact, the scapegoats banished to the organizational desert to atone for the failure.[18]

This tactic is intentional and well calculated in managerial politics, and carefully applied by the heads of organizations; yet it is used resolutely in times of necessity for their protection. Those managers who are destined to be removed from their office can usually calculate the amount of power possessed by their superior, and they know quite well the political balance of power in the ranks of the elite. They therefore tend to resign themselves to their fate and have no choice but to leave their positions without a fight. Some of them conduct secret negotiations to obtain greater compensation or alternatively to be appointed to another position in a more distant place in the organization. Those who dare to protest publicly against being blamed are usually met with scorn and derision by lower level members who expect to be shown that justice will be done in the organization and that someone will pay the price for faulty management.

Those managers who, in spite of their power and regardless of their political maneuverings, do not survive, are forced to step down from their positions against their will and pass them on to successors they have not chosen. One of the political measures often taken by managers who step into a new office is called "cleaning out the stables." This measure means the dismissal of a significant number of those who are to be their subordinates and replacing them with new people they have chosen. In order to avoid disturbances in the organization, this process of change is generally a gradual one, although it is completed within a relatively short time. Consequently, after awhile the organizational apex or the dominant coalition is filled with new faces that owe their positions to the new head. Politicians who get elected as presidents, prime ministers, mayors, general secretaries or chairpersons are probably the first ones to "change horses" in this way. Similar processes of replacing senior officers can be seen in businesses and other kinds of organizations as well.

As in every political course of action, even this systematic replacement is guided by the personal interests of the new manager. The persons destined to be transferred from their positions are those who are liable to endanger the position of the present chief and to lessen his or her power, namely, those who are declared loyalists of the previous manager; those long-term senior members of the organization who claim the right to take the place of the manager; those who do not spare words in criticizing the organizational elite; and those who are well established in the social network of the organization. In short, whoever could be a threat or become an obstacle to the new chief is fated a priori to be deposed.

In this way, every head of an organization builds around himself a court of his loyalists who man the positions nearest to his: deputies, associates, assistants, advisers, speakers, secretaries, and the like. In public administration these positions are defined as positions of trust that are generally filled by those close to government ministers. The popular term for defining people in these positions is "political appointees." A similar phenomenon prevails in one way or another in the business sector as well, in which new CEOs surround themselves with their associates, some of whom are brought in from outside the organization. From time to time, the media reports on agitation within organizations that arises from the opposition of the employees, mainly from the senior ones, against the induction of such key personnel over their heads. In sum, turnover of senior administrators in organizations is mostly an outcome of managerial politics that takes place at the top of the organization. This is a power-based political game played in the highest league for the purpose of gaining greater power with all the benefits that come with it.

Conclusion

The management hierarchy with all its ranks constitutes the skeletal structure that bears the weight of the organization and drives it towards various objectives. The managers at every level are active in carrying out the tasks of the units they are charged with, and advance the goals and objectives set by their superiors. At the same time, these managers, both senior and junior, do whatever they can to retain their positions, to get promoted in rank and function, and, above all, to receive all material and symbolic benefits in exchange for their managerial responsibilities.

To this end numerous managers accumulate personal power and exercise it more or less often, mainly against their subordinates, by means of various political tactics. In this way they take a personal and active part, some more, some less, in the managerial politics that goes on in every organization. These tactics represent attempts to influence others' behavior in ways that exceed the manager's authority, and are based on a certain degree of pretense, intimidation, deceit, and mental and emotional pressure exerted upon the other person.

Several typical tactics that are applied against subordinates as well as against colleagues and superiors were discussed in this chapter on managerial politics. Among those political tactics that managers tend to use are the tactic of simulated consultation, selective communication, delaying of implementation, and so forth. Also discussed here were the ways in which managers intentionally create a sense of rarity, of commitment, of consistency, and the like, to influence junior participants in the organization.

Managerial politics thus creates, among those who are subordinate to managers, various responses that are expressed in the form of identification and compliance; it may also raise feelings of resistance and disobedience to their superiors. As may be expected, not every tactic is effective in influencing to the same degree, and not every tactic is applicable in different organizational, social, and cultural conditions.

Organizations differ one from the other in their managerial structure. Broadly, these structures contain coercive management patterns based on the frequent use of threats and physical penalties to subordinates; remunerative management patterns based on the frequent use of enticements and material incentives to participants in the organization; and normative management patterns based on the frequent use of symbols of identification in order to strengthen the belief of subordinates in the goals of the organization and to persuade them to obey the will of its leaders.

Managerial politics in each of these types of organizations is thus characterized by different methods and tools, and so the outcome is correspondingly different. Within such management regimes, different managers choose for themselves the methods of influence that suits their character, status, and function in those organizations. Whatever the case may be, these political games played in organizational reality bear considerable profits and benefits for those who control the organization at the expense of the rank and file participants.

At all times there are some contenders, inside and outside an organization, which conduct political maneuverings to replace the incumbents of senior positions at the top of the organization. In those struggles, efforts are made to depose the heads of organizations from their posts by means of various allegations and pretexts in order to replace them with others. Research has shown that organizations in distress because of poor performance are tempting prey for those who want to drive the chief executives or administrators out of their offices.

Therefore, different kinds of chiefs and senior managers become involved in struggles for survival that are meant to guard their positions and prevent their removal. These political measures include, among others, the creation of dependence upon them and loyalty to them; the gathering of supporting blocs in voting processes related to the appointment and removal of managers in office; careful selection and appointment of board members; and the generation of power and prestige outside the organization.

Chief executives, who succeed in winning such political games and retaining their positions, tend to appease the minds of their rivals and public opinion by transferring senior managers of the second highest level from their positions. By so doing, they seemingly display an intention to change the management of the organization and lead it to recovery. Those unable to survive are forced to vacate their seats to new managers who swiftly clear out the stables, that is, they create an alternative to the senior managers who are identified with the old regime and endanger the new one, and they appoint fresh staff members who are closely associated with them. At the same time, they surround themselves with a court of loyalists who man a large group of key positions, and who protect the new chief and his deputies from the intrusion of so-called hostile elements. All those activities as well as other ones represent managerial politics at the top level of organizations.

Notes

1. Martin & Sims, 1971: 155.
2. Daft, 2001.
3. Shenhav, 1999.
4. Martin & Sims, 1971.
5. Cialdini, 1988; Pfeffer, 1992.
6. Pfeffer, 1992: 193-194.
7. Pfeffer, 1992: 203-206.
8. Falbe & Yukl, 1992.
9. Martin & Sims, 1971: 159-160.

10.   Etzioni, 1975:8-9.
11.   It is worth qualifying this by stressing that the coercive approach in an authoritative-subordinate relationship is mainly characteristic of relations between superiors who participate in coercive organizations by their own free will as officers, supervisors, or caretakers (such as permanent army officers or prison guards, psychiatrists, and the like), and between people who have been brought into these organizations against their will, for various periods of time, and who remain there unwillingly (regular soldiers, detainees and prisoners, the mentally ill, captives, etc.).
12.   Mintzberg, 1979.
13.   Daft, 2001: 74.
14.   Pfeffer, 1981: 254.
15.   Ibid.
16.   Boeker, 1992; Drazin & Hayagreeva, 1999.
17.   Fredrickson 1992: 258.
18.   Boeker, 1992.

Conclusion

The perception of organizations as arenas of power struggles and political contests allows scholars and students in this area to study the nature of organizations with the help of analytic tools that differ from the usual ones. This viewpoint sheds a different light on organizational structures and processes from that which is conventional nowadays. While today's scholars and practitioners recognize the presence of politics in organizations, they realize that it still remains a somewhat marginal issue in organization science or management.

The view of organizations as political arenas does not require the attribution of some primary mission or ultimate goals to organizations; in fact, the controversial issue of whether organizations have ultimate goals is irrelevant from this theoretical point of view. Moreover, it does not require attributing to organizational actors the kind of compliant behavior that fits in only with the rules and procedures of the organizations.

Political theory is embedded in the open systems conception of organizations. According to this approach, every organization constitutes an open social system that provides the needs of the environment and at the same time derives its own needs from the environment. This mutual exchange of resources for products enables organizations to survive for a long time. As seen from the political perspective, organizations as open systems are activated by the drive of objectives, desires, motives, and impulses of human beings (as individuals and as groups), not by some ultimate mission. They aspire to gain the most and best benefits that the organization can grant them, such as income and property, social services, power and influence, social status and prestige; and they continue to pursue such benefits as long as the survival of the organization is not jeopardized by their excessive drawing on its resources.

The theory of political shadows, first presented in this book, is an attempt to combine arguments of rational theory with those of political theory. The present theory argues that organizational behavior may be seen either as a concrete object or as a virtual shadow. Following this metaphor, the term *object* refers to any activity or mode of behavior taken by one or more actors to maintain the organization, to enhance its strength, to advance its strategies, or to ensure its survival. Such activities represent one kind of behavior, which frequently takes place in all organizations; it may be identified as organization-serving behavior. This behavior reflects the conformism aspect, which complies with rules

215

and prescriptions of the organization. On the other hand, the term *shadow* refers to any activity taken by one or more actors to gain greater and better benefits than the ones that the organization entitles them to receive, even at the expense of the organization as a whole or of some of its parts. These shadows thus reflect activities that are intended to advance particular interests of individuals and groups, to obtain extra benefits and to generate greater personal or group power. They represent another mode of behavior in organizations, namely, the aspect of opportunism, which may therefore be identified as self-serving behavior.

One may argue, then, that it is possible to find some political shadows behind many prescribed organizational activities. Sometimes these shadows are clear and prominent and sometimes they are blurred and evanescent. There are cases in which the political shadow is larger than the shape that casts it and cases when it is smaller. As a general rule, organizational behavior necessarily contains selfless intentions as well as selfish motives of the actors involved with it.

Organizational politics is neither marginal nor rare; on the contrary, it occupies a significant portion of total organizational activity in all its forms. A considerable proportion of those taking an active part in the various organizations participate in the organizational politics that take place in them to a greater or lesser degree. The political shadows can be found in organizations everywhere and at all times. Moreover, politics is neither a random nor a spontaneous element in organizational life. On the contrary, politics is actually a continuous, systematic, intentional activity performed by individuals, by groups, and by entire organizations.

The political shadows have clear patterns of behavior that may be identified, and their features can be delineated. The means chosen here to describe these patterns and to examine these characteristics is that of analogy with the world of sports. In this way, organizational politics has been juxtaposed with a variety of games of a political nature, comparable to games of sport.

Like these games of sport, political games are also conducted in a specific arena, at specific times, and by competing players. These players apply various strategies and tactics and behave according to known and accepted rules of the game with the aim of winning and gaining the spoils of victory. As in sports arenas, so in organizational arenas, various types of games can be conducted at one and the same time.

Since political activities in organizations are not usually viewed with favor, and quite often are even repelling and arouse criticism, it is no wonder that many actors tend to rationalize their selfish motives and to justify their political maneuvers. These explanations are meant to convince other members of the organization that their intentions are merely to fulfill loyally their organizational duties, to seek the attainment of the organization objectives, and to contribute to its success.

It is well understood that many actors do try to advance the interests of the organization and to support it loyally and in good faith. Yet, most of them are stakeholders in the organization and, therefore, strive to advance their own standing and improve the return on their investment in the organization, whether their investment is made in terms of money, time, skill, or effort. Therefore, they are not likely to resist adopting measures of a political nature to serve their own interests.

The main tool of the game used by most players in the organizational arena is power—physical, economic, or social power—through which they force their rivals to yield, compromise, pay the required price, or leave the playground. Every competitor who takes an active part in this game tries to influence the other competitor and alter his behavior in the desired direction. And so the weaker ones are those who yield, obey, or renounce in advance, while the stronger take over the positions of control and influence in the organization. In every organization, therefore, there are those who lead and those who follow, those who command and those who comply. As can be expected, the organizational spoils are divided among them respectively, that is, the most benefits go to the stronger minority, while the lesser benefits go to the weaker majority.

In order to increase their power and to balance their relative strengths, the weaker actors tend to group together and create coalitions of various kinds against the power-holders in organizations. The more power the weaker ones accumulate—through joint force and by political activity—increases the tendency among the stronger ones to form a partnership and to forge alliances of their own. Under such conditions, the political game rises to a higher level and develops into an intergroup contest or a wider interorganizational one, in which many and stronger players compete for much higher stakes.

The strength and weakness of social actors of various types (individuals, groups, and organizations) are a direct outcome, on the one hand, of the different resources that are at their disposal and, on the other hand, of their dependence on obtaining resources that are not at their disposal. Therefore, organizational actors do all they can to increase their reservoir of resources, which others are also interested in obtaining. In this way, they enhance their power vis-à-vis other actors and lessen their dependence upon them.

The political game that is conducted in organizations is thus based on the mutual exchange of valuable resources of which every actor tries to receive the most possible and to give the least possible in exchange. Since this does not concern simple economic trading but complex and abstract social exchanges, organizational actors are accustomed to exert their power and use a variety of political plots to influence the judgment of the other person and the way he behaves. Such attempts at influence in organizations are directed at those who are in charge of allocating organizational resources and the ways they are to be used. Therefore, political efforts are generally focused on the decision centers of every organization, and especially on those persons who are at its topmost level.

From the scientific point of view, political behavior in organizations should not be judged as either positive or negative in itself, since in this respect it does not differ from any other activity conducted in organizations. Politics is a fact of life and is unavoidable in organizational reality. The tendency of practitioners (e.g., managers, suppliers, consultants, and the like) is to deny the prevalence of politics in their organization or, at least, to decry its importance. This tendency is presumably due to the notoriety common people attach to politics in organizations.

Apparently, people prefer to believe that the organization in which they play an active part, and certainly the organization they depend on for their livelihood, is an effective and efficient organization, fair dealing and moral; and as such it is necessarily an organization that is politics free. However, there is no organization that is free of any politics. Human greed, temptation, and the need for power infuse politics into all organizations, to a greater or a lesser extent.

From the viewpoint of lower-level participants in organizations, political activities bring about some negative outcomes such as coercion by physical force; acts of favoritism; manipulation and deception; mental and sexual harassment; deprivation of various rights; imposition of idiosyncratic preferences; and corruption of morals. However, it also has quite a number of positive aspects from the viewpoint of those actors in organizations—aspects that cannot be ignored.

First, organizational politics introduces greater flexibility into rigid official rules and strict procedures that weigh heavily on organizational activity; hence, politics contributes to the improvement of organizational efficiency. Second, organizational politics places the organization's authorities under pressure to change discriminating practices between employees and other participants in the organization on sectarian grounds such as sex, age, racial origin, religion, and the like. Third, organizational politics allow line workers without authority and far away from the decision centers to fight for the improvement of their pay and their working conditions. Fourth, organizational politics allows external stakeholders to exert their influence on organizations to lessen environmental pollution; to complain about internal corruption; to struggle against the distribution of faulty or dangerous products; and to protest against the exploitation of new immigrants, foreign workers, women and children.

A necessary condition for understanding organizational politics is the recognition of its existence, as well as the proper assessment of the role it plays in organizational life. The recognition of politics as a fact of life does not require an individual to be a supporter of the political phenomenon in organizations, nor even to participate in the political game in person. However, it is worthwhile for practical people involved in all kinds of organizations, and especially those who have senior positions in them, to learn to interpret the cues of the political game that abound in the organizations in which they are interested. They should know how to identify the stakeholders within these organizations and outside them, as well as the various interests that motivate them. They have to locate the players participating in the political game, both those participating in a direct way, and those participating indirectly through their agents and those who do their bidding. The correct reading of the "political map" also includes the identification of the coalitions and oppositions in these organizations, and tracing the changes that occur in the power balance between them over the course of time. Finally, there is a need to locate the various types of political games that are conducted in different places or at different times in those organizations.

This method of analysis of the organizational dynamics is not applicable only for organizational theoreticians and researchers; it is no less useful for many practitioners, who are interested in a correct diagnosis of the organizational affairs in which they take part. After all, these practical people are part of organizational reality, and contribute to the many changes that frequently occur in it.

In sum, an unbiased approach to organizational politics, to its causes, processes, and consequences, is most likely to lead both scholars and practitioners to a much more realistic perception than many of them might otherwise possess and correct interpretation of the activities constantly taking place in organizations.

References

Acker, J. 1990. "Hierarchies, hobs, bodies: A theory of gendered organizations." *Gender and Society*, 4, 139-158.

Alker, H. 1973. "On political capabilities in schedule sense: Measuring power, integration, development," pp. 307-373, in H. R. Alker, K. W. Deutch, and A. H. Stoezel (eds.), *Mathematical Approaches to Politics*. Amsterdam: Elsevier Scientific Publishing.

Astley, W. G., and P. S. Sachdeva. 1984. "Structural resources of intraorganizational Power: A theoretical synthesis." *Academy of Management Review*, 9, 104-113.

Allen, M. P., D. L. Madison, L. W. Porter, P. A. Renwick, and B. T. Meyes. 1979. "Organizational politics: Tactics characteristics of its actors." *California Management Review*, 22, 77-83.

Allison, J. T. 1971. *Essence of Decision*. Boston: Little, Brown.

Alvesson, M. 1996. *Communication, Power and Organization*. Berlin: Walter de Guyter.

Arendt, H. 1970. *On Violence*. New York: Harcourt, Brace & World.

Axelrod, R. M. 1970. *Conflict of Interest: A Theory of Divergent Goals*. Chicago: Markham.

Bachrach, P., and M. S. Baratz. 1962. "The two faces of power." *American Political Science Review*, 56, 947-952.

Bachrach, P., and M. S. Baratz. 1970. *Power and Poverty*. London: Oxford University Press.

Bacharach, S. B., and E. J. Lawler. 1980. *Power and Politics in Organizations*. San Francisco: Jossey-Bass.

Bacharach, S. B., and E. J. Lawler (eds.). 2000. *Organizational Politics: Research in the Sociology of Organizations,* vol. 17. Stamford, CT: JAI Press.

Barley, S. R. 1991. "Contextualizing conflict: Notes on the anthropology of disputes negotiation," pp. 165-202, in M. H. Bazerman, R. J. Lewicky, and B. H. Sheppard (eds.), *Research on Negotiation in organizations*. vol. 3. Greenwich, CT: JAI Press.

Barley, S. R. 1988. "Technology, power, the social organization of work: Towards a pragmatic theory of skilling deskilling." *Research in the Sociology of Organizations*, 6, 33-80.

Bates, F. L. 1970. "The political-economy approach in retrospective," pp. 262-269, in M. N. Zald (ed.), *Power in Organizations*. Nashville: Vanderbilt University Press.

Benson, J. K. 1975. "The interorganizational network as a political economy." *Administrative Science Quarterly*, 20, 229-249.

Berger, J., and M. Zelditch, Jr. 1998. *Status, Power, and Legitimacy*. New Brunswick, NJ: Transaction Publishers.

Biddle, B. J., and E. J. Thomas. 1966. *Role Theory: Concepts Research*. New York: Wiley.

Bierstedt, R., 1950. "An analysis of social power." *American Sociological Review*, 15, 730-738.

Bierstedt, R. 1974. *Power Progress: Essays on Sociological Theory*. New York: McGraw-Hill.

Blalock, H. M., Jr. 1989. *Power Conflict: Toward a General Theory*. Newbury Park: Sage.

Blau, P. M. 1964. *Exchange Power in Social Life*. New York: Wiley.

Boeker, W. 1992. "Power managerial dismissal: Scapegoating at the top." *Administrative Science Quarterly*, 37, 400-421.

Boulding, K. 1989. *Three Faces of Power*. Newbury Park, CA: Sage.

Brass, D. J. 1984. "Being on the right place: A structural analysis of individual influence in an organization." *Administrative Science Quarterly*, 29, 518-539.

Brass, D. J., and M. E. Burkhardt. 1993. "Potential power in use: An Investigation of structure behavior." *Academy of Management Journal*, 36, 441-470.

Bura, A. 1986. *Social Foundations of Thought Action: A Social Cognitive Theory*. Englewood Cliffs, NJ: Prentice Hall.

Burawoy, M. 1985. *The Politics of Production*. New York: Verso.

Burt, R. S. 1980. "Cooptive corporate actor networks: A reconsideration of the interlocking directorates involving American manufacturing." *Administrative Science Quarterly*, 25, 557-582.

Burns, T. 1961. "Micropolitics: Mechanisms of institutional change." *Administrative Science Quarterly*, 6, 257-281.

Cialdini, R. B. 1988. *Influence: Science Practice*, 2nd ed. Glenview, IL: Scott, Foresman.

Clegg, S. R. 1975. *Power, Rules and Domination*. Boston: Routledge and Kegan Paul.

Clegg, S. R. 1979. *The Theory of Power and Organization*. London: Routledge and Kegan Paul.

Clegg, S. R. 1989. *Frameworks of Power*. London: Sage.

Clegg, S. R., C. Hardy, and W. R. Nord (eds.). 1996. *Handbook of Organization Studies*. London: Sage.

Cobb, A. T. 1984. "An episodic model of power: Toward an integration of theory research." *Academy of Management Review*, 9, 482-493.

Cohen, I. and R. Lachman. 1988. "The generality of the strategic contingencies approach to sub-unit power." *Organization Studies*, 9, 371-391.

Coleman, J. S. 1973. "Loss of power." *American Sociological Review*, 38, 1-17.

Cook, K. S. 1977. "Exchange and power in networks of interorganizational relations." *Sociological Quarterly*, 18, 62-82.

Cook, K. S., and R. Emerson. 1978. "Power, equity, and commitment in exchange networks." *American Sociological Review*, 43, 712-739.

Coser, L. A. 1976. "The notion of power: Theoretical Developments," pp. 150-161, in L. A. Coser and B. Rosenberg (eds.), *Sociological Theory: A Book of Readings*, 4th ed. New York: Macmillan.

Cropanzano, R., J. C. Howes, A. A. Grey, and P. Toth. 1997. "The relationship of organizational politics support to work behaviors, attitudes, stress." *Journal of Organizational Behavior*, 18, 159-180.

Crozier, M. 1964. *The Bureaucratic Phenomenon*. Chicago: University of Chicago Press.

Cyret, R. M., and J. G. March. 1963. *A Behavioral Theory of the Firm*. Englewood Cliffs, NJ: Prentice-Hall.

Czarniawaska-Joerges, B. 1992. *Exploring Complex Organizations: A Cultural Perspective*. Newbury Park, CA: Sage.

Daft, R. L. 2001. *Organization Theory and Design*, 7th ed. Cincinnati, OH: South-Western College Press.

Daft, R. L. 2004. *Organizations: Theory and Design*. 8th edition. Mason, OH: Thompson.

Dagan-Nissim, D. 1997. "Professional and political considerations in rendering in-house service." Master's thesis, The Technion—Israel Institute of Technology, Haifa (Hebrew).

Dahl, R. 1957. "The concept of power." *Behavioral Science*, 2, 201-215.

Dalton, M. 1959. *Men Who Manage*. New York: Wiley.

Drazin, R., and R. Hayagreeva. 1999. "Managerial power succession: SBU managers of mutual funds." *Organization Studies*, 20, 167-196.

Drory, A., and T. Romm. 1988. "Politics in organization its prevention within the organization." *Organization Studies, 9, 165-179.*

Drory, A., and T. Romm. 1990. "The definition of organizational politics." *Human Relations*, 11, 1133-1154.

Edelman, M. 1964. *The Symbolic Uses of Politics*. Urbana, IL: University of Illinois Press.

Eisenhardt, K. M., and L. J. Bourgeois III. 1988. "Politics of strategic decision making in high-velocity environments: Toward a midrange theory." *Academy of Management Journal*, 31, 737-770.

Emerson, R. M. 1962. "Power-dependence relations." *American Sociological Review*, 27, 31-41.

Emerson, R. M. 1972. "Exchange theory," Part I, Part II," pp. 38-88, in J. Berger, M. Zelditch and B. Anderson (eds.), *Sociological Theories in Progress*, vol. 2. Boston: Houghton Mifflin.

Enz, C. A. 1988. "The role of value congruency in intraorganizational power." *Administrative Science Quarterly*, 33, 284-304.

Etzioni, A. 1975. *A Comparative Analysis of Complex Organizations*. 2nd ed. New York: The Free Press.

Etzioni, A. 1988. *The Moral Dimension: Towards a New Economics*. New York: Plenum Press.

Falbe, C. M., and G. Yukl. 1992. "Consequences for managers of using single influence tactics combinations of tactics." *Academy of Management Journal*, 35, 638-652.

Ferris, G. R., D. B. Fedor, J. C. Chachere, and L. R. Pondy. 1989. "Myths politics in organizational context." *Group Organization Studies*, 14, 83-103.

Ferris, G. R., and K. M. Kacmar. 1992. "Perceptions of organizational politics." *Journal of Management*, 18, 93-116.

Ferris, G. R., D. D. Frink, M. C. Galang, J. Zhou, and J. L. Howard. 1996. "Perceptions of organizational politics: Prediction, stress-related implications, outcomes." *Human Relations*, 49, 233-266.

Finkelstein, S. 1992. "Power in top management teams: dimension, measurement, validation." *Academy of Management Journal*, 35, 505-538.

Fligstein, N. 1987. "The intraorganizational power struggle: The rise of finance presidents in large corporations, 1919-1979." *American Sociological Review*, 52, 44-58.

Foucault, M. 1984. *A History of Sexuality*. London: Peregrine.

Foucault, M. 1986. "Disciplinary power and subjugation," pp. 229-242, in S. Lukes (ed.), *Power*. Oxford, UK: Basil Blackwell.

Fredrickson, J. W. 1992. "A model of CEO dismissal." *Academy of Management Review*, 13, 255-270.

French, J. R. P., Jr. and B. Raven. 1960. "The bases of social power," pp. 607-623, in D. Cartwright and A. Zender (eds.), *Group Dynamics*, 2nd ed. New York: Harper and Row.

Gabriel, Y., Fineman, S. and D. Sims. 2000. *Organizing and Organizations*, 2nd ed. London: Sage.

Galbraith, J. K. 1983. *The Anatomy of Power.* Boston: Houghton Mifflin.

Gamson, W. 1968. *Power Discontent*. Homewood, IL: Dorsey.

Gandz, J., and V. V. Murray. 1980. The Experience of Workplace Politics. *Academy of Management Journal*, 23, 237-251.

Gargiulo, M. 1993. "Two-step leverage: Managing constraint in organizational politics." *Administrative Science Quarterly*, 38, 1-19.

Gergen, K. J. 1999. *An Invitation to Social Construction*. London: Sage.

Gils, M. R. 1984. "Interorganizational relations networks," pp. 1073-1100, in P. J. D. Drenth and B. Groenendijk (eds.), *Handbook of Work Organizational Psychology*, vol. 2. New York: Wiley.

Goldhamer, H., and E. A. Shils. 1939. "Types of power status." *American Journal of Sociology*, 45, 171-182.

Goldman, A. I. 1972. "Towards a theory of social power." *Philosophical Studies*, 23, 221-268.

Goldner, F. H. 1970. "The division of labor: Process of power," pp. 97-143, in M. N. Zald (ed.), *Power in Organizations*. Nashville: Vanderbilt University Press.

Gouldner, A. W. 1954. *Patterns of Industrial Bureaucracy*. New York: Free Press.

Granovetter, M. 1985. "Economic action social structure: The problem of embeddedness." *American Journal of Sociology*, 91, 481-510.

Gulati, R., and M. Gargiulo. 1999. "Where do interorganizational networks come from?" *American Journal of Sociology*, 104, 1439-1493.

Habermas, J. 1984. *The theory of Communicative Action. Vol. 1*. Boston: Beacon Press.

Hackman, J. D. 1985. "Power centrality in the allocation of resources in colleges universities." *Administrative Science Quarterly*, 30, 61-70.

Hambrick, D. C. 1981. "Environment, strategy power within top management." *Administrative Science Quarterly*, 26, 253-276.

Hardy, C. 1989. *Strategies for Retrenchment Turnaround: The Politics of Survival*. New York: deGruyter.

Hardy, C., and S. R. Clegg. 1996. "Some dare to call it power," pp. 622-641, in S. R. Clegg, C. Hardy, and W. R. Nord (eds.). 1996. *Handbook of Organization Studie*. London: Sage.

Hardy, C., and N. Phillips. 1998. "Strategies of engagement: Lessons from the critical examination of collaboration conflict in interorganizational domain." *Organization Science*, 9, 217-230.

Harpaz, I., and I. Meshoulam. 1997. "Intraorganizational power in high technology organizations." *Journal of High Technology Management Research*, 8, 107-128.

Harsanyi, J. C. 1962. "Measurement of social power, opportunity costs, and the theory of two-person bargaining game." *Behavioral Science*, 7, 67-80.

Harvey, E., and R. Mills. 1970. "Patterns of organizational adaptation: A political perspective," pp. 181-213, in M. N. Zald (ed.), *Power in Organizations*. Nashville: Vanderbilt University Press.

Haunschild, P. A., and C. M. Beckman. 1998. "When do interlocks matter? Alternate sources information interlock influence." *Administrative Science Quarterly*, 43, 815-844.

Henderson, A. H. 1981. *Social Power*. New York: Praeger.

Hickson, D. J., C. R. Hinings, C. A. Lee, R. E. Shneck, and J. M. Pennings. 1971. "A strategic contingencies theory of intraorganizational power." *Administrative Science Quarterly*, 16, 216-229.

Hickson, D. J., J. W. Astley, R. J. Butler, and D. C. Wilson. 1981. "Organization as power," pp. 151-196, in L. L. Cummings, B. M. Staw (eds.), *Research in Organizational Behavior, 3*. Greenwich, CT: JAI Press.

Hinings, C. R., D. J. Hickson, J. M. Pennings, and R. E. Shneck. 1974. "Structural conditions of intra-organizational power." *Administrative Science Quarterly*, 19, 22-44.

Hinkins, T. R., and C. A. Schriesheim. 1990. "Relationships between subordinate perceptions of supervisor influence tactics attributed bases of supervisory power." *Human Relations*, 43, 221-237.

Homans, G. C. 1974. *Social Behavior: Its Elementary Forms*. New York: Harcourt Brace Jovanovich.

Ibarra, H., and S. B. Andrews. 1993. "Power, social influence, sense-making: Effects of network centrality proximity on employee perceptions." *Administrative Science Quarterly*, 38, 277-303.

Kahn, R. L., D. M. Wolf, R. P. Quinn, J. D. Snoek, and R. A. Rosenthal. 1964. *Organizational Stress: Studies in Role Conflict Ambiguity*. New York: Wiley.

Kanter, R. M. 1977. *Work and Family in the United States: A Critical Review and Agenda for Research and Policy*. New York: Russell Sage.

Katz, D., and R. L. Kahn. 1978. *The Social Psychology of Organizations*, 2nd ed. New York: Wiley.

Kipnis, D., S. M. Schmidt, and I. Wilkinson. 1980. Intraorganizational influence tactics: Explorations in getting one's way." *Journal of Applied Psychology*, 65, 440-452.

Kipnis, D., and S. M. Schmidt. 1983. "An influence perspective on bargaining within organizations," pp. 302-319, in M. H. Bazerman, R. J. Lewicki (eds.), *Negotiating in Organizations*. London: Sage.

Kipnis, D., and S. M. Schmidt. 1988. "Upward influence style: Relationship with performance, salary, and stress." *Administrative Science Quarterly*, 33, 528-542.

Kotter, J. P. 1979. "Managing external dependence." *Academy of Management Review*, 4, 87-102.

Kramer, R. M. 2000. "Political paranoia in organizations: Antecedents and consequences," pp. 47-88, in S. B. Bacharach and E. J. Lawler (eds.), *Organizational Politics*. Stamford, CT: JAI Press.

Kramer, R. M., and M. A. Neale (eds.). 1998. *Power and Influence in Organizations*. Thousand Oaks, CA: Sage.

Krochmal, Z. 2000. *Brazen-faced Military Police: Personal Stories of Military Investigator*. Tel Aviv: Yedioth Ahronoth.

Kumar, P., and R. Ghadially. 1989. "Organizational politics its effects on members of organizations." *Human Relations*, 42, 305-314.

Lasswell, H. 1958. *Politics: Who Gets What, When, How*. New York: Meridian.

Lasswell, H., and A. Kaplan. 1950. *Power Society*. New Haven, CT: Yale University Press.

Laumann, Edward O., and D. Knoke. 1987. *The Organization State: Social Choice in National Policy Domains*. Madison: The University of Wisconsin Press.

Lawler, E. J., and S. B. Bacharach. 1979. "Power-dependence in individual bargaining: The unexpected utility of influence." *Industrial Labor Relations Review*, 32, 196-204.

Lukes, S. 1974. *Power: A Radical View*. London: Macmillan.

Lukes, S. (ed.). 1986. *Power*. Oxford, UK: Basil Blackwell.

March, G. J. 1955. "An introduction to the theory of measurement of influence." *American Political Science Review*, 49, 431-451.

March, J. G. 1962. "The business firm as a political coalition." *Journal of Politics*, 24, 662-678.

March, J. G. 1966. "The power of power," pp. 39-70, in D. Easton (ed.), *Varieties of Political Theory*. Englewood Cliffs, NJ: Prentice-Hall.

March, J. G., and J. P. Olsen. 1989. *Rediscovering Institutions: The Organizational Basis of Politics*. New York: Free Press.

March, J. G., and H. A. Simon. 1958. *Organizations*. New York: Wiley.

Martin, R. 1977. *The Sociology of Power*. London: Routledge and Kegan Paul.

Martin, N. H., and J. H. Sims. 1971. "Power tactics," pp. 155-161, in D. A. Kolb, I. M. Rubin, and J. M. McIntyre (eds.), *Organizational Psychology: A Book of Readings*. Englewood Cliffs, NJ: Prentice-Hall.

Mayes, B. T., and R. W. Allen. 1977. "Toward a definition of organizational politics." *Academy of Management Review*, 2, 672-678.

Mills, C. W. 1956. *The Power Elite.* New York: Oxford University Press.

Mintzberg, H. 1979. *The Structuring of Organizations.* Englewood Cliffs, NJ: Prentice-Hall.

Mintzberg, H. 1983. *Power in and Around Organizations.* Englewood Cliffs, NJ: Prentice-Hall.

Mintzberg, H. 1984. "Power organizational life cycle." *Academy of Management Review,* 9, 207-224.

Mintzberg, H. 1985. "The organization as a political arena." *Journal of Management Studies,* 22, 133-154.

Mitchell, T. R., and H. Hopper. 1998. "Power, accountability, and inappropriate actions." *Applied Psychology,* 47, 497-517.

Mizruchi, M. S., and L. B. Stearns. 1988. "A longitudinal study of the formation of interlocking directorates." *Administrative Science Quarterly,* 33, 194-210.

Molm, L. D. 1990. "Structure, action, outcomes: The dynamics of power in social exchange." *American Sociological Review,* 55, 427-447.

Molm, L. D. 1997. *Coercive Power and Social Exchange.* Cambridge: Cambridge University Press.

Morgan, G. 1986. *Images of Organization.* Beverly Hills, CA: Sage.

Nicolson, P. 1996. *Gender, Power and Organization.* London: Routledge.

Nohria, N., and R. Eccles. 1992. "Face to face: Making network organization work," pp. 288-308, in N. Nohria and R. Eccles (eds.), *Network Organizations: Structure, Form, Action.* Boston: Harvard University Press.

Oliver, C. 1990. "Determinants of interorganizational relationships: Integration and future directions." *Academy of Management Review,* 15, 241-265.

Parker, C. P., R. L. Dipboye, and S. L. Jackson. 1995. "Perceptions of organizational politics: An investigation of antecedents consequences." *Journal of Management,* 21, 891-912.

Parsons, T. 1963a. "On the concept of influence." *Public Opinion Quarterly,* 27, 37-62.

Parsons, T. 1963b. "On the concept of political power." *Proceedings of the American Philosophical Society,* June, 232-262. Reprinted in S. Lukes (ed.). 1986. *Power,* pp. 94-143. Oxford: Basil Blackwell.

Patti, R. J. 1974. "Organizational resistance and change: The view below." *Social Service Review,* 48, 371-372.

Perrow, C. 1961. "The analysis of goals in complex organizations." *American Sociological Review,* 26, 859-866.

Perrow, C. 1970. "Departmental power perspectives in industrial firms," pp. 59-89, in M. N. Zald (ed.), *Power in Organizations.* Nashville: Vanderbilt University Press.

Pettigrew, A. M. 1973. *Politics of Organizational Decision-Making.* London: Tavistock.

Pfeffer, J. 1978. "The micropolitics of organizations," pp. 29-50, in M. W. Meyer (ed.), *Environments Organizations.* San Francisco: Jossey-Bass.

Pfeffer, J. 1981. *Power in Organizations.* Marshfield, MA: Pitman.

Pfeffer, J. 1992. *Managing with Power: Politics and Influence in Organizations.* Boston: Harvard University Press.

Pfeffer, J. 1997. *New Directions for Organization Theory.* New York: Oxford University Press.

Pfeffer, J., and A. M. Konrad. 1991. "The effects of individual power on earnings." *Work and Occupations,* 18, 385-414.

Pfeffer, J., and W. L. Moore 1980. "Power in university budgeting: A replication extension." *Administrative Science Quarterly,* 25, 637-653.

Pfeffer, J., and G. R. Salancik. 1978. *The External Control of Organizations.* New York: Harper & Row.

Pichault, F. 1995. "The management of politics in technically related organizational change." *Organization Studies,* 16, 449-476.

Powell, W. 1990. "Neither market nor hierarchy: Net forms of organizations," pp. 295-336, in B. M. Staw and L. L. Cummings (eds.), *Research in Organizational Behavior*, Vol. 12. Greenwich, CT: JAI Press.

Provan, K. G. 1980. "Recognizing, measuring, and interpreting the political power distinction in organizational research." *Academy of Management Review*, 5, 549-560.

Provan, K. G., J. M. Beyer, and C. Kruytbosch. 1980. "Environmental linkages power in resource dependence relations between organizations." *Administrative Science Quarterly*, 25, 200-225.

Raven, B. H. 1992. "A power/interaction model of interpersonal influence: French and Raven thirty years later." *Journal of Social Behavior and Personality*, 7, 217-244.

Reed, M. 1989. *The Sociology of Management*. New York: Harvester Wheatsheaf.

Riesman, D., N. Glazer, and R. Denney. 1961. *The Lonely Crowd: A Study of the Changing American Character.* New Haven: Yale University Press.

Russell, B. 1938. *Power: A New Social Analysis*. New York: Norton.

Sagie, S. 1990. "Intra-organizational power and information systems unit." Ph.D. diss., The Technion—Israel Institute of Technology, Haifa (Hebrew).

Salancik, G. R., and J. Pfeffer. 1974. "The bases and uses of power in organizational decision-making: The case of a university." *Administrative Science Quarterly*, 19, 453-473.

Samia, Y. T. 2004. "Organizational climate in field units of Israel defence forces." Ph.D. diss., University of Haifa (Hebrew).

Samuel, Y. 1979. "An exchange and power approach to the concept of organizational effectiveness." Department of Sociology Anthropology, Tel Aviv University, Israel (mimeograph).

Samuel, Y. 1996. *Organizations: Features, Structures, Processes*, 2nd ed. Haifa: University of Haifa Press & Zmora-Bitan (Hebrew).

Samuel, Y. 2000. *The Political Game: Power and Influence in Organizations.* Haifa: The University of Haifa Press & Zmora-Bitan Publishers.

Samuel, Y., and M. B. Zelditch, Jr. 1989. "Expectations, shared awareness, and power," pp. 288-312, in J. Berger, M. Zelditch, and B. Anderson (eds.), *Sociological Theories in Progress*, vol. 3. Newbury Park, CA: Sage.

Samuel, Y., and C. Jacobsen (1997). "A System dynamics model of planned organizational change." *Computational & Mathematical Organization Theory*, 3, 151-171.

Savage, M., and A. Witz (eds.). 1992. *Gender Bureaucracy*. Oxford: Blackwell.

Schein, E. H. 1977. "Individual power political behavior." *Academy of Management Review*, 2, 64-72.

Schein, E. H. 1996. "Culture: The missing concept in organization studies." *Administrative Science Quarterly*, 41, 181-196.

Schmidt, S. M., and D. Kipnis. 1987. "The perils of persistence." *Psychology Today*, 21, 32-34.

Scott, W. R. 1992. *Organizations: Rational, Natural, and Open Systems*, 3rd ed. Englewood Cliffs, NJ: Prentice-Hall.

Selzinck, P. 1949. *TVA and the Grass Roots*. Berkeley: University of California Press.

Shenhav, Y. A. 1999. *Manufacturing Rationality: Engineering Foundations of the Managerial Revolution.* New York: Oxford University Press.

Stevenson, W. B., J. L. Pearce, and L. W. Porter. 1985. "The concept of 'coalition' in organization theory research." *Academy of Management Review*, 10, 256-268.

Tannenbaum, A. S. 1968. *Control in Organizations*. New York: McGraw-Hill.

Tedeschi, J. T., and T. V. Bonoma. 1972. "Power and Influence: An Introduction," pp. 1-49, in J. T. Tedeschi (ed.), *The Social Influence Processes*. Chicago: Aldine.

Tedeschi, J. T., B. R. Schlenker and T. V. Bonoma. 1973. *Conflict, Power, Games*. New York: Academic Press.

Thibaut, J., and H. H. Kelly. 1961. *The Social Psychology of Groups*. New York: Wiley.

Thompson, J. D. 1967. *Organizations in Action*. New York: McGraw-Hill.

Thompson, P., and D. McHugh. 1995. *Work Organizations: A Critical Introduction*. London: Macmillan.

Tushman, M. L., and E. Romanelli. 1983. "Uncertainty, social location, an influence in decision making: A socioeconomic analysis." *Management Science*, 29, 12-23.

Vigoda, E. 1997. "Organization Politics: Features, Factors, and Implications of Interpersonal Influence Processes on Workers Performance in the Israeli Public Administration." Ph.D. diss., University of Haifa (Hebrew).

Vigoda, E. 2000. "Organizational politics, job attitudes, work outcomes: Exploration and implications for the public sector." *Journal of Vocational Behavior*, 57, 326-347.

Vigoda, E. 2003. *Developments in Organizational Politics*. Cheltenham: Edward Ellgar

Weber, M. 1947. *The Theory of Social Economic Organization*. Trans. A. M. Henderson and T. Parsons. New York: Free Press.

Weber, M. 1964. *Religion in China: Confucianism and Taoism*. New York: Macmillan.

Weick, K. E. 1979. *The Social Psychology of Organizing*. 2nd ed. Reading, MA: Eddison-Wesley.

Weick, K. 2001. *Making Sense of Organization*. Oxford: Blackwell.

Westphal, J. D., and J. Zajac. 1995. "Who shall govern? CEO/board power, demographic similarity, new directors selection." *Administrative Science Quarterly*, 40, 60-83.

Williamson, O. E. 1975. *Markets Hierarchies: Analysis Antitrust Implications*. New York: The Free Press.

Williamson, O. E. 1981. "The economics of organizations: The transaction cost approach." *American Journal of Sociology*, 87, 548-577.

Williamson, O. E. (ed.). 1995. *Organization Theory: From Chester Barnard to the Present Beyond*. New York: Oxford University Press.

Wrong, D. H. 1968. "Some problems in defining social power." *American Journal of Sociology*, 73, 673-681.

Wrong, D. H. 1996. *Power: Its Forms, Bases, Uses,* 2nd ed. New Brunswick, NJ: Transaction Publishers.

Yuchtman, E., and S. E. Seashore. 1967. "A system resource approach to organizational effectiveness." *American Sociological Review*, 32, 891-903.

Yukl, G., and J. B. Tracey. 1992. "Consequences of influence tactics used with subordinates, peers, and the boss." *Journal of Applied Psychology*, 77, 525-535.

Zald, M. N. (ed.). 1969. *Power in Organizations*. Nashville: Vanderbilt University Press.

Index

Affirmative action, 156
Alvesson, Mats, 5
American Tobacco Company, 177
Amnesty International, 56
Arendt, Hannah, 5
Assertiveness, as political behavior, 95
Association of Russian Immigrants, 56
AT&T, 177
Attribution theory, 88-89
Authority
    constraints of, 9
    as legitimate power, 9-10
    as political behavior, 96-97
    power from, 9

Bacharach, Samuel, 34
Bargaining, as political behavior, 97
Blau, Peter, 29
Boulding, Kenneth, 33
Bribery actions
    compensation, 18-19
    symbolic expressions, 19-21
    temptation and, 17-18
Budgeting
    financial usages of, 78
    parts of, 77
    as political cycle, 78-79
    political nature of, 77
    unit power in, 77-78
Burns, Tom, 45
Bush, President George W., 18
Business subunit struggles
    coalition formation impacts, 164
    general manager's importance, 163-164
    line and staff relationships, 164-165
    unit competition, 163

Centrality, power from, 11
Certainty
    power from, 10

uncertainty and, 10
Charisma
    power from, 10
    vs authority, 10
Clegg, Stuart, 73
Clinton, President Bill, 132
Coalition formation, as political behavior, 97
Coercion
    fear use with, 7
    force use with, 7
    managerial patters and, 203-204
    organizational use of, 203-204
    organizational competitiveness as, 174
    power from, 7
Commitment, 202
    alienation, 202
Compensation, as bribery action, 18-19
Competitive dependence, 172
Competitive strategies, meaning of, 174
Conflict Theory
    as actor conflicts, 33
    conflict intensity impacts, 34
    intra-organizational coalitions and, 34-35
    mutual alternatives agreement, 34
    mutual relations interdependence, 3
    power cost in, 33-34
    power use in, 34
Cooptation
    board loyalty and, 181-182
    competition reducing with, 181
    meaning of, 181
    quid pro quo, 182
    risks from, 182

Decision-making centers
    committees, 71
    liaison teams, 71
    location political in, 136
    managerial positions, 50

nonprofit organizations and, 70-71
ownership, 70
player's influence in, 50
as political importance, 50
top management, 70
types of, 49-50
Dependence
competitive dependence, 172
meaning of, 171-172
symbiotic dependence, 172-173
vs independence strategies, 172
Dependence Theory, 139
arguments for, 26-27
assumptions of, 26
dependence level changing, 28
international examples, 27
organizational examples, 28-29
power expressing in, 27
reward vs punishment in, 27
structural relationships in, 27-28
Distributive conflicts, 32

Economic injury
corporation use of, 17
funds suspensions, 16-17
monetary fines, 16
Employees
intergroup politics and, 147-153
organization power and, 202-203
vs globalization, 185
See also Employee vs employer
struggles; Line and staff relationships; Trade unions
Employer vs employee struggles
coalition partners rivalry, 152-153
dispute resolution process, 149-151
employer attitudes, 149
ideological struggles and, 151
labor dispute cycles, 148
personal benefits and, 134-135
as power struggles, 149
privatization as threat, 152
professions and politics, 153
turnaround programs, 151-152
See also Line and staff relationships
Empowerment, 134
Etzioni, Amitai, 60, 202
Exchange, as political behavior, 96
Exchange Theory
assumptions of, 30
distributive conflict in, 32
labor relations exchanges, 31-32

power importance in, 31
social exchange transactions, 29-30
social and professional relationships,
32
sociology views of, 29
as unbalanced relationships, 30-31
Exclusion strategy
organizational loyalty, 154
origin of, 153-154
professional language use, 154
traveling requirements as, 154-155
women characterized in, 154
Expectation Theory
law of expected reactions, 38
power relationships examples, 38-39
shared awareness, 38
Subjective Expected Utility Theory,
38
Expected utility, 35
Expertise
power from, 8
social recognition of, 8
types of, 8

Familiarity, power from, 11
Feminist organizations as outside influ-
ences, 72
sexism problems and, 72
Feminist revolution, 56, 156
Flatterer style, as interpersonal politics,
142
Foucault, Michel, 4
French, John, 6
Functional centrality, 137
Functional conflicts
factors of, 133
inter-positional conflicts resolving,
133
interpersonal conflicts, 133-134
Functional differentiation, 81

Game rules
behavioral rules, 58
competitor behaviors, 59
conformist behaviors, 61
controversial problems in, 58
fairness principles, 60-61
formulation of, 57
multi-organizational networks, 60
normative rules for, 57-58
organizational violence, 58
reciprocity norms, 59-60

"red lines" in, 59
secrecy issues, 59
Games. *See* Political games
Gender equality
   affirmative action and, 156-157
   defense sector obstructions, 155-156
   gender politics, 153-155
   organizations targeted by, 156
   political struggles for, 158-159
   precedents method and, 157
   public sector acceptance of, 155
   revolutions for, 153
   secondary organization support for, 158
   status of women advisors, 157-158
   support services needs, 155
   women's organization support, 158
   See also Sexual harassment; Women
Gender politics, exclusion strategy and, 153-154
Globalization, 185
Goals
   official vs operational, 74-75
   types of, 75-77
Golden parachute, 210
Government
   agency structures, 83
   as outside actor, 55-56
   partnership strategies of, 183-185
   as takeover partner, 188-189
Greenpeace, 56
Gunslinger style, as interpersonal politics, 142

Hidden agenda, 164
Horizontal integration, 187
Hostile takeovers, 186
Human Genome Project, 183-184
Hussein, Saddam, 27

IBM, 177
In-house political actor
   elites and, 52
   identifying of, 51
   interest groups in, 51-52
   professional staff and, 52-53
Inclusion strategy, 153
Information
   demands for, 9
   harassments over, 9
   power from, 9
Ingratiation, as political behavior, 95

Inner circle, 130
Intergroup politics
   conclusions on, 167-169
   employer vs employee struggles, 147-153
   focus of, 127
   gender equality struggles, 153-159
   intergroup politics, 148
   organizational pie competing, 147148
   organizational subunit conflicts, 159-167
   research assumptions, 128
Interlocking directories
   board of director's loyalty, 180
   political games in, 180
Interorganizational networks
   advantages of, 179
   creating of, 177-178
   functional changes and, 178-179
   member interest varying, 178
   political economy from, 178
   vs changes, 179-180
Interorganizational politics
   conclusions on, 190-192
   constraint coping with, 173-174
   dependence concept and, 171-172
   focus of, 127
   interorganizational relations types, 174
   organization takeovers, 185-190
   organizational competition, 174-177
   organizational cooperation, 177-185
   organizational environment and, 171
   organizational power importance, 173
   research assumptions, 128
   symbiotic dependence, 172-173
Interpersonal politics
   action levels for, 127-128
   conclusions, 144-146
   focus of, 127
   influence styles, 142-144
   leverage from, 128-135
   location basis in, 135-139
   personal influence basis, 139-142
   research assumptions, 127-128
Involvement, 202
Israel, defense industry, 76

Job's personal benefits
   extra benefits obtaining, 129-130
   functional conflicts, 133-134
   inner circle assistance, 130

organizational units and, 128
political leverage in, 129
as power struggles, 135
as preferential treatment, 130
resource controlling, 128-129
rules circumventing, 130-131
senior position temptations, 131
sexual harassment and, 131-133
supervisor vs subordinate conflicts,
    134-135
Joint ventures
basis for, 182-183
Human Genome Project as, 183-184
meaning of, 182
political shadows and, 184
power expressions in, 183
use of, 173

Kennedy, President John F., 58

Labor disputes
employer actions during, 150
    Equality ideology, 151
    equity ideology, 151
    internal organization cooperation dur-
        ing, 150-151
    resolution process for, 149
    strike breaker punishments, 149-150
Law of diminishing marginal utility, 35-36
Lawler, Edward, 34
Lewinsky, Monica, 132
Liability
    organizational use of, 13
    sources of, 12-13
Line and staff relationships
    budget confrontations, 165-166
    hidden agendas in, 164-165
    interest conflict between, 164
    management territory trespassing, 164
    personal privileges benefits, 156
    resource controlling, 164-165
Location as political
    actor access, 136-137
    decision-making centers proximity,
        136
    information access, 136-137
    interpersonal power, 138-139
    junior employee power from, 136
    network forming and, 136
    organizational power effecting, 135
    organizational uncertainty, 138-139
    types of, 135

Manager as politicians
    authority extending by, 194
    dispute involvement by, 194
    issue framing procedures, 200
    organizational machine and, 193
    organizations controlling by, 193
    political behaviors, 194-200
    political games denying, 201-202
    political games with, 193-194
    soft tactics successes, 201
    subordinates reactions to, 200-201
Managerial patterns
    coercive organizations and, 203-204
    managerial politics, 206-207
    normative organizations and, 205-
        206
    power dimensions of, 202
    resources' personal use, 202
    subordinates orientation to, 202-203
    utilitarian organizations, 204-205
Managerial politics
    conclusions on, 212-213
    examples of, 195-200
    internal culture and, 195
    managerial patterns, 202-207
    managerial turnovers and, 207-212
    managers as politicians, 193-202
    meaning of, 194-195
Managerial turnover
    board of directors and, 209
    causes of, 207
    CEO loyalty, 211-212
    golden parachutes for, 210-211
    new manager interests, 211
    subunits effects from, 208-209
    vs manager survival, 209-210
    vs organizational performance, 207-
        208
Manager's political behaviors
    commitment creating, 199
    compromise agreements, 197
    consultation use, 195-196
    contrasts creating, 199
    distance maintaining, 198-199
    maneuvering ability, 196
    negative timing, 196-197
    rarity creating, 199-200
    selective communication, 196
    self-confidence, 197-198
    theatrical behaviors, 197
Maneuvering ability, 1969
Mega mergers, 187

Microsoft, 61, 176-177
Mintzberg game classifications
  alliance building game, 109
  budgeting game, 110
  counter-insurgency game, 108
  criteria for, 107
  empire building game, 109
  expertise game, 110
  insurgency games, 108
  line vs staff game, 111
  lording game, 110-111
  political game types, 107-108
  rival camps game, 111-112
  sponsorship game, 108-109
  strategic candidate's game, 112
  whistle blowing game, 112
  young Turks game, 113
Mintzberg, Henry, 53, 75, 88
Morgan, Garth, 41, 46

Nongovernmental organizations (NGO),
  as outside influence, 73
Nonprofit organizations, employee attitudes in, 149
Normative organizations, 203, 205-206

Observer style, as interpersonal politics,
  142
Organization subunit struggles
  budget confrontations, 165-166
  business organizations and, 163-165
  functional conflict displaying, 161
  functional differentiation of, 159
  goods and services determining, 160
  inter-unit politics, 162-163
  occupational group tensions, 166-167
  power amplifying, 159-160
  resource dependence theory and, 161
  strategic decision influencing, 160-
    161
  strategic factors coping, 162
Organizational ambiguity, 68
Organizational competition
  coercive nature in, 174
  competitive strategies, 174
  information's political uses, 176
  interorganizational competition, 175
  law suits over, 177
  resource dependence, 174-175
Organizational cooperation
  cooptation, 181-182

economies of scale benefits, 185
globalization and, 185
government partnership strategies,
  184-185
interlocking directories, 180-181
interorganizational networks, 177-
  180
joint ventures as, 182-184
political shadows, 184
reasons for, 177
Organizational environment
  actors in, 171
  interdependence in, 171
  meaning of, 171
  vs outside dependence, 171-173
Organizational goals
  goal selecting, 75-76
  ideological struggle over, 77
  importance of, 75
  stakeholder pressure, 76
  types of, 75
Organizational learning, 180
Organizational machine, 193
Organizational politics, 94
  defined, 45-46
  explanations for, 103
  motive assumptions in, 103-104
  as negative behaviors, 104
  political games as, 46
  two sides of, 103
Organizational politics attitudes
  attribution theory and, 88-89
  behavior as political, 89
  concepts of, 87
  description of, 88
  importance of, 89
  as neutral reality, 87
  power use in, 87-88
  publicly denial of, 88
  subjective side of, 88
Organizational politics perceptions
  factors contributing to, 91-92
  procedures as, 91
  underprivileged relationships and, 92
  universities, 91
Organizational structures
  academic inspired changes, 83-84
  functional differentiation advantages,
    81
  government agencies and, 83
  organization structure role, 82
  political activities, 82

political game characteristics, 82
as significant issue, 82-83
stakeholder political influence, 83
Organizational takeovers
corporate-government relationships, 188-189
foreign businesses concerns, 188
horizontal integration, 187
hostile takeovers, 186-187
illegal organizations and, 187
interorganizational confrontations, 189-190
local economy dominating, 189
meaning of, 185-186
mega mergers, 187-188
organizational power in, 187
reasons for, 186
vertical integration and, 186
Organizational uncertainty
information lacking as, 138-139
as problem, 138
Organizational politics determinates
ambiguity, 68
change resistance as, 67-68
organizational consensus needs, 68-69
rules as, 65
as unavoidable, 69
vs production technologies, 65-66
Outside political actors
board of directors, 53-54
clients, 54-55
dynamic nature of, 57
government, 55-56
identifying of, 53
media, 56-57
owners, 53
political skills requirements, 57
special interest groups, 56
supplier groups, 54

Palestinian Authority, 61
Parsons, Talcott, 4
Penalty actions
bribery actions, 17-19
economic injury, 16-17
physical injury and, 15-16
symbolic expressions, 19-21
Perceived politics
attitudes toward, 87-89
behavior types as, 93-99
conclusions on, 103-104

political behavior consequences, 99-103
situations as, 89-93
Performance gap, 102
Personal influence
emotional manipulation, 141-142
emotional use in, 141
flattery use, 141
interpersonal politics, 141, 144
interpersonal relationships benefits, 140-141
methods basis for, 142
modes of, 142-143
political style and, 143
purpose of, 142
social proof and, 140
Pettigrew, Andrew, 47
Pfeffer, Jeffrey, 61, 69, 77, 140, 159, 200
Physical injury
international relations and, 16
military use, 15-16
types of, 15
Political actors
goals of, 50-51
identity of, 51
in-house players, 51-53
outside players, 53-57
participant types in, 51
Political action
levels of, 127-128
leverage differences, 128
Political agenda
conclusions on, 84-85
financing of, 77-79
goals of, 74-77
organizational politics and, 65-69
organizational structures, 81-84
political issues, 71-74
political struggles focus, 69-71
senior appointments and, 79-81
Political arena
actor competition perceptions, 47-48
borderline defining, 49
game meaning in, 48
resources increasing, 48
rivals as partnering, 48-49
Political behavior consequences
as circular process, 100-101
damage from, 99-100
negative interpretation results, 102
positive results from, 102

power increases from, 100
psychological results from, 101-102
resource unfairness, 100
unjustified profits from, 99
unofficial behavior and, 94
vs reality, 102
Political behavior perceptions
    behavioral patterns as, 95-98
    examples of, 98
    importance of, 99
    organizational behavior types, 93
    unofficial behavior and, 94
Political game players, 113-114
Political game power bases
    kinds of, 114
    typology of, 114-116
Political game typology
    game types, 116-120
    limits in, 115
    organizational politics dimensions, 115
Political game visibility
    concealment benefits, 122-123
    continued existence of, 123
    intention hiding from, 121-122
    interorganization secrecy, 122
    as legitimate behavior, 121
    overt vs covert games, 121
    participant surveillance, 1213
    political actor intentions, 122
    secrecy reasons for, 122
Political games
    bargaining game, 118-119
    characteristics of, 82
    classifications for, 107
    coalition game, 119
    collaboration game, 120
    conclusions on, 123-124
    confrontation game, 118
    interlocking directories, 180
    manager as politician, 193-194, 201-
        202
    meaning of, 107
    Mintzberg games classification, 107-
        113
    persuasion game, 117-118
    political arena and, 48
    political games typology, 113-121
    political games visibility, 121-123
    political players, 113-114
    as politics, 46
    rules for, 57-61
    subjugation game, 119

submission game, 116
seduction game, 116-117
uniform game, 120-121
Political issues
    decision change difficulties, 74
    feminist organizations and, 72
    nongovernmental organizations, 73
    outside influences on, 71-72
    political struggle issues, 74
    stakeholders and, 73
    trade union and, 72-73
Political layout
    characteristics of, 46
    conclusions on, 62-63
    emergence of, 46
    game rules, 57-61
    organizational politics and, 45-46
    organizations as socioeconomic en-
        tity, 45
    political actors, 50-57
    political arena and, 47-49
    political goals and, 49-50
    as political organization, 45
    vs organizational structure, 46-47
Political leverage
    as job-holder leeway, 129
    power exercising, 129
Political shadows, 184
Political situation perceptions
    civil servants and, 92-93
    employee perceptions vs fact, 93
    examples of, 90
    organizational politics as, 91
    political motives attributing, 93
    procedures as, 90-91, 91-92
    situation creating, 89-90
Political struggle focus, decision-making
    center as, 70-71
Political style, 143
Political victims, 92
Pollard, Jonathan, 59
Power
    concepts of, 2-7
    conclusions on, 21-23
    defined, 1-2
    expressing of, 13-21
    organizational political goals, 1
    political goals for, 2
    social life foundation, 1
    sources of, 7-13
Power concepts
    as ability to influence, 5-6

as action's form, 5
as asymmetrical, 2
behavior change as, 3-4
communicative interpretation of, 5
deterrence principles, 3
factors defining, 3
normal life details as, 4-5
power relationship defining, 6
power types, 3
system resource as, 4
Power expressions
    bribery actions, 17-19
    penalty actions, 15-17
    symbolic expressions, 19-21
    threatening actions as, 13-15
Power sources
    authority, 9-10
    centrality, 11
    certainty, 10
    charisma, 10
    coercion, 7
    effectiveness of, 7
    expertise, 8
    familiarity, 11-12
    information, 9
    liability, 12-13
    organization's use of, 13
    reputation, 12
    rewards, 8
    status, 12
    supply, 11
Power's theoretical basis
    comparative views of, 39-41
    conclusions on, 41-43
    conflict theory, 33-35
    dependence theory, 26-29
    exchange theory, 29-32
    expectation theory, 38-39
    model testing, 25
    power and politics merging, 25
    structural vs behavioral distinctions,
        25-26
    utility theory, 35-38
Precedents method, 157
President George Bush, 27
Privatization, as employee threat, 152
Production technologies
    employee's disputes, 66
    political immunity, 66
    purpose of, 65
    services of, 65-66
    stakeholder preventions, 66

Punishment, as political behavior, 97-98

Rationality, as political behavior, 95-96
Raven, Bertram, 6
Reputation, power from, 12
Resource Dependence Theory, 161, 186
    vertical integration, 186
Rewards, types of, 8
Rotary Club, 56
Russell, Bertrand, 1

Salancik, Gerald, 69
Senior appointments
    competition for, 79-80
    selection as political, 80-81
    stakeholder benefits from, 79
    types of, 79
September 11 tragedy, coalitions from,
    179-180
Sexual harassment
    examples of, 132-133
    reasons for, 131
    relationship establishing, 132
    sexual bribes as, 133
    types of, 131-132
Slack resources, 175
Social proof, 140
Stakeholders, 73
Standard Oil Company, 177
Status, power from, 12
Supply, power from, 11
Symbiotic dependence, 172
Symbolic expression
    business use, 21
    countries demonstrating, 21
    historical use, 20
    importance of, 19
    objects as, 20
    organizational use, 20-21
    political language and, 19-20

Tactician style, as interpersonal politics,
    142
Technical core, 137
Temptation, as bribery action, 17-18
Theoretical comparative views
    political and power relationships, 39-
        40
    theory commonalities, 40-41
    theory uniqueness, 41
Trade unions
    labor dispute cycles, 148

labor disputes, 149-151
labor relations of, 58
as outside influence, 72-73
worldwide effort of, 148
Threatening actions
behavioral threats, 14-15
deterrence level of, 15
obeying choices, 13
resource controlling, 13
verbal threats, 14

Uncertainly
ambiguity and, 68
as organizational problem, 67, 138-139, 140
Universities
business changes from, 83-84
politics perceived in, 91
research grant as power, 161-162
staff persecution complaints, 91
Utilitarian organization, 203-205

Utility Theory
alternative determining, 35
approval in, 35
assumptions in, 35
business organization and, 37
law of diminishing marginal utility, 35-36
power confrontations and, 37-38
power relationships and, 36-37
state organizations and, 37

Veto bloc, 209

Weber, Max, 2
Wilde, Oscar, 17
Women
exclusion strategy against, 153-155
feminism and, 56, 72, 156
intergroup struggles, 153-159
vs manager as politicians, 200-201
See also Gender equality; sexual harassment